'Marketers who want to recharge their left and right brains can do no better than read *Marketing Genius*. It's all there: concepts, tools, companies and stories of inspired marketers.'

Professor Philip Kotler, Kellogg Graduate School of Management
and author of *Marketing Management*

'A fantastic book, full of relevant learning. The mass market is dead. The consumer is boss. Imagination, intuition and inspiration reign. Geniuses wanted.'

Kevin Roberts, Worldwide CEO Saatchi & Saatchi
and author of *Lovemarks*

'This is a clever book: it tells you all the things you need to think, know and do to make money from customers and then calls you a genius for reading it.'

Hamish Pringle, Director General of Institute of Practitioners in Advertising
and author of *Celebrity Sells*

'This is a truly prodigious book. Peter Fisk is experienced, urbane and creative, all the attributes one would expect from a top marketer. The case histories in this book are inspirational and Peter's writing style is engaging and very much to the point. This book deserves a special place in the substantial library of books on marketing.'

Professor Malcolm McDonald, Cranfield School of Management
and author of *Marketing Plans*

'Customers, brands and marketing should sit at the heart of every business's strategy and performance today. *Marketing Genius* explains why this matters more than ever, and how to achieve it for business and personal success.'

Professor John Quelch, Harvard Business School
and author of *New Global Brands*

'*Marketing Genius* offers marketers 99% inspiration for only 1% perspiration.'

Hugh Burkitt, CEO The Marketing Society

marketing genius

peter fisk

CAPSTONE

Contents

About the author   vii

Turn on   1

Play   10

PART 1 Ingenuity: The making of a marketing genius   20

     Track 1 Complexity   23

     Track 2 Expectations   55

     Track 3 Genius   85

PART 2 Thinking: The mind of a marketing genius   108

     Track 4 Strategy   111

     Track 5 Brands   139

     Track 6 Customers   169

     Track 7 Innovation   197

PART 3 Competing: The touch of a marketing genius   226

   Track 8 Propositions   229

   Track 9 Experiences   253

   Track 10 Connections   279

   Track 11 Relationships   305

PART 4 Leading: The impact of a marketing genius   328

   Track 12 Performance   331

   Track 13 Marketers   369

   Track 14 Leadership   395

   Track 15 Futures   419

PART 5 The genie: Becoming a marketing genius   450

   Genius lab   452

   Genius catalysts   461

   Genius source   469

   Recharge   484

Index   485

About the author

Peter Fisk is an experienced strategist and marketer, and has worked with some of the world's leading companies including Coca-Cola, Microsoft and Vodafone.

He joined British Airways, at a time when it was justifiably 'the world's favourite airline', after early adventures in nuclear physics. He worked across sales and marketing – including channel development, relationship marketing and brand management – and was part of a strategy team to address the challenges of globalization and low-cost entrants.

With PA Consulting Group, he led their global marketing consulting team, and worked with companies from Silicon Valley to Singapore to develop more customer-centric businesses. This ranged from innovation at American Express to market-shaping strategies for Shell, brand repositioning for Courage and leadership development at BT; helping Philips to become a customer-driven business, and Microsoft to embrace value-based marketing.

As CEO of the Chartered Institute of Marketing, the world's largest marketing organization, Peter championed professional standards and reputation, and encouraging business leaders to embrace customers and brands as the most important source of long-term shareholder value. This was supported by the launch of Knowledge Hub, an online learning product, a new journal *The Marketer*, and the Shape the Agenda thought leadership programme.

He now jointly leads a strategic innovation firm, The Foundation, helping companies to grow their businesses from the outside in. By seeing the world as customers do, he helps business leaders to see things differently, and to develop the insights and strategies, belief and capability, to do exceptional things. This has, for example, led to the refocusing of M&S retail proposition, and reengineering of Volkswagen's customer processes.

Peter is a recognized expert and commentator on marketing around the world. He is an inspirational speaker on customers and brands, strategy and innovation. He is thoughtful and considered, provocative and entertaining. He is co-author of the *FT Handbook of Management*, and *The Complete CEO*. In January 2006, *Business Strategy Review* identified him as one of the leading new business thinkers.

He combines youthful energy and inspiration with significant, practical experience. He is married with two young daughters and, having grown up in the Northumbrian countryside, now lives just outside London. He is a committed long-distance runner, Newcastle United supporter, and never far from his BlackBerry or iPod.

Turn on

Every marketer has the ability to achieve 'genius', to combine their intelligence and imagination in more strategic, innovative and effective ways. I hope this book inspires you to think and do what you might never otherwise have thought possible. **Play.**

Part 1 INGENUITY: THE MAKING OF A MARKETING GENIUS

How do you succeed in markets that are incredibly complex and uncertain, intensely competitive and fast changing, where customers and shareholders constantly demand more, and the conventional ways of marketing just don't work any more?

Track 1 Complexity

- Explore the new challenges of market space and speed, and the fundamental shifts in power.

- Consider the vision of Google and focus of Apple, the rise of Starbucks and revolution of eBay.

- Learn to map emerging markets, to create rhythms that give you an edge, and to harness customer power.

Track 2 Expectations

- Understand the demands of customers and shareholders, and how to create superior economic value for both.

- Learn from value disciplines of Microsoft and Toyota, and the strategic focus of Coca-Cola.

- Address these challenges through stakeholder mapping, and learn how to analyse the drivers of economic and shareholder value.

Track 3 Genius

- Explore what it means to be a genius, and how it applies to the world of marketing and marketers.

- Learn from the intelligence of Steve Jobs, the imagination of Philippe Starck, and the extraordinary results of Phil Knight.

- Consider and profile the attributes of genius, and how they can be applied to each aspect of business and marketing.

Part 2 THINKING: THE MIND OF A MARKETING GENIUS

Seize the best opportunities in your markets by thinking more strategically and innovatively, combining the rigorous analysis and radical creativity that led to Albert Einstein's mind-boggling discoveries, and Steve Jobs's market transformations.

Track 4 Strategy

- Embrace market strategies that give you the perspective and focus to create lasting competitive advantage.

- Learn from the market-shaping strategies of Jet Blue and Sky TV, and the bold differentiation of Enterprise car rental.

- Apply the ideas to your business through better market strategy and selection, portfolio analysis and competitive positioning.

Track 5 Brands

- Explore what creates a great brand, how it lives and evolves, and how to maximize its power.

- Learn from the brand thinking of Virgin, the passion of Pret A Manger, and the unrelenting focus of BMW.

- Develop your own brand strategy, with a clear architecture, brought to life inside and out, to build long-term brand equity.

Track 6 Customers

- Consider what really matters to customers, and how to ensure that the whole company is founded on a customer orientation.

- Reflect on the insights of Zara, the ethical approach of Café Direct, and the re-orientation of Procter & Gamble.

- Learn to do business built on genuine customer insight and foresight, which is ethical and takes genuine responsibility.

Track 7 Innovation

- Embrace innovation that is based on disruption and creativity, applied to everything from products to business models.

- Learn from the innovation of BlackBerry and 3M, and the market-redefining success of Cirque du Soleil and Ikea.

- Embed innovation in your business through disruptive and creative catalysts, and by managing innovation in a more holistic way.

Part 3   COMPETING: THE TOUCH OF A MARKETING GENIUS

Deliver more distinctive and engaging marketing, in a way that Pablo Picasso, one of the few artists to become a legend in his own time, and Philippe Starck, the French designer of hotels and watches, would be proud of.

Track 8 Propositions

- Explore what really creates value for customers today, and how to articulate your offer in a way that is distinctive and engaging.

- Consider the brand propositions of Tesco, the sub-branding of British Airways' Club World, and the re-emergence of the Mini.

- Learn to develop customer value propositions that stand out from the crowd, through compelling scripts and memic messages.

Track 9 Experiences

- Consider what creates a great customer experience, one that embraces cool design, personal service and theatre.

- Learn from the funkiness of Jones Soda, the function and form of Paul Smith, and the sexual thrill of Agent Provocateur.

- Improve your customers' experience through customer mapping, intelligent design, and more intuitive and theatrical delivery.

Track 10 Connections

- Explore why integrated communications, inverted channels and new types of networks are essential to connect with customers.

- Reflect on the direct approach of Dell, the digital revolution of Amazon, the alignment of MTV and the buzz of Krispy Kreme.

- Learn to improve your customer connections through media and channel integration, and network marketing.

Track 11 Relationships

- Consider the challenges of building customer affinity, loyalty and partnerships in today's promiscuous markets.

- Explore the infectious loyalty of Panera Breads, and the customer relationship building of Centrica and Mercedes.

- Learn to build better customer relationships through affinity branding, loyalty ladders and partner development.

Part 4   LEADING: THE IMPACT OF A MARKETING GENIUS

Unlock the real value of your brands and marketing. Learn from Warren Buffett, the world's greatest financial investor, and Phil Knight's passion for performance and profits at Nike, to do great marketing that delivers exceptional business results.

Track 12 Performance

- Consider how to embrace more rigorous marketing measurement and optimization, internal and external reporting.

- Learn from the value-based approaches of Cadbury Schweppes and Diageo, and the brand building of Stella Artois.

- Improve your performance by embracing value-based marketing scorecards and metrics, and 'customer capital'.

Track 13 Marketers

- Consider why marketers must be the organization's champions of customers, innovation and growth.

- Learn from the marketing leadership of Nestlé, the orientation of British Airways, and the sustained growth of Disney.

- Introduce a better approach to managing markets and brands, and innovation and growth in your organization.

Track 14 Leadership

- Explore the leadership roles of marketers, functionally and cross-functionally, and why marketers make better CEOs.

- Be inspired by the passion of Richard Branson, the discipline of Jim Stengel and Terry Leahy, and the leadership of Meg Whitman.

- Learn how to be a more effective marketing leader and manager, and how to influence and drive the wider organization.

Track 15 Futures

- Consider a future business world built around intelligent markets, insightful brands and inspiring marketers.

- Learn from the vision of Nike, the insight of Nokia, the innovation of Dyson and the innocence of Innocent.

- See the future of your markets and business, and how blogging, branding and the five balls might help.

Part 5   THE GENIE: BECOMING A MARKETING GENIUS

You have the potential to be a marketing genius, seizing the challenges and opportunities of today's markets in more intelligent and imaginative ways. But where should you start? How can you and your marketing deliver extraordinary results?

Genius lab

A simple diagnostic approach to understanding how you and your team can achieve 'genius': evaluating your marketing and personal strengths and weaknesses, and how you could become a genius marketer, delivering genius marketing.

Profile 1:   Genius Marketing

Profile 2:   Genius Marketers

Diagnostic 1:   High Performance Marketing Map

Diagnostic 2:   High Performance Marketer Map

Genius catalysts

Fifty challenges for every marketer today – to make sense of markets and stand out from the crowd, improve your influence and reputation in the business, and deliver exceptional business results.

Genius source

250 inspirations to provoke your thinking and inspire your action. A selection of leading brands

and marketers, the most significant innovations and informative sources, to help you think and act more intelligently and imaginatively.

List 1:   50 Genius Brands

List 2:   50 Genius Marketers

List 3:   50 Genius Innovations

List 4:   50 Genius Concepts

List 5:   50 Genius Inspirations

Play

So you want to be a genius?

The genius of marketing lies in the ability to connect outside and inside, markets and business, customers and shareholders, creativity and analysis, promises and reality. Genius marketers have both the intelligence and imagination to seize the best opportunities, and to deliver extraordinary results.

Marketing Genius is for marketers who want to make a difference.

While many people have challenged the rise of global brands, and the influence of marketing on our lives, few have come to its defence. Few have considered why good marketing matters more than ever, its contribution to our economic wealth, and why it is the most exciting place to work today. However, markets have changed; therefore, marketing is changing, and marketers need to change further if they are to achieve high performance.

Marketing Genius offers a radically new approach to marketing.

In fast-changing and competitive markets, it is not obvious where to focus investment short- and long-term, or how to create and sustain exceptional value for customers and shareholders. Business needs marketing and marketers like never before. This book gives you the ideas, insights and inspiration to build brands that are truly different, to develop more innovative solutions and engage customers more deeply.

Marketing Genius is for everyone in business today.

Whether you are a communications specialist or market researcher, a brand manager or product developer, marketing leader or CEO, this book is for you. If you work in strategy or finance, sales or customer service, you will find it useful too. It is as relevant to large corporates as to small businesses, and agencies too.

Why did I write this book?

I want to inspire you to think differently, and to do great marketing.

In recent years I have experienced some great marketing, alongside much mediocrity. I have met many stimulating and ambitious marketers, but also many others who lack the confidence to challenge the status quo, to make their great ideas happen, to seize the opportunity to lead their organizations.

I want marketing to succeed, to be the driving force of business, and to have the influence and respect as a profession that it deserves.

Marketing creates more economic value for business than any other activity, yet it is too often seen as a marginal activity, a support function and a tactical cost line. Marketing has an unmatchable power base from which to drive the business – understanding the market, championing the customer, leading innovation, building the brand, driving profitable growth.

This requires an approach that is more strategic and commercial, innovative and engaging. Marketers must embrace the analytical rigour to connect passions with profits, but they must not lose their creative spark to reach out for what is new and different. Too many businesses, and their marketers, have become blinkered servants to process and numbers, which alone are increasingly commoditized and outsourced capabilities.

In today's incredibly complicated world, every business faces enormous change, uncertainty and opportunity. The best ideas will make companies great. Customers, rather than capital, are increasingly the scarcest resources. Concept rather than knowledge management will matter more in the future.

I believe marketers are best positioned to address these challenges and others like them:

- People are more different – kids, for example, can typically do 5.4 things at once, while adults struggle to do 1.7 (and men even less).

- Traditional marketing approaches are under fire – 54% of US consumers have 'banned' telemarketing.

- Purchase decisions are made in an instant – the average decision about which brand to buy is made in 2.6 seconds.

- Markets are much more competitive than ever before – intensity has on average tripled in the last 10 years.

- Products are quickly imitated and outdated – life cycles have on average reduced by 70% in the same time.

- Customers face a confusing barrage of noise – the average person comes across approximately 300 messages every day.

- Technology has become central to our buying behaviours – the Internet is used by 42% of consumers before buying a new car.

- Yet people rely on people more than ever – 75% of consumers say they trust personal recommendation most.

- Proving the value of marketing has focused our minds on metrics – yet 60% of brand investments impact on future years, not this year.

- Businesses are still incredibly short term – yet major investors look at the potential of the business beyond the next 4 years.

- The majority of a business' value is now based on intangible assets – accounting for 78% of *Fortune* 500's market value.

- Marketing talent is essential to business leadership – 21% of FTSE CEOs are marketers, and deliver 5.9% greater TSR than others.

Marketers have the unique talents to address today's intelligent and demanding customer, to bring direction and focus to their organization, and to drive the future profits that sustain business success.

What do I know about marketing?

As a marketer, I have worked for some of the most fascinating companies in the world.

From my early days at British Airways, where we spent many hours trying to work out how to fit a bed into a business class cabin and still make money, to the brand and logistical challenges for Coca-Cola in entering emerging Eastern European markets, more radical solutions have been needed.

At American Express we recognized that the brand had to be more than a plastic friend, but had to convince the business leaders to step outside their safety zone. Then there were the significant cultural challenges in making the ultimate technology firm, Microsoft, a more customer-oriented business.

However, working with small companies has often provided the greatest learning experiences. From government agencies to small bakeries in The Netherlands, to the astronomical rise and then fall of Regus, the office service firm, small businesses have no alternative but to think differently in order to beat bigger rivals, to make the most of their strengths, and do more with less.

As CEO of the world's largest marketing organization, the Chartered Institute of Marketing, with 60,000 members in 131 countries, I was privileged to meet great marketers in every part of the world. I was motivated by the terrific energy and ideas that make marketers tick, their passion for brands and customers, to make a more valuable contribution to their businesses, and desire to succeed as a profession.

What has inspired me?

Work experiences have not been my only inspirations, and nor should they be yours. Our perceptions and ambitions, the way we think and our confidence to act differently comes more from experiences outside the workplace. All sorts of personal experiences, large and small, have inspired me.

My first real experience of a market was in the small town of Rothbury, where I grew up. Every Wednesday I watched convoys of farm trucks arrive from every direction to buy and sell their cattle and sheep, and then depart again at the end of the day.

My parents always encouraged me to try new things, and from this grew my passions. Even when I traded in music lessons for the local running club, my Mum still encouraged me, and my Dad would drive me to races every week. I would never have done many things without their support and encouragement.

I loved winning too, in whatever I did. Once you taste success, you want more of it. I will never forget the first time I won the district schools' 1500m race as an 11 year old. And from that day, I was never afraid of putting myself on the line, in the pursuit of faster times, and the pure joy of sprinting through the finish tape before anyone else.

At university I had a scientific curiosity. I studied physics, and in particular the superconductivity of atomic particles when cooled to −200 degrees Celsius. Yet, while I was fascinated by the many still unexplained properties of nature, I was quickly bored by the need to solve long and repetitive algebraic equations.

Meeting your future partner is an electrifying moment. I will never forget the excitement of getting to know my wife Alison, who over the years has become my best friend, my motivation to do what I never thought possible, and my link to reality.

Of course I had sporting heroes like everyone else. Watching Sebastian Coe defy injury and illness to win his second Olympic gold medal, Steve Cram break world records every week, and Jonathan Edwards jump to lengths he just could not believe. I can still remember the dates, times and distances.

In the business world, the opportunity to innovate was what made me tick. In particular, working with colleagues and agencies at British Airways to truly let go of our beliefs and inhibitions, to create breakthrough ideas that would seek to redefine the travel industry, shaped my attitudes and ambitions.

Sometimes just being there is important too, to observe actions and sample the atmosphere. I was fortunate to work in Silicon Valley during the late nineties, to feel the energy and ambition of the entrepreneurs and investors who clambered to make their technological fortunes.

Perhaps most important in thinking about genius was meeting the successful people inside some of the world's great brands. From the outside they were names that I was in awe of. Inside, they were ordinary folk, desperate to learn from other companies and to improve what they do.

And at the end of the day, there is nothing like two young children to bring you down to earth. They rekindle the innocent joy of play, to sing and dance, talk and laugh, like nothing else in the world matters.

These are some of the little things that have spurred me on. I am sure that you too have your own set of experiences that influence your beliefs and perspectives, guide your judgements and ambitions.

They have conditioned the way that I look at brands and their marketing, the way I read the many marketing books and learn from the companies and people around me. Books, of course, merely offer a point of view, and best practices are only one way to deliver results. The challenge is to select and apply the best ideas and insights in the right way for your business.

What will you learn?

Imagine if you could see the emerging opportunities in your markets as well as Apple's Steve Jobs, address them with the vision of Jeff Bezos at Amazon, the leadership of eBay CEO Meg Whitman, and the commercial success of Nike's founder Phil Knight.

Imagine if you could transform your industry with the direction of Michael Dell, the innovation of James Dyson and the persistence of low-cost airline king Michael O'Leary. Imagine if you could build powerful brands like Scott Bedbury did for Starbucks and Nike, with the irreverence of Jones Soda founder Peter van Stolk, and the creativity of advertising's *enfant terrible* Trevor Beattie.

Imagine if you could deliver experiences with the aesthetics of iPod designer Jonathon Ive, the passion of sandwich entrepreneur Julian Metcalfe, and the effectiveness of P&G's top marketer, Jim Stengel.

Marketing Genius describes how you can do all of this:

- Make sense of today's complex and changing markets, and distinguish the hot spots, white spaces and black holes.

- Become the driving force of your business strategy, identifying new sources of competitive advantage.

- Bring an outside-in approach to your whole business, and align the expectations of customers and shareholders.

- Balance delivering today with the need to create tomorrow, by gaining new insights into what really matters to customers.

- Build strong brands that engage and inspire people, and which also embrace a new level of ethical and social responsibility.

- Innovate products, markets and business models more radically, by harnessing technology and design in creative and unusual ways.

- Articulate customer propositions that are distinctive and compelling, and ensure that your communication is contagious and unforgettable.

- Connect with customers on their terms, in more knowledgeable and integrated ways, when, where and how they want.

- Serve customers in more personal, empathetic and human ways, delivering experiences that are compelling and enabling.

- Measure your marketing with accurate and actionable measures, optimizing your budgets and resources for a better return.

- Unlock the real economic value of your marketing, and realize your own potential as a marketer.

Every marketer has the ability to achieve 'genius', to combine your intelligence and imagination, to think more strategically and act more effectively, and to do what you might never otherwise have thought possible.

How will it help you?

I hope that *Marketing Genius* gives you the confidence to do marketing that is more strategic, innovative and commercial.

While I have included many concepts, case studies and tools to help you, this is not an exhaustive guide to marketing, or a replacement for all the excellent theoretical texts.

Instead I seek to provoke your thinking, to illustrate connections, to highlight dilemmas, to suggest alternatives, and to stimulate more thoughtful yet radical action that delivers improved business results.

I hope it encourages you to see your market and business more holistically, to challenge conventions both outside and inside, and to remove the fear of areas of business that you perhaps understand less well.

Over the years, and in researching this book, I have become convinced that:

- Markets, complex and fast changing, competitive and borderless, are the best sources of opportunities for business today. They should be the stimulus and driving force of business purpose and direction, priorities and alignment.

- Marketing is the most important and exciting activity in business. It offers an essential mindset for everyone, particularly business leaders, and is the engine of strategy and brands, experiences and relationships, innovation and growth.

- Marketers are more valuable to their organizations than ever. They bring an outside-in perspective, with the ability to think creatively and analytically, strategically and practically, creatively and commercially.

If we can achieve recognition of this through practical actions and results, then marketing will be a profession that we can all be proud of – respected by peers, valued by society, aspired to by the best young talent, and the breeding ground of future CEOs.

Marketing is the key to delivering extraordinary business results.

You have the talent and opportunity to apply the intelligence of Einstein and the imagination of Picasso, to make sense of markets and stand out from the crowd, and to deliver results that even Warren Buffett would be proud of.

You could be a marketing genius, if you want.

I will never forget the inspirational words that I learnt in my early days of marketing: 'Whatever you can do, or think you can do, begin it. For boldness has power, genius and magic in it.'

Be innovative. Be different. Be inspired.

Ingenuity:
The making of
a marketing
genius

PART 1

▶ Ingenuity: The making of a marketing genius

▶ How do you succeed in markets that are incredibly complex and uncertain, intensely competitive and fast changing, where customers and shareholders constantly demand more, and the conventional ways of marketing just don't work anymore?

▶ How do you make sense of today's markets? How do you identify the best opportunities for growth? How do you address the intensity of competition and rising power of customers?

▶ How do you meet the high expectations of customers, employees and shareholders? And indeed of society? How do you reconcile their different needs? How do you create exceptional 'value' for all of them?

▶ What does it mean to be a genius? How is a genius different? How do they combine intelligence and imagination? What does it mean to be a marketing genius, and how does it achieve better results?

'Extraordinary people visualize not what is possible or probable, but rather what is impossible. And by visualizing the impossible, they begin to see it as possible.'

Cheri Carter-Scott

'Keep in mind that you cannot control your own future. Your destiny is not in your hands; it is in the hands of the irrational consumer and society. The changes in their needs, desires, and demands will tell you where you must go ... This means that managers must themselves feel the pulse of change on a daily, continuous basis ... They should have intense curiosity, observe events, analyse trends, seek the clues of change, and translate those clues into opportunities.'

Michael Kami

Making sense of uncertain markets

Complex markets, intense competition, expectant customers and demanding shareholders require more intelligent marketing. To see the emerging form of markets and how they can be shaped, to target the best opportunities before others, to beat competitors in smarter ways than price discounting, to innovate more radically in new directions, to build brands like nobody else, to engage with customers in ways they have never thought possible, and to deliver returns to shareholders that would make analysts jump requires a new and different approach.

'Unless you are prepared to give up something valuable you will never be able to truly change at all, because you'll be forever in the control of things you can't give up.'

Andy Law

'They are playing a game. They are playing at not playing a game. If I show them I see they are, I shall break the rules and they will punish me. I must play the game, of not seeing I see the game.'

Kevin Kelly

Inside out	Outside in
Intensity. Competition comes from all angles, adjacent and distant markets. Imitation is instant, sameness is rife.	**Complexity**. Markets are incredibly complex, blurred and fragmented, borderless and unpredictable.
Possibilities. There are more diverse opportunities than ever. Businesses can compete anywhere and do anything.	**Speed**. Market change is constant and accelerating. New challenges and opportunities emerge rapidly.
Orientation. Companies continue to work inside out, with financial blinkers, seeking to improve what they've always done.	**Power**. Customers now call the shots, demanding you do business outside in, what, where, how and when they want.

Competing in fast changing markets, where borders have fallen and rules are broken, can be a disorienting experience. Take, for example, today's world of communications – to some companies they are in the telecoms business, others the broader communications market, others the IT or networking world. Your perspective determines your competitors, your solution set, your customers, and your potential for success.

Does this make a difference? The narrow-focused telecoms company may start to wonder where their customers have gone, while the communications company might struggle to be relevant to those with a specific telephony need. The guys in the IT space may pitch their pricing relative to an IT peer group, which would be perceived to be expensive relative to the niche market. However, if the target customer is in the IT mindset, then it could quadruple your margins. Yes, it makes a difference.

Making sense of complexity requires intelligence. Bill Jenson wrote the book *Simplicity*, which seeks to interpret today's world into dimensions you can get your hands on. However, as the quantum physicists realized, complex problems require complex solutions. And while the result might look admirable, the derivation is not easy. Nothing is certain; everything has a level of ambiguity about it. And everything is connected to everything else in some way.

We could do well to remember relativity and uncertainty into today's world. Not only do the old ways not work, but complexity also throws up many new opportunities if you have the right mindset. However, the director who sits round the boardroom table and recites, 'In my day, we looked at these things simply' is probably missing the point, as is the marketer who seeks to apply simplistic, conventional models to the complex challenge.

Take customers. They used to come in a range of similar shapes and sizes. We called them segments. We could predict that people with similar socio-demographic labels would behave alike and want similar things. Not so today. Not only are people more different, resulting in many more highly fragmented segments, but they are also less predictable, behaving in different ways at different times, and therefore in many different segments depending on the occasion, or even the mood.

Marketers need deeper logic and more creativity to succeed amidst complexity.

Brands must reorientate to compete within these new market dynamics. However, the first step is to choose where and how you want to compete in this new world. Only in this way can you decide the kind of company you will be, the type of audience to pursue, the type of value proposition that will make sense. Only in this way do you have a chance to define the future in your own vision, to ensure that you are part of it, and a leader within it.

The blurring of boundaries, of virtual and real worlds, and fusion of previously unrelated industries, is a daunting challenge but also a fantastic opportunity. The creative possibilities within today's connected world are endless. Almost any brand can work with any other, or against each other, in markets that used to have no connection. Whether it is Time Warner bringing together the disparate worlds of magazines, movies and networks – or a single brand like Virgin reaching out into many seemingly unrelated service offerings, there is immense potential to be realized by those who have the dreams and brains, confidence and persistence to realize it.

Inspiration 1.1 GOOGLE

'Googol' is the mathematical term for a 1 followed by 100 zeros. It perhaps symbolizes the magnitude of Google's ambition and increasing impact on the whole dynamic of markets and marketing.

In 1995 Larry Page and Sergey Brin created in their Stanford University bedroom what within 5 years would already be dealing with 100 million Internet searches every day, and make them multi-billionaires in less than a decade.

Google has a simple vision, to be 'the perfect search engine' or, as Page puts it, 'one that understands exactly what you mean and gives you back exactly what you want.' Now with over 80 million users, searching through 8 billion web pages, Google is well established as the world's leading search engine.

Indeed, most marketing today starts with 'a Google': textbooks don't include it in their theories of communication flows, and few ad agencies would dare admit it, but it really does represent the customer taking control, the customer-initiated transaction, the customer seizing power in today's complex world.

Brand awareness is achieved through word of mouth and the viral impact of click-throughs from many other sites, and revenues are driven by enabling advertisers to target online users in highly sophisticated and efficient ways.

Google argues that this makes the advertising useful to customers as well as to the advertiser placing it. It believes customers should know when someone has paid to put a message in front of them, so seeks to distinguish ads from the search results or other content on a page. Indeed, Google doesn't sell placement in the search results themselves, or allow people to pay for a higher ranking there.

Thousands of advertisers use Google AdWords to promote their products and services on the web with targeted advertising, the largest program of its kind. In addition, thousands of website managers take advantage of the Google AdSense program to deliver ads relevant to the content on their sites, improving their ability to generate revenue and enhancing the experience for their users.

The basic ranking system is a model of customer democracy – search rankings determined by the most popular sites, and assisted by those sites that encourage more open networking, linking one to another.

Google stays strong in a complex world by sticking to its philosophy built on 'ten things'. While their self-beliefs have often challenged conventions – not just in disrupting markets, but also, for example, at the time of their 2004 Nasdaq flotation when they insisted that investors should not treat them like a 'normal' company – their convictions are the empowered guidance that keeps them flexible but going in the right direction.

Google

Ten things

1 **Focus on the customer and all else will follow.** While many companies claim to put their customers first, few are able to resist the temptation to make small sacrifices to increase shareholder value ...

2 **It's best to do one thing really, really well.** Google does search. Google does not do horo-scopes, finance advice or chat. Our entire staff is dedicated to creating the perfect search engine ...

3 **Fast is better than slow.** Google believes in instant gratification. You want answers and you want them right now. Who are we to argue?

4 **Democracy on the web works.** Google works because it relies on millions of individuals posting websites to determine which other sites offer content of value ...

5 **You don't need to be at your desk to need an answer.** The world is increasingly mobile and unwilling to be constrained by a fixed location ... through their PDA, mobile phones or in their cars ...

6 **You can make money without doing evil.** Google is a business. Our revenues are derived from offering its search technology to companies and from the sale of advertising ...

7 **There's always more information out there.** Once we had indexed more pages than any other search service, we focused on information not readily accessible, such as images or PDF files ...

8   **The need for information crosses all borders.** Google facilitates access to information across the entire world ... the interface can be customized into about 100 languages.

9   **You can be serious without a suit.** Our founders wanted to a create a company not serious about anything but search ... work should be challenging and the work should be fun ...

10 **Great just isn't good enough.** Always deliver more than expected. Through innovation and iteration, we take something that works well and improve upon it in unexpected ways.

Source: google.com (annotated)

Concept 1.1 MARKET SPACE

Kodak used to know where it stood – the brand leader in the photographic film market. The markets and competitors, customers and products were all fairly predictable. Over the decades camera film came in many different formats and sizes, yet everyone knew that Kodak film was the best, better than Fujifilm or Agfa.

Ten years later, Kodak's position is increasingly unclear – what market it is in, who the competitors are, what customers want, or which products to focus on. Digital disruption has displaced traditional film, and previously separate markets of hardware devices, software and processing, imaging and printing have all converged.

Digital cameras come from Sony or Dell, images are stored on your hard drive, shared by e-mail, and if you still want the physical images then processing comes from Snapfish or Jessops, and printing from HP or Epson. Kodak has tried to respond in every direction. Kodak cameras, Kodak online wallets, Kodak printers, Kodak print kiosks. It describes itself as an imaging company, but neither its focus nor future are clear.

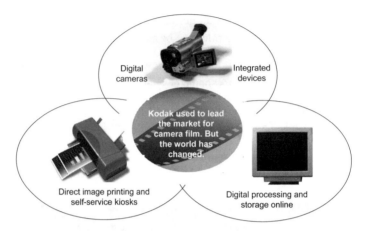

Market and technological convergence, the irrelevance of physical boundaries, the changing needs of consumers and retailers, and competitors emerging from previously unrelated markets have created complexity in every sector.

Today it is hard to know what type of business to call yourself, to distinguish a competitor from a collaborator (although they might be one and the same), and where you should bet your future. Not only is the market different, it keeps changing too.

So what are the drivers of change?

They are largely driven by technology, but also sociological and economic factors. The drivers include:

- Rise of computing power, interactivity and virtual networks.

- Compression of distance and time, and the speed of change.

- Irrelevance of geography, borders and hierarchies.

- Frictionless economics and corporate transparency.

- Rapid imitation of new products, and shortened life cycles.

- Globalization of culture, alongside religious difference.

Moore's Law emerged during the 'dotcom' boom and, unlike many of the companies it was initially associated with, it is still going strong. Gordon Moore, the founder of Intel, observed that computing power doubles approximately every 18 months while costs remain the same (or, put another way, the same power can be squashed into a chip half the size). This relentless improvement drives much of the short life cycles and obsolescence we see in products today.

However, the power of the Internet goes far beyond the devices through which we access it. More significant than Moore's Law is the related Metcalfe's Law, which explains the power of networks and the way in which they drive new forms of interactivity, and can quickly build powerful communities and achieve great scale and reach. Robert Metcalfe, who launched 3Com, suggested that the power of a network is related to the square of the nodes. Therefore, every additional member has a disproportionate impact. Think of eBay, for example, where the network of users and diversity of goods creates the proposition.

Impact of Technology =	Power		Bandwidth		Network		Diversity
	Moore's Law says that computing power doubles every 18 months	x	**Gilder's Law** says that telecom bandwidth triples every 12 months	x	**Metcalfe's Law** says that the value of a network is the square of its nodes	x	**Kao's Law** says that creativity rises exponentially with diversity
	x 1.3 pa		x 3 pa		x n x n		x exp(d)

The changing environment is accompanied by new practices, issues and regulations, present-ing business and marketing with new challenges. The rise of more aggressive telemarketing approaches, such as the highly irritating recorded messages that interrupt your home at any hour of the day with highly misleading suggestions that 'you have just won a major prize' has prompted a majority of US households to 'ban' such practices by registering at donotcall.com.

More general examples include:

- Demand for customer privacy and ownership of personal information.

- Customer backlash against the avalanche and intrusion of direct marketing.

- Rise of social issues and ethics, from environment to transparency.

- Deficit of customer trust, and prevalence of competitive promiscuity.

- Globalization of brands, leading to cultural sameness and classlessness.

- Importance of intellectual properties, and value of intangible assets.

Customers are more different and intelligent, their expectations are higher and they are more powerful than ever. Research by Martin Lindstrom in *BrandChild*, for example, shows that kids can cope with complexity far better than adults: they can do 5.4 things at the same time – watching, playing, talking, texting, eating simultaneously – while adults can manage 1.7 (men even less).

Some of the broader implications are:

- Western populations are more affluent but with less time to enjoy it.

- Older people are wealthier, with time, and want to travel the world.

- Kids grow up fast, quickly replacing baby toys with designer fashion.

- Rise of online communities, buying groups and political lobbies.

- Concerns about health and obesity, the falling standards in sports.

- Many of us have everything we need, yet we still want more.

These structural and behavioural changes fundamentally reshape markets, making profitable ones unprofitable, requiring new ways to approach existing ones, and opening up completely new spaces to compete. Indeed, it is useful to draw an illustrative map of your extended 'market space', your existing and adjacent markets, adjacent in terms of both business capabilities and customer applications.

Within this extended space you can then plot where the best opportunities are likely to be, now and in the future. And where the competition is now, and likely to be. You can then begin to identify:

Hot Spots	**Cool Places**	**White Spaces**	**Black Holes**
where the new competition is	where latest trends emerge	where nobody has ventured	where old brands die

- *Hot Spots*, where demand converges and all brands seek to play, e.g. multimedia phones, the integrated computer and TV.

- *Cool Places*, where lead users go in search of newness and difference, creating niches or the next big thing, e.g. Korean food, Smart cars.

- *White Spaces*, where new opportunities emerge, often through convergence. They have not yet been exploited, such as iTV retailing, or cashless wallets.

- *Black Holes*, where traditional markets dry up, and the lead players are blindsided and marginalized, e.g. the music industry, the car manufacturers.

While this might sound impractical, far from the conventions of your own markets today, it actually describes the morphology of every market today. From sheep farming to corner shops, from industrial manufacturing to food restaurants, markets are more connected than ever, and influenced by outside change.

Market mapping is a strategic tool that helps you make sense of your changing marketplace, to spot the challenges and opportunities first.

The rapid convergence of mobile phones and cameras is just one example where not only should the camera-less phone manufacturer be worried, but the camera manufacturers should be too. Many people upgrade their handsets every year; therefore, adoption, and obsolescence, can be incredibly rapid.

There is no one authoritative map for any market, as there is no certainty as to how it will evolve. Market maps are therefore predictions, your own view of your markets and their future. Others will have different starting points, and different perspectives. Indeed, your future competitive advantage is likely to come partly from how well you can draw the market map relative to others.

Your market map might be based on any combination of attributes – such as capabilities versus applications, products versus location of use and products versus type of customer. The levels of change will depend on the market and other factors too.

A more sophisticated approach to market mapping might therefore also embrace techniques such as Market Radar, which considers the likely evolution of markets in terms of economic, competitive, customer, technological, social and political change – each mapping what is certain, likely and possible.

Scenario development can also be used to combine different possibilities into future market scenarios, then evaluating the upsides and downsides of each, and estimating the overall likelihood. If many scenarios predict certain aspects more frequently, then its likelihood will increase.

The output, intuitive or sophisticated, is a better understanding of your 'real' market today, and the challenges and opportunities that may well not be visible from a traditional perspective. The best opportunities should then be evaluated in terms of risk and reward, as described in the next chapter.

As an example, consider a local convenience store. On one axis we might plot the range of goods the store sells; on the other we plot the reason why a customer might use the shop.

Starting at the origin, the store currently sells food and drink. However, the store could easily sell flowers and newspapers, or even books and music, or perhaps even local or utility services. Beyond top-up shopping, the customer might shop for gifts, the weekly family shop, large occasional items, or seek advice on new services.

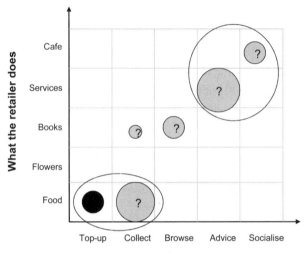

What customers do

On the resulting grid we can then plot where there might be significant demand, who the customers might be, the competitors, and innovatively how we might deliver such a proposition.

Inspiration 1.2 APPLE

Apple has long been famed for its 'think different' mindset. Founded in 1979, in the pioneering days of the personal computer, the Macintosh was the great rebel of the industry, loved by the highly demanding graphic designers who harnessed its leading-edge features, but a rebel in refusing to bow to the growing power of Microsoft Windows.

Sometimes in those early pioneering days of the technology revolution, they were first to admit that they missed the mark, thinking as product inventors rather than market innovators. The Mac was technically advanced, but resolutely niche.

Years later, Apple was back in the forefront with that iMac, proving that PCs don't have to be grey and boring, seeking to bring exceptional design both aesthetically and functionally to the user's operation. The iMac was a great hit – now compatible with Windows – yet it was still for the knowing few rather than the profitable many.

Apple is one of the leading brands profiled by Kevin Roberts in *Lovemarks*. On the book's related website, people are encouraged to rank and talk about their own 'lovemarks'. Apple, not surprisingly, figures highly on the site, with many contributions like the following:

> 'An Apple computer is the first thing I switch on every morning and the last thing to be turned off every night. Apple's computers enhance my life, and make what I do possible in a way similar products by other makers never do. Apple's story, their myth, their mystery is unassailable. I never cease to be fascinated.'

After the candy-coloured range of iMacs came the revolutionary iPod.

Recognition that the new millennium lives by new rules.

Digital music formats were struggling to move beyond the CD and the retailer. Napster was the rogue, illegal download website. Everyone could see a market flex but were uncertain where the future would go. Should record companies abandon physical formats? Should artists abandon record companies? Would network providers or phone companies seize the space?

Apple saw the opportunity and quickly made the iPod a cultural phenomenon. The complementary iTunes download site quickly became the global leader in downloadable music, selling more than 70 million songs in its first year, and for the first time a serious threat to the old physical world.

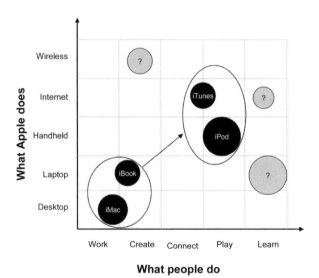

What people do

Apple's shift can be simply illustrated by a market map, showing the rapid evolution of technology – from the wired desktop to the wireless handheld, while the consumers' tolerance for such devices now went well beyond work. Apple is constantly disrupting the conventions of the market, and expectations of the customer. For example, the low-price, limited functionality iPod Shuffle was a shrewd move to ward off any low-end imitators of its iPod.

The next evolutions are probably still in the head of Steve Jobs; however, by extension of the axes, or consideration of other dimensions, we can see the possibilities.

Application 1.1 MARKET MAPPING

How do you make sense of complex markets, where borders have blurred and it is no longer clear which market you are actually in? Where are the hotspots or cool places for brand extensions? Where are the black holes?

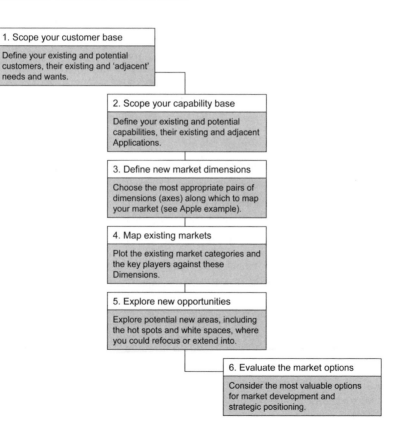

1. Scope your customer base

Define your existing and potential customers, their existing and 'adjacent' needs and wants.

2. Scope your capability base

Define your existing and potential capabilities, their existing and adjacent Applications.

3. Define new market dimensions

Choose the most appropriate pairs of dimensions (axes) along which to map your market (see Apple example).

4. Map existing markets

Plot the existing market categories and the key players against these Dimensions.

5. Explore new opportunities

Explore potential new areas, including the hot spots and white spaces, where you could refocus or extend into.

6. Evaluate the market options

Consider the most valuable options for market development and strategic positioning.

Concept 1.2 MARKET SPEED

Jack Welch argues, 'When the rate of change inside the business is exceeded by the rate of change outside the company, the end is near.'

Today's markets can evolve incredibly quickly. New ideas and structures, standards and expectations can spread in a way that was previously reserved for fads and fashions. Speed is driven by the connectivity of people through technology, the rise of non-locational communities and the constant desire of consumers to have the latest, best, coolest, smallest, fastest devices.

Whether it is the latest multi-disciplinary mobile phone, or a new range of Puma shoes, or the latest interactive game, as soon as it enters one market, it enters all markets. In the past, movies were shown in North America up to 6 months before Europe. Within weeks of release in LA, it will now be bootlegged in the shops of Bangkok or available online to people anywhere.

Similarly with products; the rapid and repetitive disruption of the data storage market shows how large floppy disks were displaced by smaller disks, and they by CD-ROMs and they by USB devices. The benefits of each new device were huge – scaling up storage capacity many times, shrinking in size, cheaper and more convenient. Once the new device hits the market, everybody wants it everywhere. And one click of amazon.com can deliver it within days.

The effect of networks, the viral impact of communication across them, the contagiousness of new ideas. Hotmail, launched by Microsoft as a free online e-mail service, went from launch to leadership within days. Without any traditional marketing to boot. The bottom of every e-mail sent by a Hotmail account holder contains an invitation to the receiver to set up their own free account. Yes, they needed early adopters to start the ball rolling but, after a few days, the snowball was enormous – 100 million people in the case of Hotmail.

The same effect can be seen in every other market too. Speed is also perpetuated by the expectation of newness and intolerance of oldness. It is spurred on by intense competition and the ability to deliver new products to market faster than ever before. Car manufacturers launch models every year, and sometimes new editions every quarter, while in the days of Henry Ford, the cycle times were more like decades.

Clothing retailers will launch new ranges at least once every season; although, now that is the convention, to be fashionable requires a new range every few weeks. Visit a Zara clothing store one week and it is unlikely to be stocking the same clothes when you return a few weeks later. Make your mind up now or it will be too late. And, indeed, to get there before anybody else, Zara's designers don't wait to see what's the latest fashion on the catwalks; they go straight to the yarn mills of Milan to find out what's emerging. You can now buy the high street imitations on the same day that the new designer range is modelled.

Cycle times are much faster and shorter, more unpredictable yet more powerful. We live in a constantly evolving state of newness. When is the best time to buy a new laptop? Never. Because whenever you buy it, it will inevitably be displaced by something better in a few months, and your own model, while completely adequate, will have its price slashed because enough people still want the latest thing. At the same time, this creates a whole secondary market for remainder items – and the rise of stores like TK Maxx in the clothing market, selling massively reduced designer clothes only a few months 'out of date', and indeed challenging the full-price unbranded items of mass market chains.

Speed can often be witnessed in the form of 'vortices' within markets, a little like highs and lows that drive our weather systems. The difference is that these vortices are typically man-made, or through the competitive and customer responses to deliberate actions. Each vortex is the result of significant change and creates a significant impact on its surroundings. As a new idea develops, the vortex builds momentum, and its increasing centrifugal force draws nearby competitors and adjacent markets into its reach.

The market-driving business, seeking to define its markets in its own vision and advantage, will often need to create such vortices, but it also recognizes the wider consequences of its own actions. In the early stages it will be more isolated, creating new opportunities fairly remotely from what else is going on. However, it then starts to affect others as competitors respond, and the business needs to step up to leading the 'game change' rather than just defining it. Ultimately new market conditions start to form, and the business must actively shape these new structures as it normalizes.

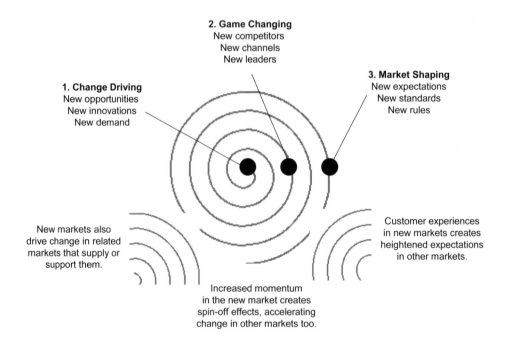

2. Game Changing
New competitors
New channels
New leaders

3. Market Shaping
New expectations
New standards
New rules

1. Change Driving
New opportunities
New innovations
New demand

New markets also
drive change in related
markets that supply or
support them.

Customer experiences
in new markets creates
heightened expectations
in other markets.

Increased momentum
in the new market creates
spin-off effects, accelerating
change in other markets too.

So how do you keep pace with the rapid pace of markets? How can you get ahead of the curve rather than behind it?

Like the athlete who is most likely to win the gold medal, the strong company will learn to control the pace, choosing when to set it, when to slow it, when to just go with it. The key to this is to align the rhythm of the business to the pace of the market. Every business already has a rhythm, usually driven by its planning cycle internally – typically an annual event, with a rolling 3- to 5-year horizon. Product development cycles are driven internally by the frequency of market research, and the complexity of product development and market entry processes. Externally, the pace might be driven by industry events – the IATA conference for airline schedules, the major fashion shows in clothing design, or the GSM World Congress in mobile phones.

Organizations can break these natural rhythms and create new ones: planning cycles once a quarter rather than annually, accelerated product development processes can radically reduce time to market, and more modular business design can enable business structures themselves to rapidly morph to exploit new capabilities and market opportunities.

However, like the athlete who is most likely to win the gold medal, the most successful companies can set the pace to their own advantage – be it fast or slower, they can exert influence that conditions how others behave. Armani can influence fashion show organizers and Nokia can influence whole supply chains, regulators are strongly influenced by leaders who drive economies, and retailers are reluctant to go without P&G or Unilever products on their shelves.

Indeed, rather than just synchronizing your business to the market, a leader might seek to create a rhythm slightly faster than the market, so that they lead rather than lag – they are the innovators rather than imitators. This might be achieved by working to a 10-week cycle rather than a 12-week cycle in fashion, by being faster to spot trends like Puma, or by having the earliest adopters hooked into your brand like Apple. And if they are effective in executing their market entries, they can define coolness and charge a premium for it, before the mass market arrives.

Inspiration 1.3 STARBUCKS

Starbuck, a character from the novel *Moby Dick*, first came ashore in 1971, having until that time been the name of a fishing boat in Seattle harbour. Instead it became a coffee house in Pike Place Market.

A decade later Howard Schultz arrived as director of marketing, moving the focus away from coffee grinding to Italian-style espresso bars, billed as the 'premier purveyor of the finest coffee in the world'. A trip to Milan in 1983 convinced Schultz that coffee bars had significant potential outside Italy, prompting him to set up his own 'Il Giornale' cafes in 1985, which then acquired the original Starbucks business and adopted its name two years later.

The roll-out of Starbucks Coffee then started. Indeed, the speed at which coffee has culturally evolved from a cheap instant drink to a premium coffee shop culture is phenomenal. Styled as 'the third place', Starbucks claims that 'there's home, and work, and then there's Starbucks'. The environment, with its sofas and music, encourages people to linger as long as they want.

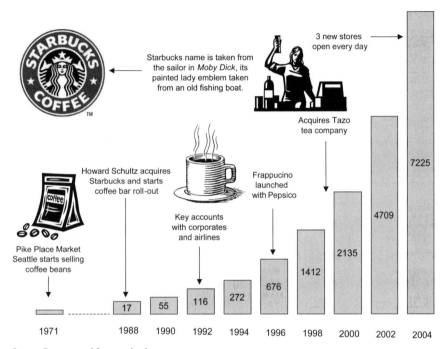

Starbucks name is taken from the sailor in *Moby Dick*, its painted lady emblem taken from an old fishing boat.

3 new stores open every day

Acquires Tazo tea company

Howard Schultz acquires Starbucks and starts coffee bar roll-out

Frappucino launched with Pepsico

Key accounts with corporates and airlines

Pike Place Market Seattle starts selling coffee beans

1971	1988	1990	1992	1994	1996	1998	2000	2002	2004
	17	55	116	272	676	1412	2135	4709	7225

Source: Data sourced from starbucks.com

Schultz recognized that corporate deals, with airlines, retailers, and corporations to offer Starbucks within their own facilities, were a fast track to growth. Indeed, the coffee bars were fuelling such a strong aspirational desire among consumers that having Starbucks as part of their airline, retail or work experience immediately offered added value and enhanced prestige.

Coffee branding was important too. The 'Christmas Blend' coffee, together with its festive paper cups, was a hit from year one. In 1994 'Frappuccino' became a best selling ice-cold blend of coffee and cream, and was quickly bottled and sold by many other retailers too.

Schultz explains that there is no hidden secret to his success:

> 'We have no patent on anything we do and anything we do can be copied by anyone
> else ... but you can't copy the heart and soul of a business. That's created by people.
> People who know what they are doing, why they are creating a special experience for
> every customer, and how to make it their personal third place.'

Every employee who works more than 20 hours per week, which is most, is given share options in the business, and so they feel even more part of its mission and share in its success. Indeed, Starbucks has created many millionaires out of its employees along its path to growth.

Customers have evolved too as Starbucks has matured. There is now a diverse mix of young and older customers, from all backgrounds, who have been attracted by the coffee and the place. Indeed, the ability to customize your coffee is important too. Most customers will have their favourite – whether it be a 'double grande skinny latte' or a 'vanilla tall no-fun cappuccino', their language and preferences have evolved too.

Schultz visits his own and his competitors' stores around the world. In his own stores, he typically drinks five coffees a day – different varieties at different times. However, he never drinks his competitors' coffee. 'I know what it's going to taste like,' he says rather dismissively.

Of course, Starbucks is not without its detractors, most famously Naomi Klein in her book *No Logo*, which, while appreciating many of the positive aspects of marketing and increasingly global brands, also cautioned against their potential for cultural arrogance and trading dominance. Indeed, Starbucks has been careful to embrace Fair Trade coffees, and ensure that it acts responsibility both locally and globally, encouraging its entire staff, for example, to get involved in local charitable projects.

Starbucks defines its purpose as 'to provide an uplifting experience that enriches people's daily lives'. It seeks to achieve this by establishing Starbucks as 'the premier purveyor of the finest coffee in the world, while maintaining our uncompromising principles as we grow'.

Application 1.2 MARKET VORTEX

How can you achieve leadership in rapidly changing markets? How can you be on the leading rather than lagging edge of the waves of change in your market? How can you drive the change vortex in your vision, rather than be left in the wake of others?

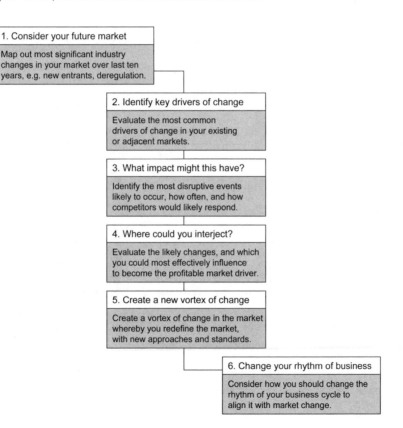

1. Consider your future market

Map out most significant industry changes in your market over last ten years, e.g. new entrants, deregulation.

2. Identify key drivers of change

Evaluate the most common drivers of change in your existing or adjacent markets.

3. What impact might this have?

Identify the most disruptive events likely to occur, how often, and how competitors would likely respond.

4. Where could you interject?

Evaluate the likely changes, and which you could most effectively influence to become the profitable market driver.

5. Create a new vortex of change

Create a vortex of change in the market whereby you redefine the market, with new approaches and standards.

6. Change your rhythm of business

Consider how you should change the rhythm of your business cycle to align it with market change.

Concept 1.3 MARKET POWER

New markets need new marketing, not just to manage the complexity, or to shape it before somebody else does, but to recognize that the fundamental dynamics of customer transactions have changed too.

Customers now call the shots. We have moved from markets of surplus demand to those of surplus supply. There is far more stuff around than customers need. And they have everything they want. So how do you sell more to them?

From powerful suppliers ...

Companies drive markets of surplus demand

Mass market of standardized products and advertising

Consumers call the shots in markets of surplus supply

Individual buyer experiences, customized and interactive

... to powerful consumers

Creative intelligence is required to develop solutions that do more for customers than their product functionality, to go beyond customers' finite needs.

In our busy lives we have little time to indulge, or to connect with communities in traditional ways. Space is limited as we keep buying more, and support is expected as our tolerance levels fall. Brands must do much more to educate, to entertain, and to inspire. Education is infinite, you can never have enough entertainment, and art has no bounds.

How can marketers develop propositions, interactions and solutions that enhance people's lives in these ways? Either as a means to help differentiate us from the competition, or to add value and thereby charge more? Such factors – time, space, education – could also become currencies, more important than money, in which we do business.

Doing business on customer terms means we must engage them differently too.

Customers are hard to reach, its difficult to get their attention, they have high expectations, and are even harder to retain. We must go to them, rather than they come to us. They are not customers of ours. They are our buyers, belonging to themselves. We need to do business how, where and when they want.

Campaigns are dead.

The idea that we can sell people a new car when it fits into the marketing department's campaign schedule doesn't work. Campaigns inevitably have a mass market, inside-out feel to them, which doesn't work in a diverse and devolved world. New forms of communication, part initiated by customers, while still retaining brand awareness, are needed.

Channels must invert.

Similarly, distribution channels were set up as extensions of the supplier, not the customer – travel agents were agents of the airline, rather than the customer. Suppliers used to define the prices; customers were required to pay. The agent was incentivized to sell on their behalf. Five minutes on eBay will show you that pricing doesn't work like that any more.

It is unlikely that many of these problems can be solved by one supplier alone, indeed few buyers know exactly what they want, or where to get it from. However, when customers are demanding, this is an opportunity to go and help. The brands that customers know best and trust most to resolve their uncertainty, who can source whatever is required and knowledge-ably customize it to the buyer, in the most convenient way, will succeed in future.

Power has fundamentally shifted from supplier to customer.

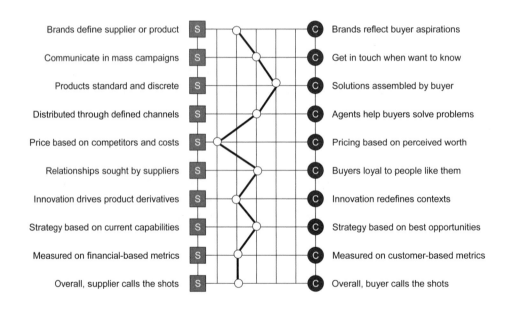

Brands define supplier or product	Brands reflect buyer aspirations
Communicate in mass campaigns	Get in touch when want to know
Products standard and discrete	Solutions assembled by buyer
Distributed through defined channels	Agents help buyers solve problems
Price based on competitors and costs	Pricing based on perceived worth
Relationships sought by suppliers	Buyers loyal to people like them
Innovation drives product derivatives	Innovation redefines contexts
Strategy based on current capabilities	Strategy based on best opportunities
Measured on financial-based metrics	Measured on customer-based metrics
Overall, supplier calls the shots	Overall, buyer calls the shots

Inspiration 1.4 eBAY

Founded in 1995, eBay has styled itself as 'the world's online marketplace … for the sale of goods and services by a passionate community of individuals and businesses'. It now facilitates transactions worth over $35 billion, as 135 million registered members buy and sell goods worth over $1000 every second.

It all started when the idealistic French-Iranian computer programmer Pierre Omidyar built a website from his Silicon Valley bedroom and auctioned off his broken laser pen for $14.

He conceived what was initially called AuctionWeb as 'a place where people can come together' – an online exchange that would never actually handle the goods sold but enable buyers and sellers to determine a fair market price. He enlisted the help of the highly experienced marketer Meg Whitman, who as CEO brought together a management team with experience from leading brands, from Pepsi to Disney.

While it is perhaps best known for its individual users who auction their junk and collectables, it soon had many business users too. From IBM to sole traders, selling cars, computers, white goods and services, they found that they could usually achieve better margins than they would when reaching a more limited market, with the physical burdens of distribution and premises, stock and discounting.

Browsing and bidding on auctions is free, but sellers are charged transaction fees for the right to sell their goods. There is a non-refundable insertion fee based on the opening bid on the item and, when the auction is complete, a completion fee that generally ranges from 1.25% to 5% of the final price. There are also additional fees if sellers want to highlight their items in various ways. Once the auction is finished, completing the transaction is left up to the seller and buyer, while eBay collects its fee.

PayPal enables any individual or business with an e-mail address to securely, easily and quickly send and receive payments online. This builds on the existing financial infrastructure of banks and credits cards, and uses the world's most advanced fraud protection systems. It is available in 45 countries and 5 currencies.

Indeed, PayPal, which was acquired by eBay in 2002, has become a leader itself, the world's number one online payment system, with over 20 million registered accounts worldwide, and is now used by many more retailers, online and offline.

To engage buyers and sellers, eBay must be more than a trading point. The community spirit is strong too, with buyers and sellers often helping each other find what they want, and reach a fair price. Through the Community Hub, members meet through participation in discussion boards, chat rooms, online workshops, user groups and the Answer Center. This community feel creates trust and more frequent visits, wraps people into the eBay world, as intimately as in previous decades they would have been loyal to their local corner shop.

eBay is one of the few Internet 'pure plays' to consistently make a profit. Indeed, it has beaten off the challenge of the likes of Amazon and Yahoo! which have tried to imitate the eBay model as part of their propositions but with little success.

Application 1.3 POWER PROFILE

How do we address the changing balance of power in our markets? How do we meet the ever-higher expectations of customers, and shareholders? How do we continue to deliver today while also having time, space and resources to create tomorrow?

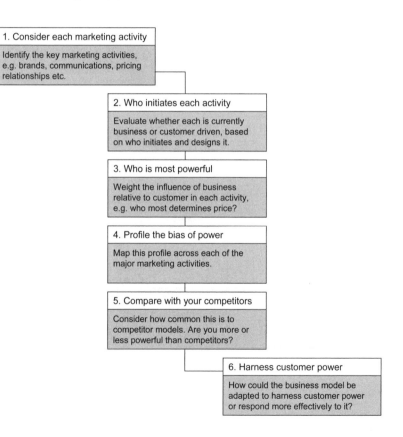

1. Consider each marketing activity

Identify the key marketing activities, e.g. brands, communications, pricing relationships etc.

2. Who initiates each activity

Evaluate whether each is currently business or customer driven, based on who initiates and designs it.

3. Who is most powerful

Weight the influence of business relative to customer in each activity, e.g. who most determines price?

4. Profile the bias of power

Map this profile across each of the major marketing activities.

5. Compare with your competitors

Consider how common this is to competitor models. Are you more or less powerful than competitors?

6. Harness customer power

How could the business model be adapted to harness customer power or respond more effectively to it?

Application 1.4 REVERSE MARKETING

How do you rethink your marketing, and for that matter the whole way you do business, to respond to the rise in customer power? What does it really mean to do business where, how and when they want? How will the conventional processes for communicating, distributing, pricing and selling change? What are the implications for strategy, brands, innovation and relationships?

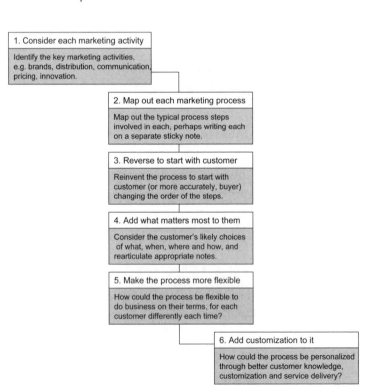

Creating tomorrow while delivering today

'The rise of an information age doesn't mean we stop producing or selling. We still need products and services. But it does mean that the business and marketing strategies that made sellers' brands powerful yesterday won't necessarily keep them tomorrow. If it's not a win-win for both sides, one side or the other will see no reason to pursue the relationship.'

Alan Mitchell

'The web enables total transparency. People with access to relevant information are beginning to challenge any type of authority. The stupid, loyal and humble customer, employee, patient or citizen is dead.'

Kjell Nordström and Jonas Ridderstråle

Markets increasingly drive the business, yet marketers are not in the driving seat. Marketing is still too often seen as a peripheral function, a specialist community, a drain on expenditure, a support to the sales team.

Marketing is much more than this: a process for the whole business, although it may require some specialist practitioners too. It drives demand in the short and long term. It fuels profits, today and tomorrow. It creates the future and delivers today, driving sales and delivery of the customer experiences, while also developing the new markets and products, and builds the brands and relationships to ensure success in them. It also typically delivers a better return on investment than any other part of business.

Delivering today	Creating tomorrow
Short-term. Pressure is on to deliver quarterly results, focusing on sales promotions to drive revenues.	**Long-term.** Pressure is on to drive future results, through strategy and innovation, strong brands and relationships.
Profit. Companies have little idea which markets, products and customers are the most profitable, now or in future.	**Value.** Economic value is the sum of future profits, rather than today's, driven by profitable growth and risk.
Inside out. Long-term value creation is what matters most to investors, and the key measure of business performance.	**Outside in.** Creating more value for the best customers is the only sustainable route to long-term shareholder value.

It is time for marketers to move from the fringes to the centre of decision-making, harnessing the momentum of market change, and the authority of the customer, to shape strategies and business priorities from the outside in, rather than inside out.

Business has been led for too long from the inside out. Accountants and operational managers have sought to improve what has always been done, rather than respond to and exploit the best opportunities in the market. The danger, of course, with incrementalism is that it can lead to irrelevance, rather than addressing the real opportunities of markets.

However, marketers must change if they want to take centre stage, and indeed if they want to survive.

The biggest opportunities in business today lie not in improving the efficiency of what you have already done, but by embracing change in the outside world. This is primarily a marketing challenge.

Businesses need marketers now more than ever.

Marketers must form the response to this change: to see the new game either being played or emerging, break out of the conventions that were designed for a previous century, exceed expectations on the high street and stock markets, and create exceptional value for customers and for shareholders, and in new ways.

Today the expectations are incredibly high on all sides:

- Customers want more than a product or service. They used to tolerate stock-outs and be happy to come back again next week, or delivery times in weeks and months, and accept that in a mainstream store there would be no negotiation, and they would expect to pay the full price. Their experiences of Amazon to Wal-Mart have changed that. They now expect the best quality products, confidence that their expectations will always be met, personalized solutions to meet their wider needs, same-day delivery, and lowest prices.

- Employees want more than a job that pays a salary. They used to tolerate menial tasks, in a sterile environment, where their role would not change over time, and as long as they got paid they did not care about the wider organization or its customers and shareholders. They now expect a more fulfilling role, a better environment and benefits beyond payment, they expect to learn and progress, care passionately about their customers; they want to influence their organization, and be proud of it.

- Shareholders want more than a return on investment. They used to tolerate ups and downs in share prices, lack of short-term profits in order to invest in future, no dividend payments some years, annual updates at the AGM. Their experiences of dotcoms and hedge funds have changed that. They expect regular and transparent information, more influence and power, constant growth in quarterly profits, regular dividends and the best returns across sector, not just among peers.

Stakeholders, more broadly, have gone from being of minor importance, through important from the perspective of compliance, to being partners in creating superior value for shareholders. This might include:

- Access to socially responsible investor capital.

- Attracting and retaining the best talent.

- Building brand loyalty and reputation with customers.

- Accessing strategic resources and capabilities through partners.

- Improved employee relations and conflict resolution with unions.

- Increased efficiency and collaboration across the value chain.

- Greater influence, favourability and flexibility with regulators.

- Mutual support and accommodation in local communities.

Similarly, a reliance on processes and systems based on facts and analysis is useful in that they add rigour and discipline, but they are not the source of new value creation.

Intelligent, logical thinking does not deliver the balanced, holistic approach that today's organizations require. Knowledge management does not usually drive creativity. CRM is rarely the route to customer intimacy or loyalty. Six Sigma and TQM do not secure innovative designs. Performance incentives do not create more fulfilling jobs. Quarterly performance targets do not secure successful futures. Maximizing shareholder value does not necessarily deliver a sustainable or responsible business.

Business today requires a more enlightened approach, a more balanced and holistic approach, one that is both creative and analytical, embraces soft and hard, customer and finance, short and long term. These are delivered through broader-thinking people who can see business through each of these lenses and have the personal attributes and awareness to take this new approach.

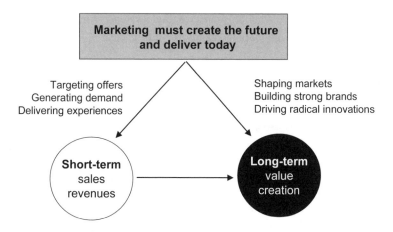

Marketers, and business in general, must learn to embrace what can often seem like contradictory objectives and expectations – to maximize sales in the short term while also investing for the long term. From a financial perspective this means maximizing revenues and profits today, but also tomorrow, the balance of which is captured by considering the economic value of actions, and thereby embracing the short and long term. Most fundamentally, marketers must bring the outside-in perspective to balance, and often lead the inside-out aspects of business.

marketing
genius

No company reflects the need to live and work in 'double time' more than Microsoft. The business, marketers and developers are constantly focused on delivering today while also creating tomorrow. Once a current version of a product is released (with all its qualities and sometimes some failings) it is up to marketers to maximize the scale of its take-up, selling as many licences as possible. However, once the product is released, the developers are immediately on to the next version, or something much more radical for the future.

> 'At Microsoft we work to help people and business throughout the world realize their full potential. This is our mission. Everything we do reflects this mission and the values that make it possible.

> At Microsoft we are motivated and inspired every day by how our customers use our software to find creative solutions to business problems, develop breakthrough ideas, and stay connected to what's most important to them.

> Just as we constantly update and improve our products, we want to continually evolve our company to be in the best position to accelerate new technologies as they emerge and to better serve our customers.'

This is then translated into value statements and straplines, such as 'Your Potential. Our Passion', consistent with the core purpose but relevant to each audience.

For businesses:

> **'We see business without borders.** You should have the ability to do business with anyone, anywhere. When business speaks a global language, the barriers disappear, and we believe technology can help. It inspires us to create software that brings companies closer to their customers and partners, regardless of language or location.'

For educators:

'We see history's great minds dropping in wherever they're needed. Exposure to great teachers, great books, and great thinking, is the most essential requirement for learning, no matter where the student or the classroom. When the world of learning opens to them, children can grow in any direction. It inspires us to create software that helps them reach their potential.'

For parents:

'We see the king of the skies. Children dream of flight, to soar. These dreams become their potential. And with the right tools and a little help, they'll make them more than their passion; they'll make them their life. This is just one of the infinite possibilities that inspires us to create software that helps you reach your potential.'

Microsoft was famously founded in Albuquerque, New Mexico, in 1975 by Bill Gates and Paul Allen. Today Microsoft sells a huge range of software products, many developed internally, and others rebranded following acquisition.

The business is organized into seven core units, each with its own financial reporting to delegate responsibility and more closely track the performance of each unit, to allay regulator fears of cross-subsidies, and probably to make survival easier if the courts ever did demand a break-up of the monolith. The business units, according to its website, are:

- *Windows Client* (managing the Windows client, server, and embedded operating systems).

- *Information Worker* (managing the office software products).

- *Microsoft Business Solutions* (managing the business services and process applications).

- *Server and Tools* (managing developer tools and integrated server software).

- *Mobile and Embedded Devices* (managing palmtop and phone devices).

- *MSN* (managing web-based services).

- *Home and Entertainment* (managing consumer hardware and software).

Microsoft openly describes its culture as 'developer-centric', even though its businesses seek to align themselves to markets rather than technologies, encouraging development against customer need rather than technical possibility.

A great deal of time and money is spent each year on recruiting the very best university-trained software developers and on keeping them in the company. Key decision-makers at every level are either developers or former developers. Indeed, the software developers at Microsoft are the 'stars' of the company in the same way that sales staff at IBM are considered the top dogs. This culture is reflected in its recruitment process which is famed for its off-the-wall questions such as 'Why is a manhole cover round?'

At a more strategic level, Microsoft is working to replicate its success on the desktop in new markets such as media players, server software, handheld devices, car navigation, web services, video games and, more recently, search engines, with varying degrees of success. Remembering Gates's early vision of 'to be in every home and office', it is now trying to establish PCs running Windows XP Media Center Edition as home entertainment hubs.

The business model is also under review; for example, moving to more of a subscription model for licensed software, rather than relying on users to buy upgrade packages every few years.

Amidst concerns from investors that it will no longer be able to sustain the historical growth rates, Microsoft announced in July 2004 its intention to implement a $30 billion stock repurchase plan over the next 4 years. It also announced a special one-time dividend in December 2004 that would pay Microsoft stockholders $32 billion, by far the largest payout by any company in history.

As customers, we sometimes grumble about being forced to pay high prices for ever-changing versions of products that frequently go wrong. And, of course, seeing the huge returns to shareholders probably frustrates some people even more. The reality though is that Microsoft has shaped its market in its own vision, while as customers we keep buying the products, and rely on them in our working lives.

Microsoft has its critics, but it is also a great marketing success.

marketing
genius

Concept 2.1 VALUE CREATION

Many organizations are confused about why they exist, and indeed there are a wide variety of reasons for organizations to exist. At the simplest level it comes down to stakeholders. These are the different groups of people who have by definition 'a stake' in the business – in some way they contribute value to the business, in the expectation that they will get a return, a 'value exchange' if you like. They include employees, customers, suppliers, partners, shareholders, governments and society.

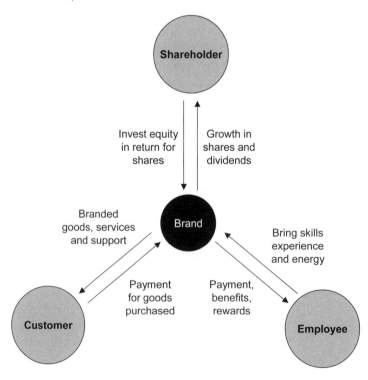

A public-listed company is owned by its shareholders, those who invest capital in the business for a financial return. Yet even in these companies, where the primary measure of success is the return on these investments, the business still exists for a higher purpose and, indeed, that is what engages employees to come to work each day, customers to grow loyal, partners to want to collaborate. The business can only succeed in delivering – and, most importantly, sustaining – a return to shareholders if it creates a model where each other stakeholder group can succeed too.

The pursuit of long-term 'shareholder value' can only be achieved by also creating value for customers, for employees and others in a virtuous circle of investments and returns. Imagine a pie chart cut by the value created for each stakeholder. There are two ways in which share-holders can gain more:

- 'Value greed' – shareholders get more value at the expense of others, who will eventually leave or defect if they feel they don't get sufficient back for what they give.

- 'Value growth' – shareholders get more, and so do all others stakeholders in similar pro-portions as before; value is created rather than redistributed.

We term this total value the 'economic value' of the business, and it is reasonable that every type of business should seek to maximize its economic value as a primary goal.

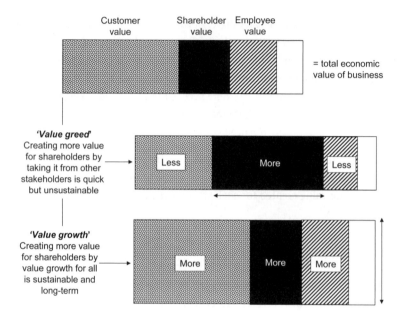

Long-term shareholder value creation should be the primary measure of success of a publicly listed company as that is why it legally exists, while recognizing that it cannot be achieved without the other stakeholders. Short-term shareholder 'greed', or indeed that of senior executives if their remuneration is only linked to short-term performance, is not sustainable (as we saw with the behaviours that it led to at WorldCom and Enron).

Sustained value creation is only achievable through growth, not greed, making a bigger cake rather than just recutting it.

Other types of organization have a different order of priorities. A charity typically exists to support the public, or at least a large section of it, and championing a particular cause, be it educational or health, religious or environmental. This type of organization still has many stakeholders, and indeed it should be commercially managed, but rather than offering a direct return to those who donate to it, it needs to ensure that the maximum possible funds can be delivered to the society it champions.

There are many other types of organization within this spectrum too.

Indeed, even the most financially oriented companies need a 'cause' beyond money. Without a sense of more meaningful purpose the company would lack the direction, difference or engagement to achieve its goals. Mission statements that 'seek to maximize shareholder value' will fail. Mission statements that seek to maximize shareholder value 'by creating the best x', or 'helping people to do y', have the makings of a clear strategy, a strong brand and a common objective which can bring people together and endure over time.

Recognizing that a business is a value exchange – a dynamic system of many different stakeholders, each giving and seeking value, where the objective is to increase value for all – opens up many doors previously closed to the blinkered financial orientation.

Inspiration 2.2 TOYOTA

Toyota is Japan's leading carmaker, with a portfolio of brands in order to reach different markets. It has a small-sized car division, selling under the Daihatsu brand, as well as a heavy vehicle division, selling under the Hino brand.

Meanwhile, the Lexus brand is used for luxury cars, the name derived from 'luxury' and 'elegance'. Lexus dealers are known to have quality customer service, creating a customer-intimate culture separate from the more operational-excellence focus of the main group.

In numbers, the business employs over 250,000 people, selling around 7 billion cars every year in 150 countries. While behind the big three – GM, Ford and DaimlerChrysler – in volume, its market capitalization is bigger than all three of theirs combined, reminding us that size and market share are not always the route to success for shareholders.

Toyota started life in 1937 as a spin-off from Toyoda Automatic Loom Works, one of the world's leading manufacturers of weaving machinery and headed by Japan's most revered inventor, Sakichi Toyoda, whose son Kiichiro was given the challenge of creating the successful company that we see today.

Key to Toyota's success is its relationships with employees and customers. Lacking the scale and capital resources of the others, Toyota looked inside to find its advantage – focusing on improving value for customers through deeper insights, continuous improvement and more creative thinking made possible by highly engaged employees.

> 'I have learned, based on my experience, that everything is dominated by the market. So whenever we are struck by obstacles or difficulties, I always say to myself: "Listen to the market, listen to the voice of the customer". That's the fundamental essence of marketing. Always, we have to come back to the market, back to the customer. That is the Toyota way.'

> Yoshio Ishiazaka, Executive Vice-President Toyota Motor Corporation

Its 'lean thinking' approach is less about operational efficiency and more about having a clear and unflinching philosophy to serve and add value to customers. This focuses on customer rather than shareholder value as the immediate objective, working through every aspect of the business to focus ruthlessly only on what adds value to customers, and eliminating anything that doesn't. This creates more flow in the organization and encourages more thoughtful problem solving, as well as improving the customer experience and business performance.

To achieve this, it also recognizes that people need more time, often unstructured, in order to solve real problems, think more innovatively and build new collaborations. 'HumanSigma' is part of the approach, measuring and managing the human difference in a company's performance.

Application 2.1 CREATING VALUE

What is the economic value of your business? How do you convert the future potential of your business into financial terms? How in principle should you distribute this value over time? How do you manage to ensure that you achieve this potential?

1. Consider your future business

Consider the drivers of your future profitability – including growth trends, potential margins and risk/uncertainty.

2. Project future profits

Project the most likely profits in each of the next years, based on trends and potential scenarios.

3. Calculate their value

Sum these profits, discounting them relative to the increasing level of uncertainty, and add a perpetuity.

4. Allocate value

Consider how you would allocate this total value between your stakeholders, e.g. customers, shareholders over time.

5. Prioritize activities

Build this into your business strategy and financial plan, and use it to help prioritize resources and investments.

6. Manage for value creation

Manage the business over time for value creation, focusing on economic profit and best long-term opportunities.

Concept 2.2 CUSTOMERS AND SHAREHOLDERS

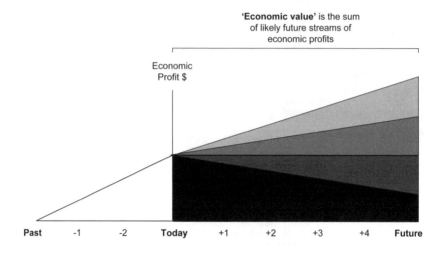

'**Economic value**' is the sum
of likely future streams of
economic profits

Economic
Profit $

| Past | -1 | -2 | Today | +1 | +2 | +3 | +4 | Future |

If we accept that the only real measure of business success is the long-term return to share-holders, then 'value' is what matters. Value is the sum of likely future profits. Revenues and profits are not enough; indeed, selling more can destroy more value than it creates if the result does not exceed the minimum expectations of investors. The reality of the commercial world is that a business exists to create value for its shareholders.

Economic value is about getting more out than you put in. If shareholders invest their money in a business then they seek a return on that investment. In fact, they seek a return that is greater than they could get by alternatively putting their money in their bank's best savings account or low risk investment plan.

The money shareholders put into a business – we call it 'equity' – gives us the opportunity to invest, to buy equipment, to develop ideas, to take them to market.

The return they expect needs to exceed what they could get elsewhere, plus a bit more to reflect the greater risk involved in a business than a bank account. We call this minimum 'hurdle' the cost of equity.

Shareholders only start to realize 'value' when they get more out of it than they need to make it worthwhile, i.e. when this hurdle is exceeded. This is the 'economic profit', rather than the operating profit, in any given year. 'Economic value' is the sum of these economic profits likely in future years. Inevitably, as we project further into the future, the certainty reduces and the profits are discounted to reflect this.

Shareholders buy shares – the demand for which is reflected in the share price and the total of which reflects the market capitalization, or the market value of the company at any given moment.

However, most shareholders are in it for the longer term, rather than buying and selling as the price fluctuates on a daily basis. Businesses take time to create real enduring value, and these committed shareholders receive their return in two ways – through dividends and growth in the price of their shares.

The total shareholder return (TSR) is typically measured over five, sometimes even ten, years. The really successful companies are not those that have the highest market capitalization at any moment – the GE and Microsoft brigade – but those that have delivered the best returns over time – companies like Quest Diagnostics and Ryanair.

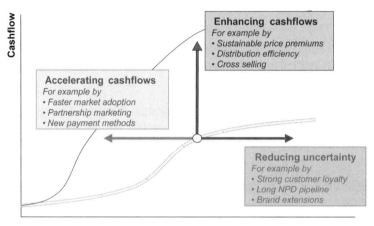

Cashflow

Enhancing cashflows
For example by
* *Sustainable price premiums*
* *Distribution efficiency*
* *Cross selling*

Accelerating cashflows
For example by
* *Faster market adoption*
* *Partnership marketing*
* *New payment methods*

Reducing uncertainty
For example by
* *Strong customer loyalty*
* *Long NPD pipeline*
* *Brand extensions*

Future

Profitable growth

Sustained, profitable growth is the foundation of value creation.

Marketing drives a sustainable cycle of profitability. Managed over time it creates profitable organic growth. Inorganic alternatives, such as mergers and acquisitions, are fraught with problems. It is hard to sustain an incremental benefit beyond the initial fusion of companies.

Many marketers might dismiss the whole notion of creating value for shareholders, not only as greedy owners in pursuit of a quick buck, but also without a care for customers. This assumes a rather clumsy reallocation of value – reducing the value of customer propositions and giving more back to investors.

Sure, there are some blinkered companies that will do this, but they are in the minority: 97% of CEOs say their number one priority is to create long-term shareholder value. Indeed, they have a legal responsibility to do so. Long term typically means over 5 years and often more. They are not after a quick buck.

Customer value

The only sustainable route to shareholder value is to create exceptional value for customers, requiring a disciplined and virtuous circle of customer and shareholder value creation. Marketing is about creating exceptional value for customers and shareholders.

The only way to sustain value growth is to create a virtuous circle of doing more for customers and shareholders. Investing in creating superior value for customers – through innovative new products and services, as well as enhancing the proposition which describes them – creates differentiation, purchase and affinity. Customers pay more, and those margins should be efficiently translated into dividends and share growth. Further investment in brands and relationships drives loyalty and repurchase.

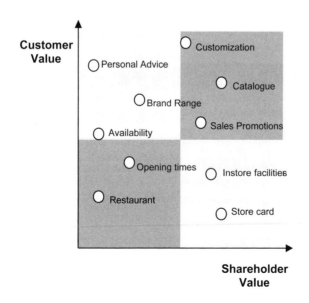

Customer value, the value to the customer as perceived by them, is harder to quantify. However, perceived value is not only a function of benefits and costs, but also of the context in which customers choose to place them. Context might mean the competitors sitting alongside on the supermarket shelf, or a change of occasion.

Consider sister companies within VAG, Audi and Volkswagen. The Audi A4 and the VW Passat are essentially the same car, with the same manufacturing base, different mouldings, unique badges, and the same cost base. Yet Audi markets itself as a peer of BMW 3 series, while the VW model is more analogous to a Ford. In the UK, the result is a £3000 price premium for Audi.

Consider Smirnoff. Smirnoff is bought in large bottles, pure alcohol. Smirnoff Ice is bought in much smaller bottles, with about one-fiftieth the alcoholic content, but with largely the same price. The Smirnoff Ice drinker is standing at the bar looking cool and sociable. Insensitive to price, far more sensitive to what the label says about him or her. Same basic product but two very different propositions, and profit levels.

Inspiration 2.3 COCA-COLA

'The Coca-Cola Company exists to benefit and refresh everyone it touches.'

The basic proposition is simple, solid and timeless.

'When we bring refreshment, value, joy and fun to our stakeholders then we success-fully nurture and protect our brands, particularly Coca-Cola. That is the key to fulfilling our ultimate obligation to provide consistently attractive returns to the owners of our business.'

Coca-Cola was created in Atlanta, Georgia, by local pharmacist Dr John S. Pemberton, who produced the cola syrup and took it down the street to Jacob's Pharmacy and sold it for five cents a glass as a soda fountain drink. He pronounced it 'delicious and refreshing', language that has stuck.

The name 'Coca-Cola' and its unique script were proposed by his friend, the local bookseller Frank Robinson, which he agreed that with its two Cs would look good on advertising bill-boards. It was registered as a trademark in 1887; by 1895 it was available in every US state, and by 1899 it had established its bottling franchise operations.

Coca-Cola's marketing chronology reads like a history of marketing, from the early oil cloths hung outside the pharmacy with the red and white logo, through the creation of the modern red and white image of Santa Claus, to the famous ad featuring 'I'd Like to Buy the World a Coke', sung on a hilltop in Italy by young people from all over the world.

'I'd like to buy the world a home
And furnish it with love
Grow apple trees and honey bees
And snow-white turtle-doves
I'd like to teach the world to sing
In perfect harmony
I'd like to buy the world a Coke
And keep it company
That's the real thing.'

Source: cocacola.com

The company now offers a portfolio of over 400 different drinks, bringing significant challenges in knowing where to focus its efforts. Which markets are the most attractive now and in the future? Which products should it invest in most?

Coca-Cola approaches this challenge in two steps: first, by understanding the global drinks market in terms of growth and profitability. This indicates that most of the current industry

– and Coke – profits come from carbonated soft drinks, yet there is little growth in the market. Sports drinks, meanwhile, show a very high growth and present a highly profitable opportunity. Water too is high growth, but with much lower margins.

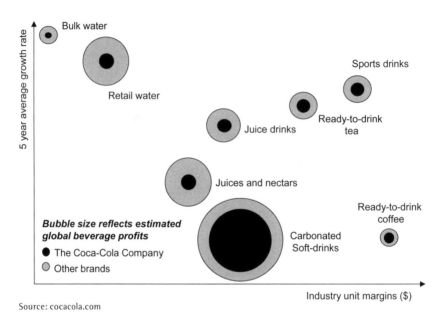

Source: cocacola.com

The second step for Coke is to understand how these opportunities fit with its own business, its capabilities and product portfolio, brand positioning and desired strategy. It can then prioritize its strategic market objectives based on the best fit in the most attractive markets. This market focus then drives the business strategy, which in its case includes the need to build new capabilities and accelerate its entry into fruit drinks, sports drinks and ready-to-drink teas.

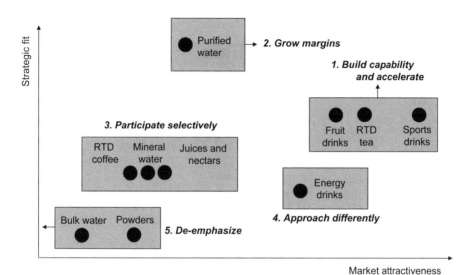

Source: cocacola.com

Application 2.2 MARKET VALUE

Why does the sum of shares, i.e. the market value, equal significantly more than the value shown on my balance sheet? Is the market value, the future worth of my business as judged by investors, good or bad? Is it more or less than what we think is the worth of the likely future streams of profits? Why are they different, and what should we do?

1. Understand economic profit

Understand the current economic profitability of business, i.e. the operating profit less the cost of capital.

2. Project future growth

Project likely market growth trends and strategic plans, and how they will Influence profits in future years.

3. Project future profits

Evaluate potential profits over next five years and a perpetuity figure to reflect how this would continue.

4. Calculate the intrinsic value

Calculate the net present value of these future profits, using a discount rate to reflect the appropriate risk.

5. Compare with the market value

Check the market value based on share price multiplied by shares, i.e. reflecting the perception of investors.

6. Address the value gap

If the intrinsic and market values differ, suggesting an over/under valuation, consider why and what action to take.

Concept 2.3 VALUE-BASED MARKETING

Marketers must create the future while also delivering today, balancing the tangible with the intangible to demonstrate how the company's biggest discretionary spend, the marketing budget, can be deployed for maximum impact.

At least two-thirds of all marketing is typically about the future, rather than today; that is, of the investment in marketing this year, around 60–70% will drive transactions in future years, rather than this year. This might come as a surprise to many finance and business leaders who expect to be able to match the vast majority of marketing costs against the same year's revenues.

However, the majority of strategy, innovation and communication will have more impact on the profits of future years than this year. That's good, as it's exactly what the shareholders are most interested in; however, it can sometimes seem far off to the CEO with the quarterly results to publish.

Marketing must therefore deliver today while creating tomorrow. Sales promotion, distribution and pricing tactics can all drive short-term sales and profits. However, the real trick is to do this in a way that also supports the future. Advertising, for example, may have an explicit sales message ('25% off garden furniture now') in order to prompt immediate purchase, or it may be about 'teaching the world to sing' which is a long-term brand-building effort, changing perceptions and building affinity.

In economic terms, marketing can typically create three times more value for a business than anything else it can do. It achieves this by improving profit margins, accelerating future cash flows, and reducing the uncertainty of them.

The real value of marketing is attained by optimizing this short- and long-term impact.

The measure of good marketing – which markets to focus on, how much to invest where, which products to develop or eliminate, how effective brand building is over time, how to optimize marketing activities, how to justify the large expenditures on the likes of advertising – is 'value'; not sales or satisfaction, share or profit, but the long-term return to shareholders, and all that that requires.

Shareholder value gives the organization a focal point through which everything else can be linked and prioritized. It provides a logical and holistic approach by which to develop strategy, make decisions, focus effort and measure performance.

'Value drivers' enable us to connect this rather abstract goal with practical activities and day-to-day decision-making, identifying and quantifying the relative importance of every action and output. A value driver analysis is typically portrayed as a horizontal 'tree diagram' showing how market-based actions lead to financial consequences.

- Market drivers

- Customer drivers

- Organization drivers

- Financial drivers

The analysis is not obvious, and while it looks intuitively simple, understanding the connections and relative importance is a significant piece of work. It will differ somewhat for every organization, given that every business has a different make-up of assets and activities, although it may be similar by sector.

It is important to start from the end-point and work backwards, as the market drivers of some other financial objective will be different. An analysis of 'operating profit' drivers, or 'revenue' drivers would lead the organization to very different conclusions as to where to focus their efforts.

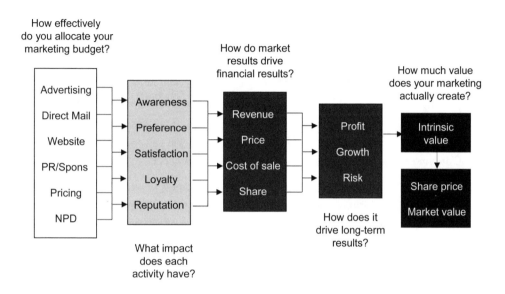

Connecting all the activities of the business can lead to surprising insights. Many organizations believe in the fundamental importance of customer satisfaction and, while a customer orientation might certainly be important, the pursuit of 'satisfaction' scores in themselves may do little for business performance. Whereas focusing effort on encouraging retention or referral can sometimes be much more significant. Of course, these value drivers will be different for every market, category and business.

Within marketing, some of the main applications of this value-based thinking are:

- Demonstrating the financial return on marketing.

- Connecting customer priorities to financial drivers.

- Justifying advertising spend with multi-year paybacks.

- Balancing short-term versus long-term objectives.

- Optimizing marketing resources and budgets.

- Focusing investment in the right places.

- Prioritizing activities across the customer experience.

- Understanding the relative importance of price.

- Clarifying which goals matter most in measuring performance.

John Sunderland, the former CEO of Cadbury Schweppes, knew what he was talking about when he took up his position in 1997 and announced: 'Within four years I will double the value of this business ... Economic profit will be our key measure of success, and building strong brands will be at the heart of achieving this.'

So if your CEO sets out an ambition like this, as a marketer what should you do differently?

- Where and how to compete ... a value-based market strategy will look very different from a conventional one, identifying which existing and emerging areas of the market offer the best long-term return on equity.

- What to focus your effort on ... a value-based portfolio analysis will identify which products are the value creators, and which are the value-destroyers and therefore where to focus effort. Taking into account the cost of equity creates a very different picture than a typical Boston Grid. A similar analysis will identify the best customers.

- How to capture the value you create ... a value-based proposition rightly focuses on creating value for customers, addressing customers' real needs and outperforming the competition. It is equally about finding ways to capture as much of this value as possible for shareholders, by maximizing the perceived value and optimizing pricing while still offering 'value for money'.

- How to get a better return on spend ... a value-based marketing programme identifies the marketing actions that will generate best returns, this year and long term. It identifies which levers to pull (e.g. sales promotion, advertising, PR) and how most effectively to leverage your marketing assets (e.g. brands, customer knowledge and distribution networks).

Value-based marketing is often dismissed as sophisticated analysis or complex performance metrics. It is much more. It is fundamentally about decision-making – choice of markets and positionings, choice of products and customers, choice of offering and price, choice of activities and investment.

Most conventional data analysis is driven by the need to create a broad range of proxy measures because there appears to be no 'best measure', or marketers are so unsure about their criteria for their decision-making that they take comfort from thick reports. So does a value-based approach to marketing create more analysis and inhibit creativity? Quite the opposite.

Great news for marketers

The great thing about value-based marketing is that it focuses on the numbers that really matter, and the right basis for effective decision-making. Invest once in the process to generate the right data, then you have less data, quicker to generate, with a much clearer focus ... and therefore much clearer scope to focus innovation, and much more time to do it creatively. And the CEO will like it too. What board will argue with a new marketing proposal that creates significantly more value for shareholders?

At Cadbury Schweppes, four years later, John Sunderland's value-based marketing approach focused on creating exceptional value for customers by investing in leading brands, and on market and product innovation. With stretching performance targets, clear marketing priorities and billion-dollar acquisitions such as Snapple, he just about achieved his targets, which in many ways was thanks to the priority he placed on brand development and marketing.

Application 2.3 VALUE DRIVERS

What are the drivers of business success or, more specifically, the drivers of shareholder value? How is improvement profitability, relative to growth and risk? How does the nature of capital investment affect this profitability? How influential is price relative to operating costs and volumes in driving profits? How important is customer satisfaction compared with preference, retention or loyalty in driving sales? And which aspects of the product, service or whole brand experience are most important to customers in driving this?

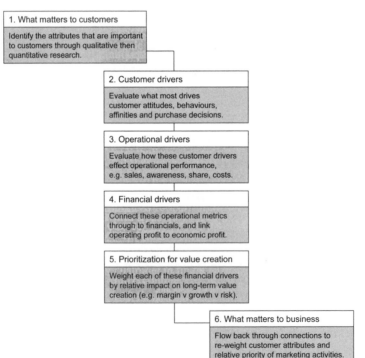

1. What matters to customers
Identify the attributes that are important to customers through qualitative then quantitative research.

2. Customer drivers
Evaluate what most drives customer attitudes, behaviours, affinities and purchase decisions.

3. Operational drivers
Evaluate how these customer drivers effect operational performance, e.g. sales, awareness, share, costs.

4. Financial drivers
Connect these operational metrics through to financials, and link operating profit to economic profit.

5. Prioritization for value creation
Weight each of these financial drivers by relative impact on long-term value creation (e.g. margin v growth v risk).

6. What matters to business
Flow back through connections to re-weight customer attributes and relative priority of marketing activities.

Marketing with more intelligence and imagination

'One is not born a genius, one becomes a genius.'

Simone de Beauvoir

'In every work of genius we recognize our own rejected thoughts.'

Ralph Waldo Emerson

Marketing matters more than ever today, yet not as it is. Marketing must be more intelligent to make sense of the complexity, and more imaginative to stand out from the crowd, to drive business outside in, as well as inside out, to do business on customer terms and grow profitably, to create more value for customers and shareholders, by delivering today and creating tomorrow at the same time.

A genius applies intelligence in an imaginative way.

More intelligent	More imaginative
Facts. Strategy, priorities and performance driven by the long-term pursuit of value creation.	**Ideas**. Sensing and responding to market opportunities, deep customer insight, and intense competition.
Analytical. Focus on best opportunities, strategic and commercial, derived and logical, evaluating to maximize value.	**Creative**. Exploring new possibilities, visionary and innovative, intuitive and challenging, connecting the best ideas.
Einstein. Harnessing the mathematical rigour and hypothetical thinking that made sense of natural complexity.	**Picasso**. Capturing the artistic passion and abstract structures that challenged convention and explored possibility.

Marketing has always been a creative discipline, yet it is surprisingly conventional in its execution. The product and packaging might be tweaked, and the advertising may tell a new story, but it is incredibly lacking in real innovative solutions to people's problems, innovative ways to reach them, innovative use of media to connect with them, innovative ways of making money from them. Marketing needs to find its creative spirit, applied in a focused and disciplined way.

A genius will find that creativity enhances analysis, and intelligence unlocks greater imagination.

Einstein struggled for years to make sense of the many complexities and contradictions of classical physics and the real world. The sheer complexity of what he was seeking to explain was mind-boggling. And for a long time, it was to him too. However, through creativity he eventually saw the light, standing back and reflecting on the patterns and symmetries, using hypotheses and deduction, he realized that the relationship between energy and matter was actually very simple, that E is equal to mc^2. And we all marvelled through the complexity, at the simplicity of the solution.

A genius creatively unleashes the power of intelligence.

We live in a world – at least in a Western world – where we generally have everything that we need. Wardrobes are full of clothes, kitchens are brimming with utensils, and garden sheds are crammed with everything we don't want inside the house. Yet we still want more. The newest, the coolest, the best. A basic human need, like hunger or shelter, which we constantly seek to satisfy in new ways. So how do marketers connect with this thirst for more?

Seeing what everyone has seen.

Thinking what nobody has thought.

Everyone in every sector is seeking to find ways to add value beyond the product and service. Shop here because it is where you meet people. Stay at our hotel because we'll take you to the theatre too. Buy a computer from us, and we'll help you to become an entrepreneur.

- Enriching the value proposition

- Extending the brand experience

- Enhancing the customer benefits

Money matters less too. If you can do something which really matters then a basic item can become a luxury item. Bottled water: from thirst quencher costing a few cents a litre to fashion accessory costing $3 a bottle. The perceived value is fundamentally changed, as is the peer group against which value is judged, and the relationship through which it is sustained. Ideas keep markets moving, and money flowing.

So what is the role of genius in marketing today?

Genius is about combining discipline and creativity to unleash innovation where it matters most. To create difference and engage people in a world where it often seems that all the best ideas have already been taken. Ideas for new solutions, ideas to exploit existing markets better, ideas to do it more effectively, ideas to compel the customer to you. Big ideas define and sustain your brand, but they need constant refreshment to stay relevant and compelling. Ideas are the source of value creation. Ideas are the basis of newness. Ideas make marketing matter, and make it the most exhilarating part of business to work in too.

Psychologists rage over whether a genius is born or can be made. Russian scientists have pursued the idea of a genius gene, which could be identified and nurtured. Others believe that the biggest influence on intelligence is the environmental stimulus a baby receives within their first year of life. Thomas Edison argued that genius was far more about hard work at any age – 1% inspiration and 99% perspiration.

Like the champion athlete, genius must require some talent. However, like those athletes who have gone on to win gold medals, and compared with the many others who have ended up by the wayside, that talent must be nurtured and directed, stimulated and stretched. Marketing genius is the same, evolving out of experiences of the workplace and the marketplace.

The stimulus for marketing genius comes from outside – from customer insight and competitive action. It comes tangentially, for example from other markets – if you were a bank, what could you learn from consumer goods, or if you were a sports shoe manufacturer, what could you learn from mobile phones? Indeed, genius is stimulated anywhere – by a documentary on Discovery channel, by an unusual experience while travelling on holiday, by a random comment that meant far more than it was meant to.

The demand from a CEO for 10% growth is likely to be greeted with a conventional response – more perspiration. The challenge from a CEO to make the impossible possible is more likely to stimulate a deeper and more inspired response.

The desire for higher performance, to do a better job comes from within, a passion to do better and be different. Inspiration. The talent for marketing genius comes from within – from the marketer who wants to be better and different from others, and to deliver extraordinary results.

Concept 3.1 GENIUS ATTRIBUTES

How does a genius think?

What is common about the thinking styles that produced the Sistine Chapel and the Theory of Relativity, penicillin and the World Wide Web?

Academics and philosophers have long tried to bottle genius. Russian scientists, through the analysis of child prodigies, claim to have identified the 'genius gene', while others argue that it is largely down to hard work – as Thomas Edison said: 'Genius is 1% inspiration and 99% perspiration'.

However, there are some clues as to what drives genius, and its extraordinary results. First, genius is widely accepted not to equate purely to intelligence. It is certainly not necessary to have an extraordinarily high IQ, to speak 15 languages by the age of eight, or to master the intricacies of quantum mechanics. It is, however, recognized that genius typically involves both intelligent and creative thought, and the combination of the two, in any combination, can create so-called genius.

There are ten characteristics of genius:

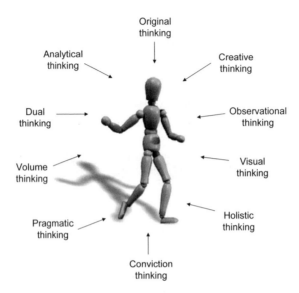

1 **Original Thinking.** A genius starts with an open mind, uncluttered by conventions, taking new perspectives, deconstructing a problem then reassembling it in better ways. Many great ideas have been rejected because they don't fit with conventional thinking, and they have been denounced as impractical or 'ahead of their time'. The Swiss watchmakers provide one such example: they rejected the idea that timepieces could be built through electronics rather than springs and gears; similar are the floppy disk manufacturers who just couldn't see the disruptive coming of the CD-ROM, and more recently the USB pen.

2 **Creative Thinking.** A genius is always open to possibility, seeking to solve problems by hypothesis, taking a mental leap and then seeing whether it proves to be true or not. Einstein often used hypothesis to jump out of his mathematical derivations, to conjure a possibility that he could then seek to prove or disprove. Logical derivation will take you down

certain avenues of thinking dependent on where you start. Constantly having the curiosity and confidence to ask 'What if?' rather than seeking safety in what is close or known.

3 **Analytical Thinking.** A genius will work through a problem or idea progressively and rigorously, as well as creatively, challenging the mathematical or scientific logic. While a genius reaches new levels or dimensions through creative leaps, there is still the need to make sense of it in practical terms. Often this requires a pure mental logic as the current mathematical formulae or scientific principles might well themselves be based on some false assumption. Breakthrough is rarely achieved by derivation of convention, but it does require proof of the new concept.

4 **Observational Thinking.** A genius has an exceptionally high state of consciousness, a greater awareness of what is going on, and looking for patterns like a forensic detective. Some of the best insights come from observation rather than enquiry, like an anthropologist watching and considering what is happening. In particular this is useful when there is no current language or logic for explaining phenomena or behaviour. Alexander Fleming found mould on his exposed medical cultures, just like many other doctors, yet instead of just throwing it away, he considered what caused it, an observation curiosity that led to penicillin.

5 **Dual Thinking.** A genius can think in parallel, to tolerate apparent ambiguities, to bring together opposites and connect the unconnected. New solutions are often contradictory, either with conventions, or within itself, and indeed Scott Fitzgerald's definition of what makes a first-rate mind is 'the ability to hold two opposing ideas at the same time'. Niels Bohr, the Danish physicist, imagined how light could be thought of as both particles and waves. This seemed entirely contradictory. Yet his discovery of 'phonons', intangible particles that behave like waves, led to his theory of complementarity. Similarly, Leonardo da Vinci combined the sound of a bell with the ripples when a stone hits water, to arrive at the idea that sound travels in waves.

6 **Holistic Thinking.** A genius can take a broader perspective, to see the holistic problem in the context of its environment and piecing together its many parts. Einstein brought together different strands of our natural world, uniting apparently diverse attributes such as energy, mass and speed of light. Picasso's abstract work sought to represent much more than a simple image. His works built personality, context, feelings and vision into his observations. He seeks to provoke more holistic and deep thought, rather than simply replicate what he sees. Indeed the ability to see the bigger picture, or to fill in the spaces, can often mean that a genius 'sees what everybody else can see, but thinks what nobody has thought'.

7 **Volume Thinking.** A genius searches for many solutions rather than just one, building on or challenging each other, constantly searching for a more perfect solution. A genius has a constantly active and fertile mind, the sheer quantity of their output can be intimidating, which is why it sometimes takes some years to identify the best from the also ran. Mozart wrote 600 pieces of music and Bach wrote one every week even when sick. Einstein published 148 papers, although he is best known for one of his earliest. The enormous work rate of Picasso in his final years was initially denounced as the senility of an old man trying to maximize his legacy; however, many years later we actually recognize this most productive period as also the most creative.

8 **Pragmatic Thinking.** A genius recognizes that ideas and solutions are of little use in the abstract, that the theory or concept must be made real, that it must be practical and useful. A genius is constantly thinking, exploring, inventing and discovering. However, genius is only genius if it can be put to practical action, can add value in some way. Edison held 1093 patents, more than anyone else to this day, and demanded of himself one minor invention every 10 days, and a major one every 6 months. Similarly, most successful entrepreneurs will have many failures behind them before they succeed and most innovators will develop far more new ideas than see commercial success.

9   **Visual Thinking.** A genius is able to express their ideas more clearly, typically visually through diagrams and analogy, to make sense of complexity in comprehensible ways. The creative explosion of the Renaissance was marked by a multitude of drawings and diagrams, as Galileo and Leonardo da Vinci graphically illustrated their revolutionary ideas. These captured people's imagination far more than words or numbers. Pictures enable connections to be made more quickly, concepts to be demonstrated far more easily, and the holistic system to be explained.

10 **Conviction Thinking.** A genius must have the inner strength, belief and confidence to stay strong to what they believe, while conventions and colleagues will challenge them. From Galileo and Leonardo, to Einstein and Picasso, genius requires an inner strength of conviction to stand by the radical ideas and actions that are at odds with received wisdom, that challenge the status quo, that could easily be compromised by a lesser-willed person. In any walk of life, it is rare for people immediately to like significant change in their surroundings, practices or beliefs. We prefer the safety and convenience of what we know than what we don't. But we gradually see the possibility, the logic, and the benefit in different thinking, and we accept it, and eventually engage in it. A genius must often reach out beyond today, and slowly people will follow and embrace what is new, different and better.

Concept 3.2 GENIUS DEFINED

Genius is about applying intelligence in more imaginative ways.

There are many definitions of genius. While some focus on the intelligence aspects of genius, for example the attainment of a high IQ, genius is typically defined, as being less about the absolute level of intelligence and more about the application of intelligence in creative ways. While some suggest that one is born with genius, or with the aptitude to achieve it, most argue that genius is primarily achieved through carefully chosen hard work that blends deeper thinking with radical creativity.

Genius uniquely combines these extremes to deliver extraordinary results.

gen·ius
noun pl geniuses

1 Exceptional intellectual or creative power or other natural ability.
2 An exceptionally intelligent or able person.
3 (pl genii/jeeni-i/) (in some mythologies) A spirit associated with a person, place or institution.
4 The prevalent character or spirit of a nation, period, etc.

Source: *Oxford English Dictionary*

The combination of intelligence and imagination is the source of this extraordinary impact, and one that is essential to marketing today.

For years marketing was overly concerned with the creative aspects of business, the source of ideas and expression that made commodities distinctive and relevant. Indeed, in most communications agencies and internal teams, creativity is still king. The power of the image or strapline matters most. Other marketers have become far more analytical – ask most today, and they will argue that they need to be even more rigorous and commercial.

Yet too many marketers see this as an either/or situation: that you can be heads-up creative or heads-down analytical, that being commercial is about finance rather than innovation, and that within agencies you are either a 'creative' or a 'planner'. This misses the point of genius. Analysis and creativity should not be seen as separate disciplines, as alternative approaches, or as compromising each other.

The source of genius is the positive combination of intelligence and imagination.

The elements of genius can be reflected in left-brain versus right-brain theory. While the brain is in reality far more complex than this, the theory reflects an understanding of extreme opposites and how to balance and combine them in a way that achieves positive reinforcement. The left side of the brain is associated with the gathering of data, analysis and evaluation. The right side is more to do with making, creativity, synthesis and exploration.

Left brain	Right brain
Interactive	Intuitive
Convergent	Divergent
Directive	Imaginative
Linear	Non Linear
Analytical	Holistic
Objective	Subjective

Genius and its combination of extreme opposites could also be reflected in the more traditional yin-yang model, where left-brain is similar to 'yang' characteristics and right-brain is analogous to 'yin' features.

Yang	Yin
Masculine	Feminine
Aggregating	Yielding
Cold	Warm
Conscious	Unconscious
Logical	Creative
Rational	Emotional

In both approaches, the opposites are not alternatives. Success requires both sides. One rein-forces the other. In education, it is recognized that the pursuit of a creative subject, such as music or art, adds to the individual's analytical capability, to appreciate the patterns within science or mathematics, and vice versa.

In marketing , we consider the implications of reconciling these opposites for each aspect of marketing – from market analysis to strategy formulation, brand development to innovation, value propositions to distribution channels, media integration to investor relations, marketing metrics to marketing leadership.

Intelligent	Imaginative
Analytical	Creative
Conceptual	Practical
Strategic	Insightful
Specific	Holistic
Promises	Reality
Financial	Operational

In *Marketing Genius* we explore how more stretching thought and actions can be brought together and applied to the key challenges of marketing today, and the many aspects that make up an integrated approach to markets in order to significantly improve customer, competitive and financial impact.

In 'Genius Lab', at the end of this book, we describe in more structured terms the attributes of genius and how they can be applied to marketing at the activity level, and to the attributes of the individual marketer. The diagnostic models apply the genius model to the challenges of marketing and business today, and illustrate how the marketer can practically embrace new approaches to each success.

Genius marketing is more intelligent and more imaginative – stretching both extremes and combining them in more powerful, reinforcing ways in order to deliver extraordinary results.

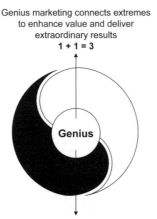

Genius marketing connects extremes
to enhance value and deliver
extraordinary results
1 + 1 = 3

Genius

Most marketing struggles to combine
more extreme opportunities
and neutralizes them
1 - 1 = 0

Application 3.1 GENIUS PROFILE

How close are you to genius? Are you more left or right brain in your natural way of working? Does your current work force or encourage you to work in a different way to your natural style? Which is better? How do you develop your or your team's marketing to be more balanced and effective? Which kinds of people would you work best with, to build the most complementary team?

1. Left and right brain

Consider the relative attributes
of left vs. right brain thinking, as one
model of different thinking patterns.

2. How you solve problems

Imagine you are addressing an
important business issue, how you
address and seek to solve a problem.

3. Profile yourself at work

Choose your preference for each
paired attribute, and profile yourself
towards the left or right side on each.

4. Profile yourself at home

Repeat the profiling for out-of-work
decisions you make, e.g. buying a car,
your next holiday, a new job.

5. Do you behave differently?

Reflect on how your work and non-work
decision-making differs, and which is
your more natural and balanced style.

6. How will you think differently?

How well do you balance and combine
left and right brain thinking? How might
you think differently in future?

Concept 3.3 GENIUS MARKETERS

Genius marketers must sense and respond to the complex challenges of today's markets with deeper intelligence and more radical imagination, to think more strategically and commercially, to implement with more focus and effectiveness. Intelligence and imagination can positively combine for more impact in competitive markets, as well as on the bottom line.

Intelligence

Everything is relative. Speed, mass and time are all subjective measures, all dependent on each other. Nothing is absolute, be it the age and motion of a human being or extra-terrestrial planet. Light has weight and speed has curves. And coiled within a pound of matter, any matter, is the explosive power of 14 million tons of TNT.

We know all of this because of Albert Einstein. In a few elegant characters he formed a simple-looking equation that governs our world and every other world out there.

In his youth, Einstein was fascinated by models and mechanical devices, yet he was considered a slow learner, possibly due to dyslexia, or shyness, while others have referred to an unusual brain structure (which was removed and examined after his death). Indeed, he credited his greatest breakthroughs to his slowness, saying that by making sense of things at a later age than most children, he was able to apply a more developed intellect.

Einstein was no quiet, subservient student. Indeed, he was difficult, prickly, and constantly annoyed his professors. They were probably relieved when he became a patent clerk in his home town of Bern, Switzerland. He was confident, arrogant, extreme and unkempt. The picture of the mad scientist, or perhaps genius. While a rigorous mathematician, his curiosity saw patterns and provoked him to hypothesize 'what if'. Indeed, these leaps in imagination, then proved through his deeply intelligent algebra, perhaps helped to achieve his extraordinary progress.

In 1905, at 26 years of age, Einstein sent three papers, scrawled in his spare time, to the leading journal *Annalen der Physik*, asking for them to be published 'if there is room'. They were all published, and went on to provide the foundation of modern physics and, in some ways, to change the world.

The papers were about:

- *Photoelectric Effect.* This described how light travels as both waves and particles, and led to the development of quantum mechanics.

- *Brownian Motion.* This explained how particles bounce around in a seemingly random way, illustrating their atomic composition.

- *Special Relativity.* 'This paper,' he modestly wrote, 'modifies the theory of space and time' by explaining how everything is relative rather than absolute.

Einstein was a genius. Only the first of the papers won a Nobel Prize, although many argued that all three should have done. The third paper, however, is perhaps the most famous and led to his subsequent explanation that energy is equivalent to the combination of mass and speed of light, $E=mc^2$, and that nothing can therefore exceed the speed of light.

Another leading physicist of the time described Einstein's papers as 'blazing rockets which in the dark of the night suddenly cast a brief but powerful illumination over an immense unknown region.'

Steve Jobs, the scientifically-trained originator of iMacs and iPods, embraces many of the attributes of the intelligence required of a genius marketer, driven by a deep understanding of his field but, like Einstein, requiring leaps of imagination in order to achieve his breakthrough solutions.

Imagination

Pablo Picasso, or to give him his full and original name, El Pablito (Pablo) Diego José Santiago Francisco de Paula Juan Nepomuceno Crispín Crispiniano de los Remedios Cipriano de la Santísima Trinidad Ruiz Blasco y Picasso López, was primarily a painter (he believed that an artist must paint in order to be considered a true artist) but also worked with small ceramic and bronze sculptures, collage, and even produced some poetry.

He was a talented painter and draughtsman, partly following in his father's footsteps, Jose Ruiz y Blasco, who was also a painter and professor of art at various Spanish colleges. However, Pablo chose to adopt his mother's name, and went on to create masterpieces in oils, watercolour, pastels, charcoal, pencil and ink.

Picasso was also a genius, challenging the impressionist conventions of his time. Having patiently absorbed the work of Manet and Toulouse-Lautrec, he combined his Spanish passion and visual talents to define the new art form of Cubism, delighting in reducing complex scenes to just a few geometric shapes, and become a rare legend in his own lifetime.

His modern art was born of visual creativity, although building on the increasing 'science' of his tutors. However, to create Cubism at a time when Impressionism was still the popular preference was bold and daring. Indeed, Pablo was a rebel from the start, a teenager who frequented the Barcelona cafés where the revolutionary-thinking intellectuals gathered. Within years of arriving in Paris he had absorbed the Impressionist genre and in his own mind had a new expression bursting to get out.

Philippe Starck, the designer of everything from the Microsoft Mouse to the Paramount Hotel, embraces many of the attributes of the imagination required of a genius marketer, driven by a radically creative, non-linear, intuitive approach but, like Picasso, also with an intelligent logic underpinning his radical solutions.

Impact

Warren Buffett is a genius. He is widely regarded as the world's greatest stock market investor, yet still lives in the same grey stucco house that he bought in his twenties for $31,000. He dines on burgers and Coke, plays bridge with Bill Gates, and frequently quotes Mae West. His only extravagance is his fondness for luxury air travel, and his Gulfstream IV-SP jet.

If his lifestyle is offbeat, then so is his investment strategy. He rejects the complex trickery of day-traders and hedge funds, instead founding his business choices on common sense and information and intuition. Buffett has a great knack of spotting undervalued companies with low overheads and high growth potential – strong market shares. He buys them on the cheap, and then watches them grow. In 1988 he recognized the strong brand, but unfulfilled financial potential of Coca-Cola. He bought shares at $10.96 and within five years, partly due to investor confidence following Buffett, they were worth $74.50.

Known as 'The Oracle of Omaha', thousands gather each year for the AGM of his company Berkshire Hathaway, to hear the great man perform, to talk about his own company, and the state of the world as he sees it. This is no usual AGM. It starts with a song from Warren, reflecting his great love of Country and Western music. There is usually a movie too, most recently featuring Warren in a version of *The Wizard of Oz*, put together by his daughter. Bill Gates even has a look in, both as a character in the movie, and by joining the company as a non-executive director.

For all this eccentricity and normality, he is one of the world's most respected business leaders, and his annual letters to shareholders of Berkshire Hathaway are read by many more millions for their insights and inspiration. His personal wealth is estimated at $36 billion, with at least one-third of that due to his significant ownership of Coke.

Phil Knight, the founder of Nike who grew his business from the back of his van to a $12 billion global leader, embraces many of the attributes of the combination and balance required of a genius marketer, to bring together the deep intelligence and radical imagination to achieve the extraordinary results of Buffett, achieved through a marketing-driven business.

Inspiration 3.1 STEVE JOBS

Steve Jobs has redefined the marketing of technology, from the early days of Apple's Macintosh to Pixar blockbusters like *Toy Story*, and back to defining our iLife at Apple. He is a market revolutionary, intelligently making sense of markets and applying technologies to existing and emerging customer needs.

He grew up in the Californian apricot orchards that later became known as Silicon Valley, at a time when technological innovation and psychedelic music were competing local influences. He studied physics and literature but dropped out to found Apple Computer with his friend Steve Wozniak in 1976, based in his parent's garage and financed by the sale of his VW campervan. By the age of 23 he was worth over $1 million, over $10 million by 24, $100 million by 25, and now a fully fledged billionaire.

He grew the business by focusing on niche markets, charging a premium for his novel products. However, 1985 saw him lose out in a power struggle with John Sculley as Apple began to crumble under the competitive might of Microsoft. This led him to Pixar animation studios, which has since created some of the most successful and loved animated films since the early days of Walt Disney. From *Monsters Inc.* to *Toy Story* and *Finding Nemo*, they have earned well over $2 billion at the box offices.

Back at Apple Computer, with Jobs reinstalled as leader, Apple recognized that the computing world had changed. In the same way that Pixar had transformed movies, the likes of Dell had disrupted the computing world. But Jobs saw the future differently. He re-engaged his passion for well-designed computers, this time with open systems, and the launch of his funky-coloured iMacs. More significantly, he recognized that the music industry was in desperate need of innovation. The iPod was born to a new generation of devices, and iTunes closely followed.

Jobs is on a high – with over 15 million iPods in circulation, downloading more than 1 billion iTunes, plus the sale of Pixar to Disney in return for $7.4 billion and, intriguingly, a seat on their board. His annual performances at MacWorld are still watched by millions, eager to hear his perspectives on fast-changing landscapes, and specifically about his latest ideas and innovations.

Jobs takes a deeply personal approach to business – a visionary and a strategist, with a hands-on style to the detail of customer needs and product design. He is a marketer and leader who inspires superlatives. His staff describe him as a 'reality distortion field'.

Inspiration 3.2 PHILIPPE STARCK

Philippe Starck is the *grand fromage* of design. From architecture to furniture, utensils to fashion, Starck puts his mark on around 100 products every year.

'Everyone should be pondering, asking themselves questions about life, money, desire, war, themselves,' he believes.

His childhood days were spent underneath his father's drawing boards, playing with paper and glue, taking anything to pieces and rebuilding it, usually in a different way. Remaking the world around him.

After dropping out of school, he founded his design firm in 1968, initially specializing in inflatable objects. Then after a brief role as art director with Pierre Cardin, he moved on to independent interior and product design. He started by redesigning two Parisian nightclubs, which caught the eye of President Francois Mitterand who asked him to refurbish the Elysée Palace.

Much of his early work was more akin to fashion and novelty, whereas he has now moved on from throwaway artefacts to more serious design, and pieces of timeless value.

Clocks, vases, door handles, toothbrushes, watches, food, cutlery, lamps, lemon squeezers, desks, motorcycles, taps, baths and toilets are all in his portfolio.

You can wake up to his alarm clock, use his Target toothbrush, wear his space-age Puma boots and Fossil wristwatches, carry his Samsonite luggage, work with his Microsoft Mouse, dine at Asia de Cuba restaurant, drink the stylish bottled beer from Kronenbourg 1664, and sleep in his new classic hotel, The Paramount.

Starck champions creativity with purpose, art that is practical, and insight that is innovative. His collaborations turn average products into practical and essential objects of desire, and can easily triple the profit margins of the brands he works with.

At his drawing board he works with purpose and passion. He inspires us with his striking reinterpretations of the world around us. He is subversive, intelligent and always interesting.

He thinks without boundary, rejecting our conventions and challenging our tolerance, creating objects that are practical and beautiful.

Inspiration 3.3 PHIL KNIGHT

Oregon USA, 1962: Phil Knight was selling running shoes out the back of a van at the local university track meeting. The young business student had a passion for running, although he was never the most talented in his team. He therefore pursued his other passion, making money. He was creative too, importing Tiger running shoes from Japan, and became as well known for his fast shoes as his own speed.

He trained hard all the same, seeking to get the best out of his talent, guided by the elderly university coach Bill Bowerman. One day they were in Bill's kitchen making waffles after a hard morning training run. Phil took his shoes off, and by accident put one down on the hot waffle iron.

The smell of burning rubber caught everyone's attention.

It caught Bill and Phil's imagination, and soon they were making their own running shoes with a unique waffle-patterned sole. More traction, less weight, more speed. A few years later they added a swoosh logo, created overnight by a young designer called Carolyn Davidson for $35, and a sporting giant was born. The flash of inspiration that created a marketing idea, and business success.

Nike. The ancient Greek goddess of victory.

Phil grew the organization with attitude and passion. He turned his own athletic frustrations to business, and with an accounting degree he created Nike as a company passionate about sports and profits.

By 1979 he had gained 50% of the US running shoe market, at a time when the jogging boom was taking off. He and Bowerman constantly innovated with waffle soles and air cushioning. Through the next two decades, largely through highly creative marketing – the advertising, the endorsements, the 'just do it' cult – he turned Nike into the global brand leader, in every sport, in every land. Nike's portfolio now extends to Converse sneakers, Hurley surfwear and Cole Haan formalwear.

As an intuitive marketer he knew that the inspiration came from his customers – helping them to achieve sporting excellence, as written on the inside of every pair of shoes. He also under-stood that deep insight, strong branding, relentless innovation and strong relationships are essential to achieve success in the short and long term.

One senior Nike executive described Knight's style as unusual but inspirational. Few managers have ever entered his office at Beaverton, and those who have are always required to remove their shoes first, even their Nikes. Even fewer journalists have managed to probe his enigma, and those who have learnt little. Yet the mediocre miler, who always aspired to more than his physical talent would allow, certainly has a knack for results.

When asked by his managers, for answers or advice on a diversity of business issues, executives would usually get the predictable and obscure guidance to 'run faster'. Just like his coach Bill Bowerman, who replied similarly to Knight's own questions about how he could become a better athlete. His managers turn away puzzled but often inspired.

'Run faster' has had a remarkable impact on Nike over the years.

More than four decades later, Phil recently decided to hang up his CEO running shoes, after successfully developing a business from scratch to $12 billion, with a passion for marketing, as well as sport, at its heart. He is a genuine marketer and business leader who combined his passion with profits, creativity with commercialism, intelligence with imagination – as you can read in Nike's unique annual reports – in the pursuit of personal, marketing and business excellence.

While Phil's best known marketing tagline 'Just Do It' is a sentiment that reflects his personal approach to business success, he leaves with one of his other well-known taglines – 'there is no finish line' – much in mind, because he and Nike know that their world is moving at a faster pace than ever, and only by constantly accelerating their ideas and innovations, markets and brands can they ensure leadership and success.

Knight is certainly a radically creative, visionary and empowering marketer, but also a disciplined accountant. He has been portrayed as mysterious, inscrutable, eccentric, unpredictable, enigmatic, idiosyncratic, shy, aloof, reclusive, competitive and a genius. He shuns publicity, although he is never far from his desk – or the gym – at Nike Campus. However, his passion continues in his products and his people, as well as making Nike one of the most profitable and respected companies in the world.

'Genius' is the one attribute on the list that Knight himself questions:

> 'Other than that, I'm all of those things, at least some of the time'.

However, surely a genius is far too intelligent to call himself such a thing.

Thinking:
The mind of
a marketing
genius

PART 2

► Thinking: The mind of a marketing genius

► Where are the best opportunities for your business today? How do you stand out in crowded markets? How do you deliver the best solutions for customers, and the best returns to shareholders?

► Where should you focus amidst this complexity? What is your competitive advantage? Which markets, brands, products and customers should you prioritize in order to maximize value creation?

► What is your defining purpose? How do you reflect the aspirations of your stakeholders? How could you make more of your brand, in new markets or applications? And how do you capture its full impact over time?

► Who are the customers for your business? How do you gain real insight into what they want? How do you embrace CSR, and address wider ethical issues? How do you create a truly customer-centric business?

► How do create more radical innovation? How do you disrupt the existing market conventions in order to create a significant and sustainable difference? How do you innovate markets and business as well as the solutions themselves?

'Discovery consists of looking at the same thing as everyone else and thinking what nobody has thought.'

Albert Szent-Gyorgi

Designing your business from the outside in

'What do you want to achieve or avoid? The answers to this question are objectives. How will you go about achieving your desired results? The answer to this you can call strategy.'

William Rothschild

'Ultimately, we wanted Nike to be the world's best sports and fitness company. Once you say that, you have a focus. You don't end up making wing tips or sponsoring the next Rolling Stones world tour.'

Phil Knight

Most business strategies are inadequate for today's markets. They lack context and difference, flexibility and engagement. They often miss the bigger opportunities, and avoid the more difficult but important choices for business. They are more about consensus than competitiveness, standing still rather than moving forwards.

More intelligent strategy	More imaginative strategy
Driven. Defining business priorities outside in by the market opportunities, competitive challenge and customer needs.	**Driving**. Defining markets in your vision, challenging conventions, and shaping them to your advantage.
Focused. Focusing on the best value creating markets, products and customers, doing few things better.	**Visionary**. Creatively defining future markets, driven by what you could do rather than what you can do.
Differentiated. Ensuring that strong and sustainable competitive advantage sits at the heart of the business.	**Innovative**. Ensuring that innovation drives both today and tomorrow, driving demand and profitable growth.

Marketing should be the driving force of business strategy, ensuring that it is driven by the challenges and opportunities in markets, and defining where and how to compete, and how to win.

- Strategy is about direction: clarifying vision and objectives, enabling clarity of organizational purpose, alignment and momentum.

- Strategy is about choices: deciding where and how to compete, prioritizing which markets and customers, which brands and products to focus on.

- Strategy is about differentiation: finding a sustainable source of competitive advantage, and how to deliver it in a compelling, profitable way.

However, most business strategies are inadequate for today's markets. They are developed without sufficient context, they are developed inside out rather than outside in. They promote evolution rather than revolution, avoiding hard decisions, seeking to do what is currently done, even if it is increasingly out of synch with the market. They lack the stretch to see the future better than the conventional industry wisdom, and the flexibility to adapt to changing markets. They are often developed remotely from those who must be engaged to make them happen. They fail to make the difficult choices of audiences or products or priorities – choices which people are not often fond of making, and are unlikely to be favourable to everyone. They forget to put competitive advantage at their core.

As a result, strategies are devalued as a paper exercise to justify budget submissions, compromised as soon as the people are asked to stop doing what they have always done, but don't want to, and end up being rather similar to the strategy of every other company in the sector. They lack the decisiveness, direction and focus that a business needs today.

Types of strategy

Strategy itself is a widely misunderstood term. As a word it is often misused as tactics – 'What is our strategy to win this sale?' – or as a plan – 'What is our strategy for next year?' The reality is that strategy is about a sustained approach, requiring flexibility and review in a fast-changing world, but typically scoped over at least three years.

- Corporate strategy is about the overall organization's purpose, the mission of the company, and the vision of what such will look like. This drives what business areas we should be in. It sets the context. Brand values and culture should align to this, providing a clear articulation of the purpose in a way that captures the difference from others, and how it is relevant to the audience.

- Business strategy typically refers to a specific business unit, e.g. sports cars, trucks, aerospace. At its simplest it defines where and how to compete in each chosen market, and the business model and resources which will be required in order to achieve this.

- Market strategy is the core part of the business strategy, and offers marketers a 'higher domain' in which to influence the business direction, focus and priorities.

- Marketing strategy is then more functional and operational – defining how brands, products, channels and communications must be developed and deployed in order to achieve success.

Novartis provides a great example of market thinking driving the business. R&D companies, like technology companies, are typically driven by their products rather than their audiences. A drug development pipeline could last for 10 years, for example. In Novartis, the marketing team drive the strategy, and thereby the strategic prioritization of new investments and innovations. While the pipeline is determined by highly technical inside-out opportunities, it is the outside-in market perspective that drives its priorities.

Outside in

Strategy development so often starts with where are we now, rather than where could we be? 'Where are we now' thinking is typically an internal perspective of what products and capabilities do we have, and how can we use them at less cost to drive more revenues? Yet, while the blinkers are on improving current performance, the market and the best opportunities might be passing the organization by. In fast-changing markets, improvement is increasingly a route to irrelevance.

Markets are the source of change, disruption and possibility today. Markets change at a far greater pace than companies. Therefore, the best opportunities, the best strategies and best performance are typically arrived at by anticipating and responding to external change.

The demand for improved results, faster growth and higher margins merely shapes the challenge rather than provides a solution. The solution comes by thinking 'outside in' – where are the best markets? What is the best fit with our brand? How can we seize these opportunities better than others? What products and services will we need? Will it deliver a superior return for our shareholders in the long term?

While 'core competence' thinking used to be the foundation of where to focus, 'market opportunity' thinking now matters more. Of course, there is a balance between the two perspectives and the point is that where you start defines the frame of reference for everything that follows.

Market strategy

Markets should be the driving force of business strategy, embracing market insight to define how the external environment is changing, and to identify the biggest challenges and opportunities for business.

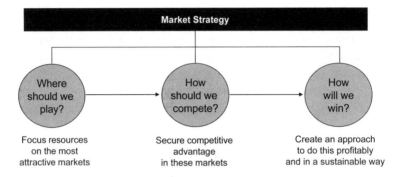

There are three dimensions to a market strategy:

- Where to play – a rigorous analysis of emerging and existing markets, future profit streams and competitive intensity, leading to choices of which markets to focus on, and which not.

- How to compete – in terms of what to offer customers, how to offer it, and how to be different from competitors, and thereby how to secure lasting competitive advantage.

- How to win – identifying the most appropriate ways to win, even considering new business models and new criteria for success.

This requires a more stretching vision for the market and what success looks like in it, a more considered evaluation of what will create and sustain advantage and a more disciplined focus on the few best opportunities.

It demands tough choices: 'How can I choose between so many great opportunities?' you might cry after considering the many new areas in which you could grow your business.

Indeed, when markets have no frontiers, when brands increasingly reflect lifestyles rather than any particular product, and when the relentless pace of technology outruns our ability to apply it, there is no shortage of choices.

- Which of the many creative ideas should we make happen?

- Which of our customers should we focus our effort on?

- Which products should we promote ahead of others?

- Which channel partners should we build relationships with?

Making choices

While decision-making at corporate level is typically driven by financial criteria, in marketing we often fail to apply similar rigours to our decisions. Of course, we fear that the financial criteria will create short-term, non-customer blinkers. In most cases this is unlikely. It certainly does not mean doing whatever it takes for 'a quick buck'.

Similarly, marketing decisions are often based more on logic and fit, insight and attractiveness. These are equally important criteria, which in reality should drive the financial analysis. Of course, the ultimate criteria for any decision, to decide strategic direction, to approve investments, or anything else for that matter, should centre on the question 'will this increase the long-term value of the business?'

In companies owned by shareholders, this typically means 'what will increase the long-term return to our investors?' which is achieved by growth in the value of their investments, and dividends they might receive at various intervals.

From the internal perspective this can be addressed in the form of 'will it deliver a return to shareholders that exceeds their expectations?' or in financial language, 'will it deliver a stream of economic profits greater than the cost of capital?'

This question is answered by evaluating the likely future profit streams deliverable by the chosen strategy, in terms of:

- Accelerating growth (that is, growth in profits).

- Improving margins (ideally economic profit).

- Reducing risk (and thereby the lower % by which these future profits are discounted).

Marketing decision-making needs to develop a set of criteria that are realistic and appropriate to the business goals. The choice of criteria can make a huge difference to the decisions you make, and judgements about what will be successful and what will not.

Marketing choices are often complex, comparing not only alternative approaches – such as how much to spend on advertising relative to direct mail – but also between dissimilar initiatives – e.g. how much to spend on advertising versus investment in new product development which may not pay back for many years.

The decisions might come in all shapes and sizes:

- Strategic choice of new markets.

- Product portfolio rationalization.

- Targeting the best customers.

- Allocation of marketing budgets.

- Structure of brand architecture.

- Pricing changes.

- Optimization of media mix.

- Capital investments.

- Performance rewards.

We are still tempted to think that biggest is best – however, market share or sales or profits are not necessarily the best thing to have; and small companies focused in economically profitable niches can often deliver far better returns than others.

Imagine the European car market where identifying the 'market leader' depends on your criteria for success. Ford might be a clear leader in terms of volumes and revenues. Lexus might lead the field on customer satisfaction, while Mercedes gains the highest level of loyalty. Volkswagen might come out tops measured on profit. However, if Porsche delivers the best economic profit, and the best return to shareholders, then it is the rightful market leader.

We jump to the assumption that volumes, market shares and even customer satisfaction are the key measures of business performance yet, while all are often useful to achieve, there is no guarantee that any of them will lead to success.

Indeed, the impulsive desire to serve everyone and, worse, to be all things to everyone is the downfall of many a company. Trying to be all things to everyone, but ending up not being special for anyone.

Inspiration 4.1 JET BLUE

Jet Blue is the revolutionary airline that has brought style to a price-discounting market, offering spacious leather seats, each equipped with 36 channels of live satellite entertainment, while most of its competitors crumbled around it. Launched by David Neeleman, Jet Blue now serves 30 carefully selected US and Caribbean destinations with a fleet of 68 new, environmentally friendly Airbus A320 aircraft.

The airline succeeds competitively and financially by combining innovative, high-quality service with low fares to build a loyal following. Neeleman followed his previous successes with

Morris Air, which he sold to Southwest, and Open Skies, a simple yet powerful reservation system sold to Hewlett Packard. In 1999 he secured $130 million capital funding, rejected the thinking that 'no-frills' was the only future for airlines, and judged that the time was right to 'bring humanity back to air travel'.

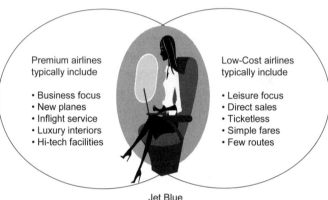

Premium airlines
typically include

• Business focus
• New planes
• Inflight service
• Luxury interiors
• Hi-tech facilities

Low-Cost airlines
typically include

• Leisure focus
• Direct sales
• Ticketless
• Simple fares
• Few routes

Jet Blue
combines the alternative conventional
approaches to create a new, distinctive
and profitable airline

The success of Jet Blue has been in choosing what to offer and what not to offer. Instead of thinking in dimensions of 'full service, high fare' or 'low service, cheap fare', Neeleman has created a different approach. He offers some aspects of full service better than anybody else – while at the same time eliminating in-flight meals, paper ticketing and the complexity of round-trip bookings. It is this unique combination that attracts customers, enables radical differentiation and sustains a high margin.

When asked how he has done it, Needleman identifies four priorities:

1   Start with lots of money – Jet Blue is the best capitalized airline start up in history, able to invest leading-edge products.

2   Fly new planes – Jet Blue's new fleet of aircraft are more reliable and more fuel efficient, and have faster turnaround times.

3   Hire the best people – Jet Blue screens new employees rigorously, trains them well and gives them the best tools, enabling and motivating people.

4   Focus on service – offer the best experience you can, driving customer retention and word of mouth recommendations among target audiences.

Source: jetblue.com

Jet Blue, rather than Southwest Airlines, is now winning all the customer satisfaction awards, a rare beacon of profitability in a struggling sector, and an inspirational case study for achieving both customer and business success.

Application 4.1 MARKET STRATEGY

Which markets should you be in? Where are the hot spots and white spaces? How should you be positioned in these markets? How will you deliver long-term value creation in them?

1. Business context

Understand the wider business strategy and objectives, and their implications for markets and marketing.

2. Evaluate the opportunities

Having mapped the broader markets consider their relative competitiveness and potential economic value.

3. Where to compete

Choose which markets or sub-domains the business should focus on to deliver goals and long-term value.

4. How to compete

Find sources of sustainable competitive advantage in this markets, and what it means for products, channels etc.

5. How to win

Design a business model that will maximize value and relative price positioning in each market.

6. Strategies for action

Develop marketing and innovation, brand and customer strategies to achieve this.

Concept 4.1 MARKET PERSPECTIVES

Strategy is about direction.

Direction depends on where you start. Constantly reshaping the markets where you start makes a big difference to what you see, and where you might end up. It therefore also requires perspective (a viewpoint on the potential landscape around you) and posture (how you will engage with it).

Markets can no longer be put in boxes, drawn with clear borders, and brands don't operate in singular domains – witness Nike's huge range of watches and eyewear, Burberry offering a wide range of shoes in partnership with Dr Scholl, and Stella McCartney's swimwear for Adidas. Brands and partnerships, fashions and consumers all break down the traditional boundaries for competition.

Having perspective

Every player is likely to have a different perspective on a market. A key aspect is to understand market adjacency. The markets adjacent to one player might be different from a competitor depending on the perspective. Adjacency can be described on any axis, but most typically in dimensions such as the following:

- Customer – who else could the same products be sold to, in their existing or some derivative form?

- Product – what additional products and services do customers seek when they buy ours? Somebody who buys coffee also wants to buy milk, sugar, biscuits and cakes.

- Capability – what other kinds of products and services could we develop using our skills and knowledge? A paper manufacturer may get into packaging, a restaurant into outsourced catering.

- Networks – what other kinds of services could use our distribution network?

This will likely generate a high number of adjacent market possibilities, while also demonstrating how many markets are in close proximity, and therefore contain brands probably just as interested in reaching into your own sector, perhaps creating new forms of competition as they link previously unrelated capabilities and applications.

Having a posture

Market posture depends on how you relate to others. As markets change, you can either shape your own destiny or be shaped by somebody else's.

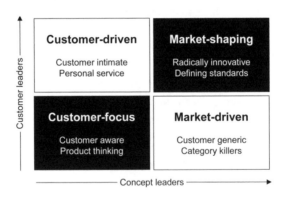

As conventions, standards and regulation rapidly evolve, they are shaped by those who are the leaders, the innovators, and the most influential. In the simplest terms, you can be a leader or a follower:

- Leaders can shape new markets on their own terms. They can establish new ways of working, new formats for products, new pricing structures. They can grab the best customers and seek to retain them. They can charge more for new solutions, while also building barriers to entry or imitation.

- Followers can learn from the mistakes of leaders. They can observe which aspects of innovation work, and avoid those that don't. They can imitate and evolve even better ideas. They can catch the second wave of customers, who are typically more numerous. They can undercut the leaders, and sometimes make them irrelevant.

Land Rover created the first sport utility vehicle (SUV) almost 40 years ago. However, it never made the most of this leadership, perhaps because it didn't see what it had with sufficient perspective, and it was those that followed that made the category attractive and profitable. Meanwhile, Apple strongly influenced the future market for download music through its hardware and software, establishing a business model that music companies find acceptable, and competitors find hard to compete against.

On top of this 'leader versus follower' approach is whether you take a market-wide or customer-specific approach. Do you seek to drive or be driven by the market as a whole, or do you more intimately want to drive or be driven by the need of individual customers? The customer approach is good in that it is more focused on the niche audience that you specifically seek to serve, but limited in that it is driven by their needs, while the market itself might be moving in a different direction.

In the B2B market, where a company may only have a small number of customers, working to the requirements of the individual customer might build a strong relationship; however, if the customer loses sight of the market then your own fate is very much in their hands. In reality you need to pay attention to customers *and* the wider market.

Bringing these postures together – leading and following, broad and narrow-focus – creates options for your 'playing style' in the competitive marketplace.

Inspiration 4.2 SKY TV

Sky has changed our viewing habits, and our social behaviours too. With more than 17 million viewers in 7 million UK households, Sky now offers an unprecedented choice of movies, news, entertainment and sport. Not only that, but it has also been smart in signing up the content that is most in demand – not least Premiership football – in order to entice terrestrial viewers, and charges a premium for it.

Sky sees the main benefits of digital technology as the ability to provide greater choice and flexibility. James Murdoch, Sky's youthful CEO, argues that 'Customers are demanding more and more in the way they consume media, the way they consume entertainment in the home with their family.' Sky sees this trend continuing to grow, with more connectivity between devices, and two or three set-top boxes in many homes.

Sky+ has been the most successful innovation, a personal video recorder, even if the ability to skip ads could damage more traditional revenue streams for the business. Advertising represents an important 8% of total revenues, and so sees the challenge as 'to think about different ways and innovative ways to continue to bring brands to consumers in more engaging ways'. Resolving this dilemma requires more experimentation into interactive forms of advertising, making them more contextual to programmes, and more valuable to customers.

Now that it reaches 30% of homes, the focus has moved from land-grab to profitable delivery. Sky+ has brought personal choice and recording in a way that Tivo failed to achieve, while the licensing of its own channels – such as Sky News and Sky Sports – to cable and digital networks has extended its reach. James Murdoch now has the challenge of sustaining the relentless growth demanded by his father.

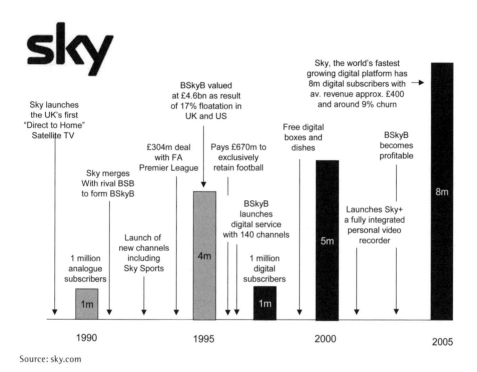

Source: sky.com

Application 4.2 MARKET SELECTION

Which markets should you choose to play in? Where are the best emerging opportunities to create value through a compelling and distinctive proposition for customers that achieves our strategic goals and delivers value to shareholders?

1. What is adjacent to you?

Consider your current market and the 'adjacent' markets to it, both current and emerging.

2. Mapping adjacent dimensions

Map out axis from your current position based on 'what' (propositions), 'how' (capabilities) and 'why' (applications).

3. Defining evolving activities

Apply a scale of related activities along each of these axes, e.g. showing how an existing proposition could evolve.

4. Connecting the markets

Connect the axes along lines of decreasing practicality, for example using high, medium and low.

5. Evaluating their potential

Evaluate possible new markets along or across the axes in terms of profit, growth and competitiveness.

6. Selecting new markets

Identify the existing and adjacent markets best fit and potential as part of your market strategy.

Concept 4.2 MARKET FOCUS

Strategy is about choices.

Strategy demands a focus of effort, deciding where your priorities lie and, by implication, deciding what you will not do. This is where organizations become unstuck. They hate saying no to opportunities and, even more, they hate stopping what they currently do. Many times has a CEO said, 'We must focus on doing fewer things better', but then finds it all too difficult to dispose of a long-standing part of the business, or a heritage brand, or to say no to entering a certain market, or serving particular segments of customers.

We shy away because we aren't completely convinced it's the right thing to do? Because there might be strong reasons for and against it or, with eternal optimism, one might believe that an under-performer will come good again. And even if we had total clarity, we still need the guts to do it, to reject an audience that we have always served, to endure the backlash of a diminishing audience that hankers after an outdated product. Then there are the implications for employees, intermediaries and suppliers.

Unilever, the consumer goods company with brands ranging from Persil to Knorr, boldly announced how it would reduce its brand portfolio from 5000 to 500, and then eventually to 50 brands. While initially these brands were local by-products of acquisitions and easy to substitute without loss of business through mainstream rebranding, it then got harder as whole businesses with significant cash flows were stood down.

While rationalizing your portfolio by 99% might seem a little optimistic, most companies could probably find that 60–80% of what it does is fairly marginal to its overall business performance – the creation of long-term shareholder value.

Which portfolios should you be considering?

- Markets – by geography or sector.

- Customers – intermediaries and consumers.

- Brands – business units or product ranges.

- Products – products and services.

While a conventional marketing approach to portfolio analysis would be to consider the 'life cycle' of products (using the classic revenue growth versus market share Boston Matrix, for example), this needs to be enhanced with a financial understanding of the likely short- and long-term returns.

However, while considering the profitability of each entity (market, brand, product, channel) within the portfolio is useful, this does not identify the real value creators. Considering 'economic profitability' raises the bar to incorporate the minimum expected return by shareholders – i.e. they expect a return of say 9–10% (depending on your business and sector), and 'value creation' only happens beyond this level.

Economic profit, which is operating profits less the 'cost of capital' (i.e. the minimum expected return), therefore 'rebases' the criteria for real success.

This enables you to focus on the real 'value creators', and to halt further investments in, or efforts to sell more of, the 'value destroyers'. Of the latter, even if they appear somewhat profitable, every additional sale will generate revenue, but destroy value. The challenge in these cases is to re-engineer or reposition the brands or products so that they do deliver an economic profit, or otherwise to dispose of them in some way.

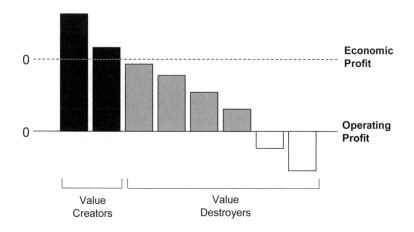

Inspiration 4.3 ENTERPRISE

Enterprise Rentacar prides itself on being 'a big company with the feel of a small business'. In less than 50 years the company founded by Jack Taylor has rocketed from a single car dealership to the top of the rental car industry.

Taylor's values were to treat employees and customers like family, and never compromise on the commitment to superior customer service.

Enterprise has quietly grown to become the largest car rental company in North America by rejecting the conventional wisdom of focusing on holiday and airport locations.

Instead Enterprise and its 57,000 staff, who all share in the business success, have grown up in the inner cities, focusing on short-term and replacement rentals. The company now generates over $7 billion from its 600,000 cars. Previous car rental leaders Hertz and Avis now need to try even harder.

Enterprise people share an incredible entrepreneurial spirit more associated with a small company, working customer by customer, car by car, to be the best rather than the biggest. Their service culture and market focus enables them to charge a market premium, and to rapidly enter new markets that to the conventional eye would appear saturated.

These principles are the focus of every action, every day, and are captured and sustained through Enterprise's 'Cultural Compass'. The compass ensures that all employees are focused on engaging the communities in which they operate, improving diversity throughout the business, and contributing 'hours and dollars to the causes that matter the most'.

Along the way, Taylor has created thousands of millionaires out of employees who work hard and share in Enterprise's success, by tying rewards to long-term value creation: 'We are not entitled to our success. We have to earn it, each and every day'.

Enterprise has recently set about reshaping its business to ensure more success in the future.

Now the largest car rental firm in the US, it is rapidly moving into new markets, particularly Europe. While the target customer remains those seeking short-term hires for weekends or while their car is getting repaired, Enterprise is at last testing the airport market too.

Car rental is still its focus, and indeed it recently spun off its non-automotive businesses that somehow grew with its success – an unlikely portfolio of balloons, footwear, golf courses, hotel amenities and prison supplies – to form the Centric Group.

Application 4.3 PORTFOLIO ANALYSIS

Which products should you have in your portfolio? What are your evaluation criteria to understand their short- and long-term value potential? Which should you focus on, remove, and add? What difference would this make to the coherence of the portfolio? Similarly, what is the best make-up of your portfolio of markets, your brand portfolio, and your customer portfolio?

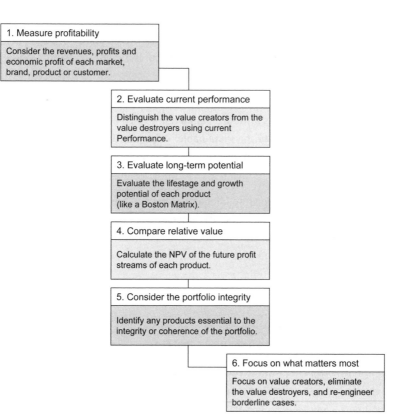

1. Measure profitability

Consider the revenues, profits and economic profit of each market, brand, product or customer.

2. Evaluate current performance

Distinguish the value creators from the value destroyers using current Performance.

3. Evaluate long-term potential

Evaluate the lifestage and growth potential of each product (like a Boston Matrix).

4. Compare relative value

Calculate the NPV of the future profit streams of each product.

5. Consider the portfolio integrity

Identify any products essential to the integrity or coherence of the portfolio.

6. Focus on what matters most

Focus on value creators, eliminate the value destroyers, and re-engineer borderline cases.

Concept 4.3 MARKET ADVANTAGE

Strategy is about differentiation.

Competitive advantage, as most non-marketers call it, or differentiation, as termed by marketers, sits at the heart of any strategy and is the source of business success. In a perfect market, a commodity will never deliver a return to shareholders beyond their expectations.

Differentiation is the source of added value, of exceeding expectations, of achieving market and financial performance. It is far more than a name, a colour, a strapline and a few added extras. It needs to be meaningful and sustainable, strong enough to define the types of people and capabilities required by the organization, and strong enough not to be imitated by competitors.

'Value disciplines' were developed by Michael Treacy and Fred Wiersema to understand the orientation that the whole business must embrace in order to achieve leadership. Their theory provides a simplistic but useful thinking model, and argues that there are three disciplines through which any company can become a leader in any sector:

- Product leadership – these companies have an obsessive focus on innovation and quality in order to offer the best products. Sony or Coca-Cola are examples.

- Customer intimacy – these companies have an obsessive focus on service and relationships in order to offer the best solutions. Dell or Lexus are examples.

- Operational excellence – these companies have an obsessive focus on efficiency and consistency in order to offer the best price. Aldi or Toyota are examples.

The model requires that a market leader must be 'good' at all three, but must specifically choose one area in which to truly excel, to be better than anybody else, and to be known for this as its source of competitive advantage. Of course, most companies will argue that today they

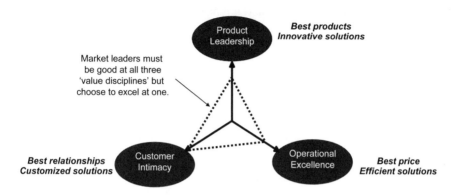

Source: Adapted from *The Disciplines of Market Leaders* by Treacy and Wiersema

need to be exceptional in all three areas; however, this is unlikely to enable focus and truly unmatchable difference.

Another reason why differentiation so often seems obvious yet inadequate in organizations is due to the primacy of the customer. If each competitor does the same market research, and seeks to meet the same customer needs, then they are likely to end up doing exactly the same – commodities that meet needs but cannot sustain a price premium. Marketers must work much harder to interpret and apply strategic thinking, competitive and customer insight, in a distinctive way.

Application 4.4 COMPETITIVE POSITIONING

How can you stand out in highly crowded markets, find a source of differentiation which is meaningful and difficult to imitate? What are the implications of this positioning for your whole business in its core competencies, its strategic priorities and its business model? How will you deliver it in words and actions? How is it manifest in your brand, and how will it tangibly add value to customers throughout their experience with you?

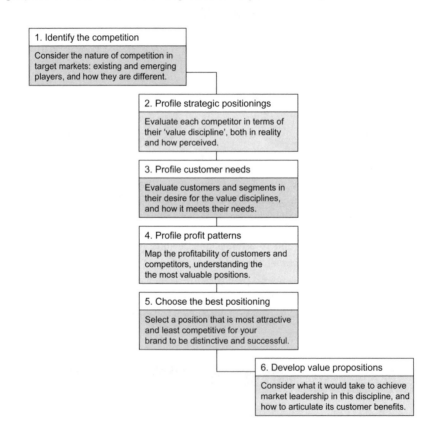

1. Identify the competition

Consider the nature of competition in target markets: existing and emerging players, and how they are different.

2. Profile strategic positionings

Evaluate each competitor in terms of their 'value discipline', both in reality and how perceived.

3. Profile customer needs

Evaluate customers and segments in their desire for the value disciplines, and how it meets their needs.

4. Profile profit patterns

Map the profitability of customers and competitors, understanding the the most valuable positions.

5. Choose the best positioning

Select a position that is most attractive and least competitive for your brand to be distinctive and successful.

6. Develop value propositions

Consider what it would take to achieve market leadership in this discipline, and how to articulate its customer benefits.

Inspiration 4.4   JOHNSON & JOHNSON

Our Credo

We believe our first responsibility is to the doctors, nurses and patients,
to mothers and fathers and all others who use our products and services.
In meeting their needs everything we do must be of high quality.
We must constantly strive to reduce our costs
in order to maintain reasonable prices.
Customers' orders must be serviced promptly and accurately.
Our suppliers and distributors must have an opportunity
to make a fair profit.

We are responsible to our employees,
the men and women who work with us throughout the world.
Everyone must be considered as an individual.
We must respect their dignity and recognize their merit.
They must have a sense of security in their jobs.
Compensation must be fair and adequate,
and working conditions clean, orderly and safe.
We must be mindful of ways to help our employees fulfil
their family responsibilities.
Employees must feel free to make suggestions and complaints.
There must be equal opportunity for employment, development
and advancement for those qualified.
We must provide competent management,
and their actions must be just and ethical.

We are responsible to the communities in which we live and work
and to the world community as well.
We must be good citizens – support good works and charities
and bear our fair share of taxes.
We must encourage civic improvements and better health and education.
We must maintain in good order
the property we are privileged to use,
protecting the environment and natural resources.

Our final responsibility is to our stockholders.
Business must make a sound profit.
We must experiment with new ideas.
Research must be carried on, innovative programs developed
and mistakes paid for.
New equipment must be purchased, new facilities provided
and new products launched.
Reserves must be created to provide for adverse times.
When we operate according to these principles,
the stockholders should realize a fair return.

Source: jnj.com

Finding the big idea that defines you

'A great brand taps into emotions. Emotions drive most, if not all, of our decisions. A brand reaches out with a powerful connecting experience. It's an emotional connecting point that transcends the product.'

Scott Bedbury

'Image is a reality.
It is the result of our actions.
If the image is false and our performance is good, it's our fault for being bad communicators.
If the image is true and reflects our bad performance, it's our fault for being bad managers.
Unless we know our image we can neither communicate nor manage.'

David Bernstein

Brands are about you, not me.

Brands are about people not products.

Brands are about customers not companies.

A great brand is one you want to live your life by, one you trust and hang on to while everything around you is changing, one that articulates the type of person you are or want to be, one that enables you to do what you couldn't otherwise achieve.

More intelligent brands	More imaginative brands
Purpose. Having a big idea that defines everything that your brand does for people, as a business or a product.	**Passion**. Having a passion that captures the mission and spirit, culture and values of the brand.
Compelling. Engaging target audience through functional, comparative and emotional dimensions.	**Reflective**. About your audience not about you. Reflecting them, the benefits they seek, and the dreams they have.
Realization. Managing the brand to drive the business and its people, current and future markets.	**Activation**. Bringing the brand to life for employees and customers, and one then reinforcing the other.

Brands were originally developed as labels of ownership. However, today it is what they do for people that matters much more, how they reflect and engage them, how they define their aspiration and enable them to do more. Powerful brands can drive success in competitive and financial markets, and indeed become the organization's most valuable assets.

Yet there are few great brands around.

Most brands are still labels, relying too strongly on brand names and logos, and focused too heavily on the companies and products that they help identify. They are articulated through superficial straplines and delivered through generic service. They make promises that the organization struggles to deliver, often failing to even attract attention, and rarely gaining the trust of sceptical customers.

Powerful brands have the ability to cut through the noise and competitiveness of markets, and to engage and retain the best customers in a way that delivers superior financial results in both the short and long term.

A powerful brand is one that:

- Defines a compelling purpose, a big idea that stands out from the crowd, that goes beyond the product or industry, and really matters to people.

- Reflects the customer, builds an image and reputation in the mind of the customer that has personal relevance, even if it alienates others.

- Engages customers in together achieving the big idea, delivered in a style through which people say, 'This is my kind of company'.

- Enables customers to do more, reinforcing the benefits and supporting their application, but also enabling physically or emotionally to do even more.

- Anchors customers around something familiar and important, while all else in the market, or in their personal world, continues to change.

- Evolves as markets and customers evolve, with the portability to move easily into new markets, and the glue to connect diverse activities.

- Attracts the target customers, building preference, driving purchase behaviour and sustaining a price premium.

- Retains the best customers, building their loyalty, introducing new services and encouraging advocacy.

- Drives shareholder value, not only through profits, but also by improving investor confidence, credit ratings and reducing cost of capital.

A powerful brand does all of this. However, a brand that attracts great attention because of its impressive ads, and that is perceived to be cool and desirable, and drives huge demand, is still not 'powerful' unless it can also convert this demand into sustained profitability.

Reflecting and engaging people

If brands are about people rather than products, then the big idea around which they are formed is more to do with what it does for people rather than the company.

There are a million models of a 'brand' – however, in common are three simple components – rational, comparative and emotional. By collectively defining what it does for people, differently from anything else, and how it makes them feel, we articulate 'the essence' of the brand. To be compelling and enduring, this is typically a far more profound idea than product, company or even sector-related benefits. It reflects aspirations rather than just needs; it provokes rather than just informs.

The brand idea is then delivered through every possible medium that the organization can utilize – from names and logos to leaders and buildings, products and services to advertising and brochures, colours and packaging to uniforms and interiors, culture and behaviours to training and rewards. Every aspect of the corporate or product 'experience' can deliver the brand in tangible and intangible ways. As Jan Carlson, former CEO of airline SAS said, 'every person, every promise and every action is a moment of truth'.

While business strategy will typically include logical mission statements and objectives, corporate brands capture the essence of why the business exists, and what it does for people. They use language and symbols that capture the essence of business concepts and customer promises; they use these symbols as more compelling shorthand to convey them. There should, of course, be strong alignment between the strategies and brands – both define the business rationally and emotionally.

Howard Schultz set up Starbucks out of frustration at the coffee quality in his native Seattle; however, the brand he created is much more than coffee. Schultz explains that he 'identified a *third place*, which I really believe sets us apart ... not work or home, it's the place our customers come for refuge'. This drives the product range, the interior design, the service philosophy, the communications: the tall skinny latte is good, but the known routine and comfortable environment mean more.

Similarly, other brands give their organizations a core, engaging purpose, which connects all audiences emotionally in 'why we do business'. Internally, brands stir emotions and energize people internally and externally to reach for the higher-order benefits that they are working towards:

- For Nike ... 'to do your best'.

- For Coke ... 'to refresh'.

- For Microsoft ... 'to help realize your potential'.

Even the most dull, boring industrial sector, dealing in so-called 'commodities' like cement or fertilizer can still create strong and compelling brands – look at Cemex or BASF, bringing real differentiation to the worlds of cement that dries faster, or fertilizer that makes your grass greener.

However, the brand is more than what you do – in fact it is not even what you do. In reality a brand is defined by how it is received and perceived – the image and reputation that forms in people's minds. A corporate brand is the reputation of the company. A product brand is the reputation of the product. Whether you think you are more likely to achieve a personal best with Nike rather than Adidas, or whether you believe that Coke is more refreshing than Pepsi.

A brand that does more for people, that reflects their personal needs and ambitions, that stirs emotions inside and tingles the hairs on the back of their necks has the making of a powerful brand. And, of course, if you seek to be special for some people, you will inevitably not engage others.

A great brand is therefore rarely liked by everyone – it stirs up passions, it polarizes people, it alienates some, but is loved by others. As Kevin Roberts, worldwide CEO of Saatchi and Saatchi and author of *Lovemarks*, says about a brand and its core audience, 'a truly strong brand is one that you love deeply and unconditionally'.

Enabling people to do more

Powerful brands enable people to do what they couldn't otherwise do. They must do more than simply endorse functional products, either by helping them to do something physically, or by building confidence and belief in their minds. Sony, for example, is all about helping people 'go create', encouraging their innovation and inspiring their action, helping them to do what they couldn't previously achieve.

Brands can typically help people to do more in four different ways:

- *Do* what they seek to achieve better, through improved functionality or support.

- *Be* how they want to be perceived, through a strong identity that gives recognition and is admired by others.

- *Belong* to a community that they seek to be part of, through improved real or perceived connections.

- *Become* somebody more than they are, adding personal esteem or the capabilities and confidence to do what they couldn't otherwise achieve.

Once a brand creates such a strong attachment with people, one that they find emotionally or practically essential to their lives, then the brand becomes an 'anchor' that can be more trusted, more permanent and more desired than many other things. Without anchors we can easily become lost in the maelstrom of competitive intensity. Imagine the drinker who can't get their favourite drink, or the weekly shopper whose visit to a certain supermarket becomes part of their routine, or the high-fashion wearer who stays loyal to their favourite designer label.

Anchor brands give people something positive to hang on to, while their markets or even their personal worlds are constantly changing. This rollercoaster of desire and choice can destabilize even the most confident buyer, creating confusion and anxiety, prompting expense and insecurity. More messages, more alternatives, more functionality, more versions, more incentives ... it can all become too much.

Brands that reflect people more personally, and do more for them, are likely to be the best anchors.

Graphic designers hang on to Apple, serious runners hang on to Nike and business leaders continue to rely on McKinsey. However, brands that seek to serve mass markets, to mean something to everyone, and therefore struggle to have strong bonds with discrete audiences, are unlikely to become the chosen anchors. Brands like Marks & Spencer, Reebok or Budweiser have succeeded by trading on mass popularity, convenience and ubiquity. What made them great could easily become their biggest handicap.

Levi's is another company trying to find relevance in today's world. When Nick Kaman took his jeans off in the famous 1983 TV commercial, the world wanted to buy his jeans. It was cool to be the same. However, in recent years the brand has seen a 65% decline in revenues, despite its increasingly frantic efforts to revive itself. In the past it was cool to be the same. Everyone wanted to be like him. Today, to be cool is to be different, and for young people that is likely to exclude wearing the same jeans as their parents, or even their peers. Today, people are more different, and therefore brands must reflect these greater differences and recognize that to be king of a niche is better than foolishly trying to conquer the world.

Driving short- and long-term value

Brands attract and retain the best customers and, as a result, are able to charge more, sell more, more often. This drives improved margins and creates greater certainty of future incomes too.

Indeed, brands are increasingly one of the most significant drivers of shareholder value, incredibly valuable intangible assets, increasing the quantity and likelihood of future profits.

These future potential profits, driven by the loyalty of customers to the brand, are often termed 'brand equity', and, indeed, a true reflection of the return on investment in a brand is only achieved by considering the brand equity that can drive current and future profits, rather than just comparing costs against short-term gains.

However, brands can do even more than this. A strong corporate brand doesn't just drive improved profits from customers; it also drives employee and shareholder behaviour too. Corporate brands have a strong and direct impact on employee morale, recruitment and retention, which can obviously flow through into better service for customers, ideas and productivity, and human capital.

Sears, the Canadian retailer, according to an article in *Harvard Business Review*, is able to demonstrate that a 5% improvement in employee attitude drives a 1.3% increase in customer satisfaction, which drives a 0.5% increase in revenue growth. Sears reflects this employee–customer–profit chain in their business objectives, to create 'a compelling place to work, a compelling place to shop, and a compelling place to invest'.

For shareholders, as well as the effect of more profitable sales, a strong brand can improve confidence through a better awareness and understanding of the organization, and a stronger view of future performance. This perception and reality of reduced risk can lead to improved credit ratings and lower cost of capital, both of which can have a significant impact on the economics of the business, as well as encouraging more investment and subsequent improvement in the share price.

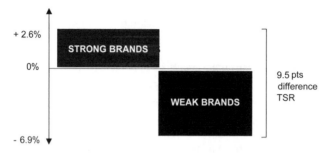

Research concluded that companies with brands that delivered both tangible and intangible benefits generated TSR (total shareholder return) that were 9.5 points higher than the TSR of weak brands.

Source: McKinsey, Compustat

Inspiration 5.1 VIRGIN

Virgin is one of the most diverse brands in the world. Led by their intrepid founder, chairman and owner Sir Richard Branson, Virgin believes in making a difference, standing for value for money, quality, innovation, fun and a sense of competitive challenge.

Virgin began in the 1970s with Branson's first venture, a student magazine and small mail order travel company.

Virgin searches for market opportunities where it can offer something better, fresher and more valuable than others. It often moves into areas where the customer has traditionally received a poor deal, and where the competition is complacent. With rapidly growing e-commerce activities, Virgin often looks to deliver 'old' products and services in new ways. It is pro-active and agile, leaving bigger and more cumbersome organizations in its wake.

When Virgin starts a new venture, it is based on hard research and analysis. It puts itself in the customer's shoes to see how it could make things better.

Virgin asks some fundamental questions: Is this an opportunity for restructuring a market and creating competitive advantage? What are the competitors doing? Is the customer confused or badly served? Is this an opportunity for building the Virgin brand? Can we add value? Will it interact with our other businesses? Is there an appropriate trade-off between risk and reward?

Today Virgin's travel operations, led by 51%-owned Virgin Atlantic Airways, are among its biggest breadwinners. Virgin Atlantic is complemented by lower-priced cousins Virgin Express in Europe and Virgin Blue in Australia. The group also operates two UK rail franchises and sells tour packages through Virgin Holidays.

Some of the group's 200 other businesses include retail stores, music, video, computer games, balloon flights, beverages, bridal stores, cosmetics, financial services, health clubs, Internet services, mobile phone services, publishing, and a record label.

The Virgin Group is a family of businesses sharing the same brand, and therefore attracting similar types of customer, but run independently. Most of these businesses are joint ventures with other companies, combining skills, knowledge and market presence, as well as investment and risk. The power of the brand, the network of businesses, and the management style all contribute to the success of each business.

Virgin sees its role as the consumer champion, with a set of brand values based on the six principles that Branson defined as what he wanted Virgin to be about when he first started.

Every Virgin company works hard to make these values mean more, bringing the brand to life in relevant and innovative ways:

1   **Value for money.** Simple, honest and transparent pricing – not necessarily the cheapest on the market, e.g. Virgin Express and Virgin Blue – low cost airlines with transparent pricing where you only pay for the basics.

2   **Good quality.** High standards, attention to detail, being honest and delivering on promises, e.g. Virgin Atlantic Upper Class Suite – limousine service, lounge, large flat bed on board, freedom menu, etc.

3   **Brilliant customer service.** Friendly, human and relaxed; professional but uncorporate, e.g. Virgin Mobile, which has won awards for its customer service, treats its customers as individuals, and pays out staff bonuses according to customer satisfaction survey results.

4   **Innovation.** Challenging convention with big and little product and service ideas; innovative, modern and stylish design, e.g. Virgin Trains' new 'Pendolino' fast tilting train with shop, radio, digital seat reservations and new sleek design.

5   **Competitively challenging.** Sticking two fingers up to the establishment and fighting the big boys – usually with a bit of humour, e.g. Virgin Atlantic successfully captured the public spirit by taking on BA's so-called dirty tricks in the mid 1990s.

6   **Fun.** Every company in the world takes itself seriously so we think it's important that we provide the public and our customers with a bit of entertainment, e.g. Virgin Mobile UK launch was naked people in a transparent phone to show Virgin Mobile had 'nothing to hide'.

Source: virgin.com

Application 5.1 BRAND DEFINITION

What is your big idea? What do you do for people? Who? How? Why is it better and different from any other brand? How do you cut through the many complex and psychologically bewildering models of brands to articulate your brand concept in a clear, practical and compelling way?

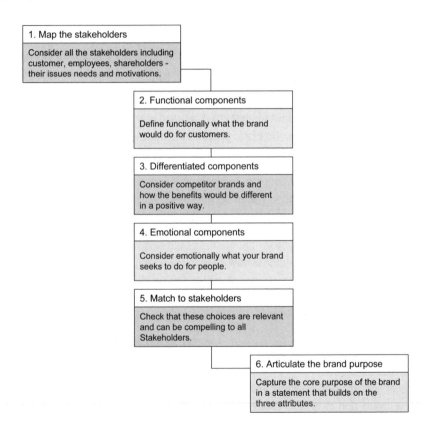

1. Map the stakeholders

Consider all the stakeholders including customer, employees, shareholders - their issues needs and motivations.

2. Functional components

Define functionally what the brand would do for customers.

3. Differentiated components

Consider competitor brands and how the benefits would be different in a positive way.

4. Emotional components

Consider emotionally what your brand seeks to do for people.

5. Match to stakeholders

Check that these choices are relevant and can be compelling to all Stakeholders.

6. Articulate the brand purpose

Capture the core purpose of the brand in a statement that builds on the three attributes.

Concept 5.1 LIVING THE BRAND

Brands increasingly define the business and, in doing so, what the overall business does for people. They connect the business to its context, to its customers and all other stakeholders.

Strong brands connect companies with people, both emotionally and practically and, most importantly, by ensuring the promises become realities over time. Brands define the purpose of business: they are the glue, the face, the relationship, and the reputation of business.

Disney's former CEO Michael Eisner suggests that 'a brand is a living entity – and it is enriched or undermined cumulatively over time, the product of a thousand small gestures'.

While brands used to be the domain of individual products, corporate brands are today the more significant form of branding, more valuable and important entities for customers and businesses. This is partly due to the rise of service-based business, the increasing awareness and transparency of the companies behind the products and services we buy, and the need for higher-order differentiation across the portfolio as well as for individual products.

Even the majority of consumer products now contain the strong endorsement of parent brands. Whereas in the past many consumers may never have heard of P&G and Unilever despite using their products daily, today the corporate brand marques appear prominently on the packaging of everything from washing powder to ice creams.

Organizationally, this means brands take on a broader, higher, non-functional role, rather than being a functional responsibility of the marketing department.

The brand defines the organization, and all the many stakeholders who work with it. It should reflect the needs and motivations of employees and shareholders, as well as customers. It overlaps and complements the business strategy and cultural values, and the business should ensure consistency and alignment between these. It is delivered through HR and investor relations as well as marketing.

While some companies, particularly when there is a strong corporate affairs department, get confused between brand and reputation, they are one and the same. The corporate reputation is the corporate brand

The brand is increasingly the most important business asset, often accounting for anything from 5 to 50% of the overall market value of a company, and in some businesses (be they luxury goods or not-for-profit) even more. It also becomes a far more complex and essential management challenge. BP, for example, considered how to harness the power of its brand across all its business units and all its stakeholders; it recognized that there was only one person who could lead this task. CEO John Browne recognized that this was his challenge, and his opportunity, to create a focused, cohesive and energized business, where his leadership could directly connect to the desired culture internally and the image and reputation externally.

Corporate brands align the inside and outside, employee and customer, culture and reputation, behaviours and differentiation, promises and reality.

Branded businesses are therefore about people. Their brand gives them a purpose that also becomes the organizing idea, the reason for coming to work each day, and a common mission that brings people together. Logos and identities, straplines and colours become mere shorthand for a much bigger and more powerful force.

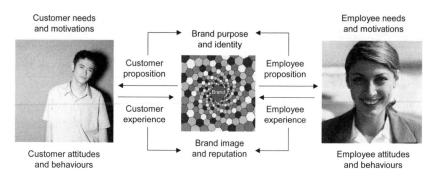

Brands are brought to life through people. Brands shouldn't be passive labels and images; they should be living experiences, where the values and beliefs are demonstrated in relevant and practical ways for customers, and equally for every other stakeholder group.

This is not simply about focusing on the customer audience, and then requiring employees to deliver it; it is about making the brand real in relevant ways for employees – and shareholders, suppliers, governments, etc. – too.

For customers a brand is made relevant through customer propositions, unique to each different customer segment and situation, which are then delivered through customer experiences that ensure that the promises of the brand and proposition become reality.

Similarly for employees, the business should develop employee propositions for each segment (some will be motivated by career progression, others more by job satisfaction, and others purely by money). Appropriate employee experiences should then be developed to match the promise and expectation of each audience.

Once staff are treated in an on-brand way, they are far more likely to respond in a positive way, i.e. to want to, to be able to, and to be motivated to put in that extra effort to 'live the brand' and deliver a personal and engaging experience for every customer.

Inspiration 5.2 PRET A MANGER

Pret is a sandwich shop. Indeed, its aluminium interiors, accessed through a doorway heralding that it is 'passionate about food', makes it unlike a normal sandwich shop.

College friends Sinclair Beecham and Julian Metcalfe set up Pret A Manger in 1986 with woefully little experience in the world of business. They created the sort of food they craved but couldn't find anywhere else. They have succeeded too, as the chain has since grown to over 130 shops, mostly in the UK, but also in New York and Hong Kong.

'It's important our sandwiches and sales taste better than anyone else's.'

To achieve this Pret builds a full kitchen at the back of every store. Suppliers are required to deliver fresh ingredients late every night and then, early the following morning, Pret's chefs get busy making the best sandwiches, wraps, pastries and cakes. There are no 'shelf life' or 'display until' dates on Pret sandwiches, as everything is fresh and made on the day, for the day.

> 'Pret creates hand made, natural food, avoiding the obscure chemicals, additives and preservatives common to so much of the 'prepared' and 'fast' food on the market today.'

> Source: Label on a Pret sandwich

Passion lies at the heart of the brand. Passion for the food they make, and people they employ. Indeed, go to their website and their 'Passion Facts' describe their passion for natural quality foods that are free from additives and preservatives, for freshness by ensuring that all food is made fresh in the shop, and for improvement, constantly seeking to make a better sandwich with the help of customers.

Despite a minority investment in the business by McDonald's, Pret rejects the conventions of most fast food brands. Not only does it not offer 'with fries', but it also rejects the mass-marketing concepts such as advertising, franchising or even focus groups. Indeed, Pret has learnt by trial and error what works best. In the USA, for example, Pret found no demand for its all day breakfast sandwich and had to swap butter for cream cheese with smoked salmon. However, the very-British coronation chicken with mango chutney sandwich was a big hit in the Big Apple.

Pret offers good jobs to great people who want to make and sell fabulous food. They invest in their people through training, incentives and rewards, paying them well above the average wage for the sector. Working at Pret is fun. They work as a team, they enjoy what they do, they play funky music all day, they wear their own jeans, and they love what they sell.

The service passion of Pret is established by a culture that treats and rewards employees as equals. Walk into a Pret store at 8 a.m. on a Monday morning and the funky music immediately captures the mood of the staff. The service is frantic but friendly and personal. Staff are taking orders, brewing coffee and taking the latest bread and pastries out of the oven simultaneously. It's a great buzz, which is contagious for customers too, and one that continues throughout the week to the infamous staff Friday nights out. Although customers aren't invited to those.

The Pret culture isn't scripted or engineered. It is just real and human, frantic and fun.

Application 5.2 BRAND ACTIVATION

How do you bring your brand to life? How do you replicate what you do for customers for internal audiences? How do you ensure that the inside and outside work together? How do give the brand depth and coherence? How do you make it impossible for anybody else to copy?

1. Start with the customer promise

Review the Customer Value Proposition(s) and Experience(s) that deliver the brand.

2. What do employees want

Understand the needs and motivations of employees when at work.

3. Make the brand relevant to them

Develop Employee Value Proposition(s) to engage them in tune with the brand.

4. Make the brand tangible to them

Design Employee Experience(s) to deliver this in tune with the brand.

5. Connect them to customers

Identify where and how employees can enhance the Customer Experience.

6. Encourage brand behaviours

Develop, encourage and reward these behaviours, and evolve them over time.

Concept 5.2 BRAND EXTENSIONS

As brands become ever more important, companies seek to get more out of them. John Browne, the CEO of BP, for example, recently made the development of the BP brand a key strategic objective, creating a new central team to manage and develop it, reporting directly to him.

As competition intensifies, organizations recognize that brands give them a bridge to other markets, new geographies or categories, and the ability to sustain a competitive position, particularly if their existing markets become over competitive or begin to decline.

While brand extensions might seem a no-brainer in terms of making more out of an existing asset, they can be full of pitfalls. They can jeopardize previously strong reputations, reduce trust and create confusion in the customer's mind. Some of the more famous stretches too far include:

- Bic, the disposable pen maker, branding underwear and perfume.

- Levi's, the jeans company, seeking to enter into men's suits.

- Colgate, the toothpaste, with a bizarre move into ready meals.

However, there is a positive side too. When companies do see the potential of new markets, brand extensions are usually a more successful route than trying to create a completely new brand, involving less cost and risk. According to David Taylor's research in *Brand Stretch*, an extension is typically 23% more successful than a new brand in prompting trial, 34% cheaper, and 61% better at driving repeat purchase.

When considering how to extend the brand, consider:

- *Where to extend*: reaching new customer groups, or geographical markets, with the same or new products, such as Tesco entering Eastern European markets, as well as convenience shoppers.

- *What to extend*: offering related or unrelated products and services under the same brand to existing or new customers, such as Virgin offering everything from planes and trains to drinks and phones, often to the same audiences.

- *How to extend*: doing it yourself, or with partners, for example by licensing your brand into new categories where others have skills, or franchising your existing business concepts to new markets in return for a royalty fee.

In each of these cases, there is a need for clarity of strategic thinking to ensure that the extension fits the objectives of the business, to evaluate the potential risks, benefits and value impact of such moves, and to manage partnerships and new market entries with effective controls.

Some companies have embraced brand extensions with a strategic objective of diversifying their business into a broader range of categories (such as Disney), sometimes to spread their bets in fast-changing markets (like Microsoft), while others have used it as a fundamental stepping stone to move the core of the business from one activity to another (e.g. GE), and sometimes because their existing markets are drying up (e.g. Kodak). Other examples include:

- BMW was always known for its executive saloon cars, but eventually recognized that the high-growth sport-utility vehicle (SUV) market was too good to miss, and it has even developed a premium range of mountain bikes.

- IBM, once known as 'big blue' for its leadership in mainframe computers, stretched into personal computers, and eventually moved away from hardware altogether into services and consulting.

- Gillette constantly evolves its range of razors, extending them to women, then further into a full range of bodycare products too, from shaving gels to deodorants and hair products.

Of course, if you define your brand around your customers, based on a belief or attitude, a benefit or aspiration, rather than it being a descriptor of your existing business or product, then it gives you far more scope and flexibility in the future.

Indeed, in fast-changing markets, 'extensions' are often no longer extensions – they simply reflect the moving centre of gravity of your business as markets and consumers evolve.

Extensions, of course, need to fit somehow with the brand structure – either using the existing brand strengths as a platform to launch into new markets, or perhaps using a different or evolved brand in order to give more flexibility and reach new audiences.

There are a number of different brand architectures to consider.

The architectures might be 'monolithic', in that there is total use of the single brand throughout, a family of different brands, as has typically been the case in consumer goods companies, or endorsement branding, where a corporate brand 'underpins' more niche-targeting brands.

In the case of a family of brands, these might reflect the different market segments (for example, Toyota's development of Lexus to target a wealthier audience with a distinctive proposition), different business activities (as in Time, AOL and Warner Bros) or use individual product brands to strengthen or even reposition the corporate brand (as iPod has so successfully made Apple cool and desirable again).

Family of product brands

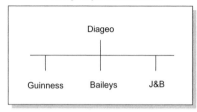

Family of business brands

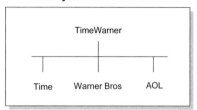

Family of segment brands

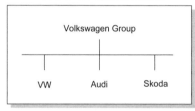

Monolithic corporate brand

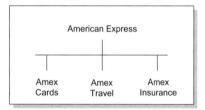

Application 5.3 BRAND ARCHITECTURE

How do you bring together the different parts of your business, and different audiences, through brands? Should you seek to fit everything under one brand? Or are a number of brands more appropriate to support your different businesses or markets?

1. What you do

Consider the current portfolio of
business and products.

2. How inside reflects outside

How do they reflect market and
customer structures.

3. Optional structures

Consider the architectural options –
from 'monolithic brand' to
'house of brands'.

4. Adding value through structures

Identify where sub-brands or
endorsement can increase the
relevance to specific audiences.

5. Choosing the right structure

Map out and articulate this structure,
ensuring that it is practical and
distinctive.

6. Rearticulating what you do

Develop identity and nomenclature to
capture this in a logical and
compelling way.

Concept 5.3 BRAND IMPACT

Brands are most conventionally evaluated through the impact of their advertising, and most typically by the amount of awareness they generate. This is misleading in that it is a measure of the advertising rather than the brand; second, there is no guarantee that awareness will lead to sales, and there is rarely a correlation between volume of coverage and profitability.

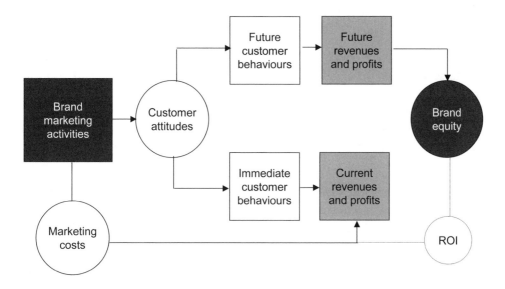

If we go further and try to relate brands to the sales they generate, then again we are only getting part of the picture. It is generally accepted that around 60% of the investment in communicating brands will drive future revenues, making a correlation between cost and revenue difficult. We therefore need something else which captures the impact of brand building today, and its potential to drive future business results. This is the role of brand equity.

Brand equity seeks to capture the future potential of the brand, that is, the likely sales that will be derived in future through the impact the brand has on customers today. We do this by understanding the attitudes and behaviours that the brand drives in its target audiences, then seek to correlate how these build up and translate into future sales. Of course, their actual behaviour will also be driven by the future context, and additional sales and marketing activity at the time of purchase.

Brand equity is typically expressed as an index, an amalgam of measures of what you initially find to be the key drivers of customer behaviour. Market research would be used to identify the prioritized customer attitudinal drivers (for example, for an airline this might be convenience, availability and service levels), then to understand how these drive which behaviours (e.g. purchase, price tolerance, referral). These are likely to differ by market, by segment and by product. Ongoing performance against these attributes can then be tracked and collated as a brand equity score.

To make this most tangible to business, we seek to connect it to financial implications, and specifically to the likely future revenues, and the costs of generating these. This future cash flow analysis can then lead to a business valuation, which captures the total likely profits in subsequent years.

For marketers, value-based analysis of brands and their marketing enables them to reflect the true return on their investments in brands, and to justify significant investments in areas that may not yet seem the most lucrative, but may well be in the future. It also helps the marketer to demonstrate to the business, and the business to investors, a significant driver of the business's overall future potential, and thereby help support its market value.

'Brand value' is often talked about, and seized upon as a key result. In most cases, this refers to the proportion of the overall value that can be attributable to the brand trademark, i.e. rather than all the other associated aspects of the brand proposition, including the product and service benefits. One way to calculate this value is to imagine that the business does not own its trademarks, and instead has to pay a third party a fee for its use, and to calculate what this fee would be over the coming years relative to the potential future profit streams.

A brand's value in this sense is a smaller but still significant proportion of a business's overall value. At an operational level, knowing the brand value has little direct application, it being far more useful either in justifying the business's value in an acquisition or disposal situation, or in justifying the value of the intangible asset for tax purposes.

As the value of intangible assets continues to rise (now at around 75% of the market value of the *Fortune* 500), businesses increasingly seek to articulate the value of their intangibles, and indeed recognize that a business whose value is largely intangible – i.e. tied up in intellectual properties that will hopefully drive future cash flows – requires a very different style of management and measurement.

At present international accounting standards only allow such assets to appear on the balance sheet if they have been acquired rather than organically developed, although these assets can now be defined more specifically rather than just lumped together as goodwill. Acquired intangible assets can also now be retained on the balance sheet, as long as the acquiring company can demonstrate that they have not decreased in value each year. Of course, this still means that the majority of brands and other intangibles that have been developed organically cannot be accounted for in a formal way.

Inspiration 5.3 BMW

The famous blue and white BMW logo represents the sky and a moving propeller, and reflects its early days since 1916 spent building aircraft engines. However, the Bayerische Motoren Werke quickly moved on within a decade to making motorbikes and cars. And, indeed, the emphasis has been on creating 'the ultimate driving experience' ever since.

There is perhaps no other brand that has retained such an unrelenting focus and consistency in what it stands for over time. It is a luxury and elitist brand that not everyone can afford, appealing to people who won't accept second best. While for many years there was just BMW – no sub-brands, no model names – today it is also the parent company of the Mini and Rolls-Royce brands.

BMW is a model of branding consistency, not only over time, but in everything it does. The 'ultimate' theme has captured the product excellence of the brand through products and services, communications and showrooms. Indeed, a BMW showroom is more like a brand temple, exuding the values of the brand both visually and experientially. However, it looks beyond the showroom to engage potential customers, not all of whom are keen to drive the same car as their parents drove.

BMW Films, for example, has become an award-winning innovative marketing campaign. BMW was relatively new to the US market, and also associated with the older rather than younger executive market. It produced eight beautifully-shot short films, each less than 10 minutes long and made them available only online. TV and press teaser campaigns highlighted their existence, creating curiosity in its target markets, and letting them find out more if they wished. The underground campaign became viral as people referred others, and BMW became a branded designer cult for a new generation.

The unusual approach of restricting access defied the classic rule that you need mass-coverage, image-based TV and press campaigns to build a brand. Instead, they offered an invitation to people to find out more on their terms, when they wanted and recommended by their friends. It also recognized that the same BMW brand needed to be articulated in very different ways to appeal to different audiences. While the technology-based personalization of messages is important, it is also the manner of the interaction that matters, in physical relationships; just because somebody talks to you about something of great interest to you, if they do so in the wrong manner then you are not interested.

Application 5.4 BRAND EQUITY

How do you measure the level of engagement that audiences have with your brand, based on their awareness, their attitudes and behaviours? How do you quantify their future propensity to purchase, based on their current affinity to the brand?

1. Understand brand perceptions

Research the brand's perceived attributes and their relative importance to customers.

2. Connect brand to attitudes

Map the customer attitudes (e.g. preference) that the brand drives, and the brand's relative impact on them.

3. Connect behaviours to purchases

Understand how these attitudes drive behaviours that lead to current and future purchases.

4. Quantify brand's current impact

Quantify the performance of brand attributes driving current sales.

5. Quantify brand's future impact

Quantify the performance of brand attributes driving future sales.

6. Measure and track brand equity

Articulate these brand drivers of future sales as a 'brand equity index'.

Getting inside the heads of intelligent customers

'I am irresistible, I say, as I put on my designer fragrance. I am a merchant banker, I say, as I climb out of my BMW. I am a juvenile lout, I say, as I pour an extra strong lager. I am handsome, I say, as I put on my Levi jeans.'

John Kay

'Diversity defines the health and wealth of nations in a new century. Mighty is the mongrel. The hybrid is hip. The impure, the *mélange*, the adulterated, the blemished, the rough, the black and blue, the mix and match – these people are inheriting the earth. Mixing is the new norm. Mixing trumps isolation. It spawns creativity, nourishes the human spirit, spurs economic growth and empowers nations.'

G. Pascal Zachary

Customers ... consumers, intermediaries, influencers, decision-makers, distributors, users, beneficiaries. The focus of business has long been on the people who generate the demand for our products and services, and who make the sales that keep us in business.

More intelligent insights	More imaginative insights
Research. Understanding customers qualitatively and quantitatively to find new and distinctive insights.	**Insights**. Observing patterns and trends, to predict how customers and their needs are likely to evolve.
Segments. Finding clusters of similar people, understanding them better, and targeting those of highest value.	**Individuals**. Recognizing that every customer is unique, with distinctive needs, motivations and aspirations.
Responsible. Marketing in legal, ethical and socially responsible ways, positively contributing to their societies.	**Transparent**. Recognizing customers as intelligent people, through more open and collaborative relationships.

Customers today are more different and individual, more discerning and demanding than ever. While 100 years ago, a new car buyer would be more than happy to buy a Ford Model T, a model that hardly changed in decades, in 'any colour as long as it's black', today customers are intelligent, expectant and pedantic. Their stated needs may well be true, but their unstated needs and wants often matter more.

Consider the BMW parked outside while the driver secures the best prices at Aldi, or the Gucci bag found on the discounted shelves of TK Maxx.

Their motivations and aspirations are complex and personal, and it takes a highly intelligent marketer to decipher them.

Indeed, classic marketing techniques such as segmentation have increasing difficulty in making sense of such markets, as customers no longer fit into simple boxes – where there is relative homogeneity within each box, and difference between them. Some companies find that they need to break their customers down into 4–500 clusters before they can get any relevant segmentation. Indeed, such groups rarely follow simple physical or demographic descriptors – postcodes, socio-economic groups and occupations are less relevant than ever in describing who we are.

Additionally, the increasing complexity of lives means that we are probably in different segments for different activities – prepared to pay a premium for the best car, but wanting to save every penny on our weekly shopping, too lazy to change energy supplier, but ready to travel double the distance to get a lower-cost flight, and even depending on our mood when doing such activities.

Our life patterns are less predictable too. With 500 channels of TV, 24 hours a day, it is hard to tell who will be watching what or when, how to target advertising, or schedule programmes. Similarly, our life stages are more complex, with more events and more unpredictability – we move house more often, we marry more often, we change job more often.

What are some of the ways consumers have changed?

- We value products less than ever before, and instead how we engage with brands is far more important.

- We respect youth more than age, we aspire to be youthful at every age, rather than looking up to our elders.

- We value life more than money, preferring to deal in currencies such as knowledge, friendship or well-being rather than cash.

- We seek to enhance the things we enjoy or value, and to minimize the things that we don't enjoy or are not important to us.

Our attitudes to brands and marketing have changed too. We live in the age of the intelligent consumer, where prior to a transaction, the consumer has probably done far more product research and price comparison than the sales assistant.

Transparency means that promises have to be realized. Consumers make choices about brands based on their CSR performance, or their attitudes towards their staff, more than the quality of products. Indeed, trust in companies and their brands has suffered as a result. Few companies manage to be whiter than white.

Trust, however, is a relative concept. According to research by the Henley Centre:

- A US consumer has on average 69% trust in Starbucks, while a UK consumer has 36% and a French consumer 12%.

- We trust our banks more than we trust lawyers, despite the fact that banks lock us into accounts with incredibly low returns.

- We trust global brands more than local brands in developing countries, but trust local brands more than global brands in developed countries.

The challenge for marketing, in these respects, is as it has always been. To understand customers, to develop solutions to their needs, and to connect with them in appropriate ways that result in their satisfaction, and a profit for the business.

It is just a million times more complicated than it was 100 years ago.

Application 6.1 CUSTOMER FORESIGHT

How do you understand what customers want when they don't know what is possible? Or they just haven't articulated the need? Or there simply isn't a word for it? How do you look at what will happen next?

1. Market evolutions

Hypothesize the evolution of next
10 years of major contextual trends
– social, economic, and technological.

2. Key junctions

Identify major future 'junctions' where
each of these contexts may
create divergence.

3. Customer trends

Consider existing measured or
perceived customer trends.

4. Extrapolate customer trends

Extrapolate these forwards
across the contexts.

5. Turning points

Develop a divergent 'tree diagram'
of the options at each junction, and
which way trends might turn.

6. Cluster potential futures

Identify all the potential end points,
and which are most common,
and more likely.

Concept 6.1 CUSTOMER INSIGHT

There is no lack of market research.

Most organizations are weighed down by research reports, tracking data, analytical spread-sheets and the like. The research industry is consequently huge too, perpetuating the myth that more data is good for you. Yet most information collected by organizations is useless. It doesn't address the issues important to them, it is quickly aggregated and averaged so that any useful knowledge is smoothed out, and it is more often than not requested by managers who have already decided what they want to do, irrelevant of the research findings.

Despite these mountains of data, or perhaps because of them, companies have very little insight into their customers' real needs, motivations and aspirations. Sometimes they will have information, but in the form of market averages it is pretty meaningless. Which customers today conform to an average, and as a result would be happy with a solution that has some-thing for everyone, but is not special for anyone?

So how do you achieve insight?

Data is not information, information is not knowledge, and knowledge is not insight. Insight is more profound. It tells you something new and useful, it considers aspects that you have not thought about before, which are not described within the conventions of markets. It puts knowledge into context. It describes why and how, as well as who and what.

The first steps in achieving insight are to stop using research 'like a drunk uses a lamp post', that is, to stop collecting more data than you need, resisting the desire to research everyone constantly, and to ask every possible question. There is also a temptation to jump into research without clarifying objectives, often finding that it has no particular purpose, or cannot answer the most important questions. Answers are then often predefined, prejudicing or limiting the responses by the questions asked or options given.

Too much research asks customers to say what they want, when they can rarely describe unfulfilled needs. It is also tempting to use the same techniques for everything, because it is the easiest method, or the most preferred by the incumbent research agency.

Another problem is the interpretation of the research through averages and, as a result, generated with little meaning to anyone. And adding to this, biasing results with preconceived wisdoms, lazy interpretation of results which trots out the same old phrases, prejudices and assertions. And to round off all these inaccuracies, researchers have a habit of seeking numbers rather than colour, wanting an absolute answer, to 2 decimal places, rather than looking deeper for more subtle differences.

Marketers need to adopt more thoughtful approaches to research, interpretation and decision-making that enable and demand real insight. These would include:

- Defining research requirements with the end in mind. If it is to improve profitability then understand what would drive this.

- Look for the deviants, the extremes, the anomalies rather than eliminating these through summarizing and averaging.

- Use a broad range of research techniques, from concept testing and mood boards to neural networking and psychographics.

- Embrace ethnography, observing what customers really need, or struggle to do, rather than asking them to describe it themselves.

- Use every source of customer knowledge as research; complaints, for example, are one of the best sources of insight and relationship.

- Find different language to describe the insights – use customer language, metaphors, analogies, symbols, cartoons and role play.

- Stay open-minded and ensure that interpretation is fact-based rather than embracing any assumption or assertion.

- Give decision-makers raw information rather than interpretation, take the boardroom to the customer, use anecdotes, stories and video.

Remember too that the recipients, the decision-makers, might seek the insights presented to them, but are even more engaged if they can be insightful themselves, understanding the analysis and drawing conclusions.

Ultimately an insight is only valuable if it leads to practical and commercial action; therefore, the insight process must be closely aligned to the innovation and delivery processes.

Analysis and ordering frameworks are useful to make sense of the data, for example to understand which factors are essential hygiene factors compared with others which are not essential but nice to have, compared with those in between which are the domain of the functional differentiators. Understand what it is that customers simply require, versus what it is that energizes them at a far more emotional level.

Brand Energizers
Building affinity and loyalty

Brand Differentiators
Building relevance and preference

Brand Essentials
Building awareness and trust

Use more rigorous analysis techniques to understand the relative importance of factors, rather than just assuming that everything is important. Perhaps utilizing more technologically-enabled techniques to trade-off complex sets of options, from the intangibility of image to the elasticity of price, understanding the preferred levels of performance, and relative performance to competitors or other benchmarks.

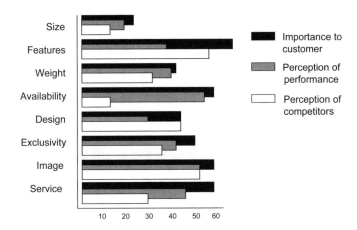

Customer research, information and insight should not be hoarded in the market research department, but freely accessible to everybody across the business and, indeed, the best insights might come when unexpected teams make use of the knowledge, connecting it to other issues and activities, driving innovation and improved performance.

One recent approach at the Neuroimaging Lab at Baylor College of Medicine, and described on its website, was to use functional magnetic resonance imaging (fMRI), a non-invasive scanning technique, to understand consumer behaviours.

As an example, they tried the 'Pepsi Challenge' on volunteers while scanning the reactions of their brains. When given Coke and Pepsi unlabelled, the response to Pepsi was five times stronger – most significantly seen in the ventral putamen, one of the brain's reward centres.

However, when the brands were revealed, nearly all volunteers preferred Coke. Coke stimulated a different part of the brain – the medial prefrontal cortex, an area more associated with thinking and judging, and with our 'sense of self'.

The brand, or at least some aspect of it, was clearly resonating with people at a much higher level and overriding more functional responses.

Inspiration 6.1 ZARA

It was in a shop window in the northern Spanish port of La Coruña that Amancio Ortega and his girlfriend spotted a beautiful silk negligee, but with a price tag well out of reach of the shirt maker's budget.

That night he went back to his workshop and reproduced what he had seen for a fraction of the price and, with the approval of his girlfriend, launched his own fashionable but affordable nightwear and lingerie business. The public reaction was so positive that he quickly moved into broader fashion and opened his first shop in the quiet, slightly dull fishing town in 1975.

Ortega pursued his vision of 'ready-baked' clothes, as he called them, translating the latest ideas from the catwalk and trends on the street into new ranges faster than anyone else.

The business grew rapidly through the eighties and, in 1989, he opened his first international stores in Paris and New York. Perhaps one of the more interesting approaches has been the different competitive positions that Zara has adopted in different markets – in Spain Zara is low-cost high-fashion, in the USA it is more premium-priced, and in UK mid-priced.

Zara is now the largest brand within the Inditex group, which with a turnover of £3 billion and 40,000 employees also includes supporting brands such as Pull and Bear and Massimo Dutti. With Ortega still very much at the helm, the group's headquarters is only a short ride from La Coruña, where its large and minimalist campus is full of designers deeply immersed in their market research and fashion magazines, or back from the catwalks and yarn mills, ready to take the latest ideas to the high street in record time.

Speed and efficiency are the real source of Zara's success. Everything is streamlined to ensure that Zara can be the first to market with the latest fashions at affordable prices. The concept depends on the continuous creation and rapid replenishment of new designs. Zara's 'sense and respond' approach enables it to occupy the leading edge of the fashion cycle, when demand and prices are highest and, coupled with its highly efficient supply chain, margins are greatest.

Visit any one of the 750 Zara stores in 55 countries, and the same fashions are unlikely to be in store for more than a few weeks. With new products arriving every day, and around 11,000 products a year, there is no wonder that customers are impulsive buyers, and regular visitors to their stores. Indeed, on average, customers visit Zara stores 17 times a year.

The Zara in-store experience is also the primary marketing platform, rejecting the typical fashion approach to image-based TV and press advertising. The company believes more in finding the best retail locations, with spacious and contemporary interiors, and its stylish navy carrier bags rather than a few seconds of overcrowded, two-dimensional airtime. Indeed, Zara spends around 0.3% of its revenues on marketing, yet has still managed to build one of the most desirable and talked about brands on the high street.

Similarly, Amancio Ortega, the old shirt maker from Galicia, may not be the best-known name in the fashion world compared with the likes of Armani, Klein or Dolce and Gabbana; however, he is one of the wealthiest. With a personal fortune of over $9 billion, only Bernard Arnault of luxury goods firm LVMH outranks him in the *Forbes* rich list, and, indeed, it also makes him Spain's wealthiest man.

Pablo Picasso might well have been impressed.

Application 6.2 CUSTOMER INSIGHT

How do you bring structure and order to understanding the needs of customers? Which needs must you meet? Which are just nice to have but could make an emotional difference? Where are the best opportunities for differentiation?

1. Consider target customers

Consider the needs, motivations and aspirations of target customers.

2. What are 'essentials'?

Identify the non-negotiable 'essentials', What is legally necessary or customers expect as given.

3. What are 'energizers'?

Identify the emotionally motivating 'energisers', the small 'nice to haves' that can make a difference.

4. What are 'differentiators'?

Identify the more rational needs that could be 'differentiators', which are more discretionary but useful.

5. Select what to focus on

Select the key attributes by level and how likely they are to vary by individual.

6. Align to your brand promise

Match this needs hierarchy against the proposed brand structure.

Concept 6.2 CUSTOMER RESPONSIBILITY

The increased transparency of organizations, the rise of more sophisticated and personalized marketing techniques, the aggressive behaviours of organizations and social implications of our highly branded, marketing-driven world should all be of concern to the marketer.

While marketing-related legislation is growing at a faster rate than ever before, in response to the concerns of individuals and regulators, it also requires the proactive responsibility of marketers to consider the broader consequences of their actions, even if they are 'just doing their jobs'.

The backlash against arrogant, blinkered marketing is gaining momentum. Naomi Klein's *No Logo* fuelled the fire, but more recently a young traveller writer, Amaranta Wright, was hired by Levi's to travel through Latin America to look at the needs of teenagers. However, she became increasingly frustrated by what she found and instead wrote the book *Ripped and Torn* about the arrogance with which Western brands address developing countries and seek to turn people into consumers.

Some of the most significant concerns of marketers should be:

- Privacy – in a world where we are constantly bombarded by media, phone, mail, text and e-mail, we seek to protect our information and ourselves.

- Debt – we are encouraged, enabled and cajoled to spend ever more money, to aspire to luxury brands, with easy payment terms and credit on tap.

- Environment – the enormous volumes of waste through packaging, indulgent over-purchase and pollution is a direct consequence of our consumerism.

- Health – obesity is reaching epidemic proportions, driven by our soft spots for sugar and fat, and marketers charging a premium for nutritious foods.

- Children – marketing the enormous range of products to kids, the irresponsible role models, and the relentless desire it promotes.

- Integrity – the need for honesty, for a sense of morality and respect, the need for ethics, and for positive role models.

Marketers individually, and as a community, have a responsibility to address these issues and many others. While we can each put on our blinkers, and pursue our business objectives, the negative consequences on our customers and society will ultimately come back to bite us – either damaging brand reputations or creating markets that are unsustainable. Nike was forced to ensure that its third world factories had the highest standards, and responded to the wake-up call. McDonald's is fighting for survival, hoping that a switch to being the health conscious crusader will save it.

However, it requires more than last-minute responses. Responsibility should be at the heart of organizations and their brands. This includes companies that embrace an ethical positioning as their differentiator – like the Co-operative Bank or skatewear company Howies – or those who simply recognize it is good business practice – witness the importance given to CSR reports and the so called 'triple-bottom line' by companies such as Cadbury Schweppes and even Nike.

Marketers should be the driving force of a more responsible approach to their businesses and customers, and this responsibility should be core to the brand. The four sides of the 'responsibility compass', addressing both internal and external challenges, requiring both physical and attitudinal changes, should help companies to serve their markets and communities with eyes and ears open rather than closed.

Inspiration 6.2 CAFÉ DIRECT

For a brand that is focused on growers, Café Direct is doing an impressive job of growing itself. The UK Fair Trade drinks company is the sixth largest coffee brand in the UK, with around 25% of the Fair Trade sales.

Indeed, Café Direct is now one of the world's leading Fair Trade manufacturers. Its brands, Café Direct, 5065, Tea Direct and Cocoa Direct are sold through most supermarkets. Café Direct was recently voted favourite coffee by *Which?* the UK's leading consumer magazine

The company was founded in 1991 by Oxfam, Tradecraft, Equal Exchange and Twin Trading in response to the collapse of the International Coffee Agreement two years earlier. The collapse sent coffee prices spiralling to a 30-year low and the livelihood of many small coffee farmers was seriously under threat.

The 'Gold Standard Fair Trade' policy guarantees a fair price for the growers' crops, well above market rates. Café Direct also puts a percentage of gross profits (8% in 2003) back into producer partners' organizations to support a wide range of activities including market information, management training and any other elements required to grow their business.

The result is significant – for a normal jar of coffee, farmers receive around 5% of the price paid in stores, while with Café Direct they receive 20%. Café Direct now buy from 33 producer organizations in 11 countries, which means that at least 250,000 coffee growers are guaranteed a decent income. Additionally, they fund a number of educational and support programmes.

However, Café Direct is no charity; it is a profitable business, but based on its strong principles. It is also not backwards in coming forwards. The '5065 Lift' marketing campaigns for the 5065 brand, with live events held everywhere from Brighton beach to the Edinburgh Festival, have been radical and hilarious, giving people a caffeine and adrenalin boost.

Sylvie Barr, the marketer behind the brand's ethical marketing and financial success says, 'The growth is remarkable when coffee and tea markets overall are static or in decline'. Indeed, the company's double-digit growth has bucked the trend seen by Nestlé, where its instant coffee sales have fallen by a similar amount.

Café Direct believes it is doing today what many will do tomorrow, seeing beyond profits to build a business with a higher purpose. Customers clearly see this too, recognizing that there is more to their purchase decisions than price.

At the heart of the business model is an approach that balances financial success with the business of making lives better.

Application 6.3 RESPONSIBLE MARKETING

How do you ensure that you are marketing responsibly to customers? With ethics and integrity? Where are the biggest areas for concerns, and how will they evolve in the future? What should we do now? And how could these concerns become opportunities for differentiation?

1. Evaluate responsibility

Map out your current business model and initiatives against the 4 responsibility dimensions.

2. Identify issue areas

Identify where there is positive or negative performance, or an opportunity to do more or better.

3. Prioritize gaps

Address negatives and priorities improvements, based on what is essential and important to stakeholders.

4. Embrace differentiators

Address positives and consider how they might contribute to differentiation.

5. Anticipate future issues

Identify emerging challenges across the 4 dimensions, and their potential impact.

6. Plan, be and improve responsibly

Develop a responsible marketing plan, embracing these initiatives into mainstream marketing.

Concept 6.3 CUSTOMER COMPANIES

'Customer focus' has been a core principle of business for decades. Exactly what it means, and how a customer-focused business differs from any other, is open to interpretation. It has become a loudly acclaimed hygiene factor for business – the objective of a thousand change programmes and a million CEO mantras.

Yet, how many companies know who their customers are, organize their business around them, really understand their motivations and aspirations, define their brands by what they do for them, focus on the propositions to them, want a relationship with them when it doesn't involve a sale, make decisions based on them first, put them top of their boardroom agendas, talk about them first in their annual reports, and measure their success on customer terms?

- Marketing programmes are still largely designed for the convenience of companies rather than customers, communicating their messages to customers when they want to in order to drive short-term sales.

- Most people in organizations are measured and incentivized on their operational rather than customer tasks: the sales manager is urged to maximize revenues, the call centre manager to maximize throughput.

- The whole concept of CRM, of building customer relationships, has been hijacked as a sales automation tool, targeting individuals to sell more to them, regardless of whether they want it.

Very few companies are truly focused on their customers, even fewer have developed customer-centric organizations, connected to customers, driven by customers and intimate with customers.

Indeed, the simple language of 'customer' can be a minefield too.

Consumer goods companies refer to consumers, while their 'customer' is the retailer. This is misleading and can create a blinkered mindset where satisfying the intermediary matters most. Similarly, B2B companies will use the word customer, or maybe client in professional services firms, while most business decisions are taken by a network of people. And, of course, Total Quality Management gave us the notion of 'internal customers', which was fine in terms of creating an outward orientation, but could easily allow people to forget that they are all working together to serve the external customer.

Most fundamental is the need to ensure that promises are delivered, to 'close the gap', as the leading customer-centric consultants the Foundation put it, between the good intentions and the operational reality. While this sounds easy, it requires significant rethinking, realignment and even a fundamental reversal of ways of working.

The starting point should be to design the organization from the 'outside in'. To collectively agree on the target customers, the promise to them and the totality of the customer experience that will deliver this. And then to design the organization in a way that most effectively delivers this.

We have already explored the radically different customer-initiated ways of doing business that are today essential to business – to respond to the power shift in markets, to the fragmentation of audiences and to the intensity of competition and sameness.

- Strategies that focus on the best market opportunities, and then the best customers within them.

- Brands that define what the companies do for customers, rather than what it does itself, and that are built around communities rather than capabilities.

- Propositions that articulate benefits rather than features, capturing the uniqueness of the offer, creating superior value for customers.

- Experiences mapped out from the customer perspective, bringing together all the direct and indirect interactions with the brand and the business.

- Relationships that customers want, that are based on mutual benefits and achieved through understanding, collaboration and ongoing dialogue.

- Measures that are customer-based and linked as the drivers of financial results, shared across the business with boardrooms and investors.

Underpinning this must be a customer company, one where customers are fundamental to everything, and where marketing's role is to be catalyst, facilitator and manager in championing the customer.

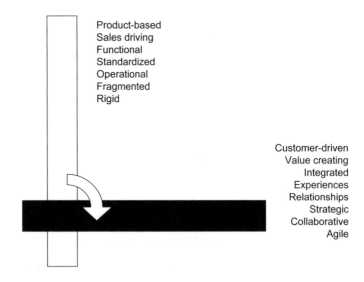

Product-based
Sales driving
Functional
Standardized
Operational
Fragmented
Rigid

Customer-driven
Value creating
Integrated
Experiences
Relationships
Strategic
Collaborative
Agile

In essence, a customer orientation is achieved by 'turning the organization sideways'.

- From vertical, functional silos, each serving the customer separately and with little seamlessness, continuity, sharing of knowledge or responsibility ... to an organization that works collaboratively and horizontally.

- From product and service thinking that is delivered in fragmented and standardized ways ... to proposition and experience thinking where solutions and personalization are the objective.

- From operational and transactional thinking, focused on productivity and sales ... to more strategic relationship thinking where the purpose is to create lifetime value of customers, as well as the first-time trial.

- From category, product and sales management that controls and measures in the vertical ... to segment, customer and relationship management where budgets are allocated and results measured along horizontal lines.

- From functional and rigid processes, structures, systems, information, resources and people ... to a more agile, integrated and aligned approach that enables people to work together for customers.

At the end of the day, it is far more motivating to get up in the morning and work for a company that is energized by what it does for customers, by its higher purpose and the people it touches, rather than just by making money.

Inspiration 6.3 PROCTER & GAMBLE

The front door of a house stands next to the entrance to P&G's innovation centre. Inside is the Consumer Village, where P&G meet the people who buy their products. On one side is a mocked-up supermarket aisle, what they call the 'first moment of truth', and on the other is six kitchens and bathrooms – complete with the cooking facilities, washing machines, dishwashers and so on, where consumers can try out P&G's products – the 'second moment of truth'.

P&G recognized that while they had always focused on customer benefits – making clothes wash whiter, or nappies more absorbent – they were less successful at understanding the unarticulated needs – how to make packaging more convenient for home storage, or nappies stretchier around the sides. Sterile focus groups tended to focus on what was prompted as opposed to what participants actually did. The Village enables them to get closer, for scientists to talk to users one to one and observe how they buy and use the products, as well as listening to what they actually say that matters.

In 2002 P&G reached $40 billion sales while employing over 100,000 people in 80 countries. It produces many of the world's most famous household brands, selling them to at least 5 billion people in over 140 markets: Tide, Ariel, Pampers, Crest, Pringles and Olay are just a few.

According to the book *Rising Tide: Lessons from 165 Years of Brand Building at Procter & Gamble*, there are a number of enduring themes to its success:

1   Focus on branded consumer products, with an unrivalled expertise in consumer marketing, and avoidance of B2B markets or own-label manufacturing.

2   Business approach to brand building, recognizing that only the whole business, not marketing activity alone, can create and deliver successful brands.

3   Rigorous experimentation and innovation, constantly seeking to analyse, test and prototype new ideas, or existing ideas in new contexts, driving innovation in the market.

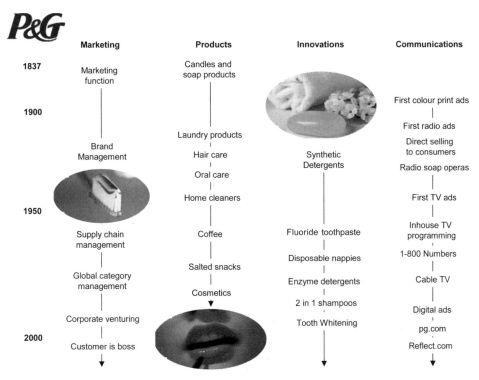

	Marketing	Products	Innovations	Communications
1837	Marketing function	Candles and soap products		
1900				First colour print ads
		Laundry products		First radio ads
	Brand Management	Hair care	Synthetic Detergents	Direct selling to consumers
		Oral care		Radio soap operas
		Home cleaners		First TV ads
1950				
	Supply chain management	Coffee	Fluoride toothpaste	Inhouse TV programming
		Salted snacks	Disposable nappies	1-800 Numbers
	Global category management		Enzyme detergents	Cable TV
		Cosmetics	2 in 1 shampoos	
	Corporate venturing		Tooth Whitening	Digital ads
2000				pg.com
	Customer is boss			Reflect.com

Source: Date sourced from Procter & Gamble

4   More effective in execution – while many of its peers have similar insights, and can develop similar new ideas, P&G is far better at making them happen, first and more profitably.

5   Balancing many business priorities and thriving on the tensions and paradoxes that they create:

- Long-term focus vs short-term priorities.

- Controlling culture vs empowerment.

- Few big ideas vs many small ones.

- US perspective vs being international.

- Product mindset vs customer need.

- Organic growth vs business acquisitions.

Since 2000 AG Lafley has created something of a revolution at the classical marketing leader, which had begun to lose its way during the 1990s. However, in the last few years, as arch rivals Unilever and Colgate Palmolive have struggled, and the rise in retailer power and own-label products have become the more serious threat, P&G has sustained double-digit growth and improved margins by refocusing its business on customers and innovation.

The rallying call for the revolution has been simple: 'The customer is boss'.

While customers were always important, products were previously king. This has been reversed, with innovation now driven by needs rather than capabilities. While there was always an arrogant view that only P&G could develop the best products, it now looks to third parties and even collaborates with competitors in order to find the best solutions to customer needs. Crest's Whitestripes is an example of successful external collaboration. Design has also become more important, as P&G seeks to extend products into experiences, such as Kandoo's funky frog-like boxes containing children's toilet wipes.

Indeed, P&G work through a number of web-based communities that bring together ideas and innovators and from which better ideas and solutions can emerge, which P&G then take to market. Ninesigma, for example, connects P&G to around 500,000 researchers, all eager to respond to a P&G brief. Innocentive.com is a similar R&D party spun off from Eli Lilly, while Yourencore.com taps into a highly experienced community of retired developers who are still keen to respond to an interesting challenge.

AG Lafley explains: 'Anyone in a garage anywhere in the world can come up with an idea that could be important to one of our businesses. We want them to bring it to us.'

One of the biggest handicaps in the past was too much data. P&G was struggling to stay afloat in a sea of quantitative research. Now, it has moved to observational methods such as ethnography, and then using these insights to focus quantitative analysis. Lafley argues thus: 'If you want to understand how a lion hunts, you don't go to the zoo, you go to the jungle.'

The work environment has evolved too. P&G's removal of product-thinking blinkers has recognized the need to work together to address markets, understand customers more deeply, and develop more meaningful and distinctive solutions. The new environment encourages collaboration and openness, with open-plan team spaces and escalators between floors to encourage movement. Perhaps most radical of all, the marketing and finance teams now sit next to each other.

Application 6.4 CUSTOMER ETHNOGRAPHY

How do you cut through the mountains of research data and gain a deeper insight into what matters to customers, and how can you solve their problems in a more satisfactory and innovative way?

1. Observe customers

Observe a specific customer activity, without them knowing, for one hour.

2. Note behaviours

Note objectively all customer actions, behaviours and impacts.

3. Compare observations

A second person should do the same in parallel, then compare notes.

4. Map behaviour patterns

Map out behaviours sequentially – identify key moments and problem areas.

5. Compare with current wisdom

Compare with existing conventional research for consistency with articulated needs.

6. Take action

Articulate the learnings, expected and unexpected activities, positive and negative, and act accordingly.

Thinking what nobody else has thought

'Innovation – any new idea – by definition will not be accepted at first. It takes repeated attempts, endless demonstrations, and monotonous rehearsals before innovation can be accepted and internalized by an organization. This requires *courageous patience*.'

Warren Bennis

'We don't have a good language to talk about this kind of thing. In most people's vocabularies, design means veneer ... But to me, nothing could be further from the meaning of good design. Design is the fundamental soul of a man-made creation.'

Steve Jobs

Innovation is the driving force of competitiveness, of growth, of profitability and sustainable value creation. While it can easily be put into the rather narrow box of product development or technology, it is a fundamental challenge for the whole business. While it can quickly become a buzzword of the times, and then quickly forgotten when times get harder, it must be an ever-present, continuous process.

More intelligent innovation	More imaginative innovation
Disruptive. Challenging business or market conventions, finding stress points ripe for removal or change.	**Creative**. Radically exploring all possibilities, and ways in which they could become reality.
Developing. Managing innovation as a strategic process, risk and reward, product and market development.	**Applying**. Innovating the product, the delivery and applications, so that it has maximum impact with customers.
Business Models. Rethinking how business works, how it adds value to customers and shareholders.	**Market Models**. Rethinking how markets work, customers and partners, channels and pricing.

It is also one of the biggest opportunities for marketers to put their mark on the organization – to take fundamental action based on their deep understanding of market opportunities and customer needs, to reach beyond their functional blinkers and work across the business, to step up to more strategic challenges and opportunities with lasting impact.

Indeed, in most companies, nobody is specifically responsible for innovation – tasked with developing an innovation strategy, with managing the innovation portfolio, with prioritizing where investment and resources should be focused, and designing the future of the business, as well as what it offers to customers.

Innovation is a natural part of the marketing mix, and is there for the taking.

Of course, the phrase 'innovation' can have different interpretations too – it can mean every-thing and nothing. Some might see it as the creative opening up of bright ideas, others as the process-based activity of new product development, others as business strategy and renewal and still others as incremental improvement in day-to-day tasks. Of course, they are all right.

Innovation is about the commercial implementation of the best ideas, be they new products and services, new ways of working, or even the fundamental business model by which you do business.

Examples of innovation in each aspect of marketing include:

- Markets – Starbucks defining the premium coffee shop market.

- Products – Dyson's vacuum cleaner sucking better without a bag.

- Service – Ritz Carlton's empowering people delighting customers.

- Channels – Nike's Niketowns as temples of brand as well as purchase.

- Pricing – Paying as you go extended the reach of mobile phones.

- Application – the iPod that became the ultimate photo album.

- Models – IKEA, where customers collect and assemble themselves.

Peter Drucker argues that there are seven basic sources of innovation: the *surprise* of unexpected success or failure; *inconsistencies*, when things don't add up according to conventional wisdom; *desperation*, where there is a crying need for a better way; *outdated* industries or processes overdue for change; *lifestyle* or demographic changes such as the rise of affluent retirees; *attitudinal* changes such as customer perception and expectations; and *discovery*, where new knowledge or capability promotes new opportunities.

Harnessing one or more of these sources typically helps a company challenge traditional thinking and explore new approaches, from which point the trick is to turn the best opportunities, fast and effectively, into commercial reality.

Innovation is an opening up and closing down process.

Innovation is also about the market. Innovating the application as well as the product.

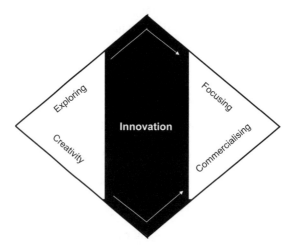

Market-shaping companies most fundamentally innovate their markets – the needs of customers, the structure of players, the channels that connect them, the rules by which they work. Indeed, business and product innovation will rarely have the dramatic impact that they seek unless they are associated with fundamental market innovation too.

And not least, marketing itself must be innovative, in the design and delivery of brands and propositions, in its use of channels and media, pricing and service, promotions and rewards.

Geoffrey Moore's *Crossing the Chasm* is a fabulous reminder as to why so many innovative products and services fail, not just in technical markets but in all categories. The 'chasm', into which so many great ideas fall and never get out of, is the gap between the early adopters and the mass market.

While the geeks in the know will queue up, waiting for the new product with blind faith in its quality, there are many more consumers who will not rush to your door. It will take them many more months to become aware, convinced and provoked to join those early adopters. If companies can't move from the initial niche to the mainstream, they will rarely secure the critical mass and the volumes that are often essential to pay back the initial investments in product development and market entry.

Consider the limited success of Apple's early Macintosh, and even its more recent iMac. Even if they were fantastic innovations, they never quite managed to make it to the mainstream. In comparison, the iPod and its derivatives have leaped over the chasm on to every high street, a must-have fashion accessory, as well as a great innovation.

Moore argues that new solutions should be carefully and differently marketed at each stage of their maturity – to engage the early adopter will require very different messages, channels and pricing to what will eventually engage the populace. Yet so many marketers switch off once a product is launched, hoping that it will ride on its launch hype, and that one message, one proposition, even one form of the product will engage everyone.

Marketing must innovate the market not only at a strategic level, but also at a tactical level– creating the right context, the right attitudes, the right infrastructure and the right appetite to ensure that the best ideas achieve competitive and commercial success.

Inspiration 7.1 BLACKBERRY

BlackBerry, the essential device to keep in touch with your e-mail on the move, has been dubbed 'crackberry' because of the umbilical cord by which users tie themselves to the tiny black machines. They have become essential and addictive to working life, and life beyond work, taken everywhere, into every meeting, on the bus, on the beach. It takes a strong will to switch off your BlackBerry.

BlackBerry is made by a low-profile Ontario-based company called Research in Motion. RIM's rather shy, serious and slightly offbeat people spent a decade experimenting with the gadget before launching its initial version back in January 1999.

BlackBerry has had to be patient. The technologies that support it have been around for some years, yet it judged that people were just not ready for e-mailing on the move. However, the massive popular growth in mobile working, and indeed for connectivity demonstrated by the rise of SMS, showed that people were now ready to be permanently connected to their e-mail.

BlackBerry focused on knowledge-worker audiences to introduce its products. A favourite technique was to target major conference events and distribute BlackBerrys free for the day to the executives, who then spent the majority of the sessions in their inboxes rather than listening to speakers.

While it might have been disconcerting for the speakers, the delegates were hooked. On Black-Berry. Once you've tried it, there is rarely any going back, and indeed many executives paid on the day, before referring their procurement managers to do a corporate deal too.

Within months, many large firms – from Credit Suisse First Boston to Intel – had jettisoned the standard issue PalmPilots for all staff and replaced them with BlackBerry devices. Even through the tech bust of 2000, when, like most other tech stocks, RIM's share price temporarily fell by 90%, its revenues kept rising at a phenomenal pace.

RIM's founder, Mike Lazardis, describes its mission statement as 'to push data packets to your hip', which, while not necessarily the most eloquent statement, has succeeded in grabbing a significant 'white space' and turning it into a 'hotspot' that established players have found difficult to compete in.

1. Define the challenge

Identify the innovation challenge
or opportunity in terms of objectives,
issues to address and timescales.

2. Explore creatively

Explore and stretch a wide range of
creative ideas within defined context.

3. Shape ideas

Connect and articulate these ideas
in more powerful ways, fusing whole
ideas or elements of them.

4. Focus commercially

Filter ideas against rigorous but flexible
Criteria, e.g. potential attractiveness,
risk, cost and return.

5. Choose best ideas

Resolve on best ideas, including
possible prototyping, articulate
how could profitably be delivered.

6. Innovate the market too

Consider innovation of market entry
and customer application
(by repeating process).

Application 7.1 INNOVATION PATHWAY

How do you innovate? What is the role of creativity, and how far should you open up before you start choosing the best options? How do you filter ideas to find the best ones? How do you ensure that the market is ready for your innovations?

Concept 7.1 CREATIVE DISRUPTION

Every vacuum cleaner manufacturer automatically assumed that a dust bag was a prerequisite within their designs. Until James Dyson came along. Every airline thought it unrealistic to put a bed on a transatlantic aircraft. Until British Airways met a yacht designer. Every analyst thought it was impossible to make money out of free information online. Until Google created a fundamentally different business model.

Innovations disrupt conventions.

The disruption might be a challenge or even a reversal in the received wisdom of the market – in the ways in which companies make money, in the assumed needs of customers, and the types of solutions that most effectively fulfil them. Hotbeds of disruption might be something that creates a high level of customer frustration (e.g. how to remortgage your home), complexity (e.g. how to integrate your many computing devices), or paradox (e.g. how to shop in bulk when you have no space in your home to store it).

Clay Christensen, Harvard professor and author of *The Innovator's Dilemma*, describes the frequent appearance of 'disruptive innovation' in today's markets where a market leader, until then, usually well respected and profitable, is quickly humbled by a lower cost entrant offering an inferior product. The new entrant has typically paid much closer attention to the priorities of customers and found ways to deliver against them at lower cost, rather than seeking to do more than is necessary as the incumbent (and indeed most brand leaders) is so tempted to do.

Imagine your DVD, your phone, your camera, your PC – it has far more functionality than you will ever need. What if we remove all the non-essentials, and thereby significantly reduce production costs and offer a much lower price?

Prior to 1960 handheld electric tools were heavy and cumbersome, designed for heavy-duty professionals and very expensive. Black & Decker then created plastic encased tools with universal motors that only last 25 to 30 hours, long enough for the lifetime of the occasional hobbyist or gardener and, at a tenth of the price, far more affordable too.

Technological innovation can often get the better of companies. Once the macho focus on product specifications takes over, the business can become blinkered by the competitive race for ever-more sophisticated solutions – bigger, stronger, faster – and can easily lose focus on what matters to customers.

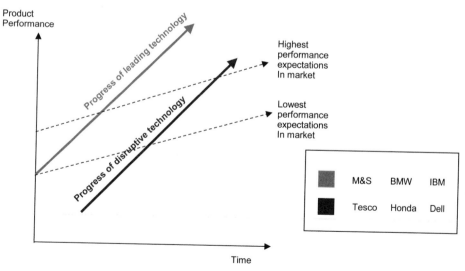

Source: Adapted from *The Innovator's Dilemma* by Prof. Clayton Christensen

Technology doesn't help: its constant ability to do more – faster processors, smaller components, more memory capacity – simply urges companies to embrace them in its next generation. Yet customers will only use technology up to a point – most electronic devices do far more than you ever do, most software on a PC remains largely unutilized, most new gizmos are reflections of aesthetic aspirations rather than functional need.

'Disruption', as Christensen describes it, happens when this tech progress is far ahead of what customers need and can use. This overshoot creates the opportunity for a new entrant to come in with something that is cheaper, simpler and 'good enough' for a significant number of customers.

Once this new entrant has carved out a niche at the lower end of the market, they can rapidly persuade more customers that they are good enough for them too. The disruption might be product related, as in Dell's disruption of the PC market, or market related, as in eBay creating an entirely new marketplace.

The phenomenon can be seen in everything from complex data storage devices being 'disrupted' by smaller, cheaper ones to doctors often being displaced by nurses, and similarly in markets as diverse as airlines and insurance.

Commercially, it is not really about technology, but about the business model. Small agile companies can succeed with business models unattractive to larger companies. An existing company may need to deliver a 40% margin in order that a new product is attractive, yet to a smaller company, a 20% margin might make them extremely profitable.

Larger companies don't only have financial blind spots to such opportunities. Capabilities and culture are also limiting factors. If BMW prides itself on its design and manufacturing excellence, it is difficult to accept 'inferior' products, not because they don't work but because they are not the best they can be. Similarly, British Airways struggled to compete against the new low-cost entrants such as Ryanair and easyJet, partly because a full-service airline that prides itself on its customer service finds limited service a difficult concept to grasp culturally.

Yet larger companies that do embrace disruptive thinking can be successful too: the rise in corporate venturing and 'intrapreunership' is as much focused on replacing the existing paradigms of the core business as it is in utilizing existing capabilities or IP in new ways. Jack Welch's parting gift to GE was a programme known as 'destroy your business', where he encouraged staff across the monolith to think like Internet entrepreneurs would, and probably are thinking, to disrupt its own business before somebody else blows them out the water.

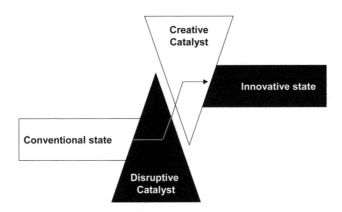

Of course, creating a disruption is only the starting point, as it then requires creativity to exploit it in some useful and different way. Thinking radically about why markets exist like they do, and what they shouldn't accept. Thinking radically about future market models, and how they should work. Pure creativity is fun and energizing, but must be structured in order to deliver meaningful results.

There are many different creative techniques, some of them high-tech and requiring significant preparation and equipment, others requiring none at all. However, creativity needs effective facilitation and structure. The development of long lists of ideas might be useful but can fragment and annoy people if they are not quickly grasped, distilled, connected and taken forwards. The worst scenario is that because of a lack of 'getting to the answer', executives compromise on easy options or do nothing.

Disruption Catalysts		Creative Catalysts	
Value Mapping	Where is business and customer value created and destroyed? How is it created? Who, what, when and why?	Trend Architects	Extrapolating, applying, building on available trends of social, economic, political and technological changes.
Hot Spotting	Identifying overlaps and waste, sites and sources of complexity, confusion. Where are the cost/time 'basins'?	Futurist Visions	What are the possible visions of the future state – what doe they have in common and what is different?
Heritage Hunt	What made you great? What are, or were you famous for? How was it earned? Could you create a new 'heritage'?	New Horizons	Designing an inspiring future in words, pictures and multi-dimensional forms. Simulating the journey over the horizon.
Rule Breaking	What are the explicit/implicit rules, inside/outside the business? There are no others? Test/stretch to limits.	Parallel Tracking	Learning from other places, e.g. different sectors or markets, and from beyond business (education, law, nature etc.).
New Perspectives	Taking different perspectives, from stakeholders, competitors, unrelated viewpoints. What if you use inversions?	Creative Fusions	Combining new ideas and conventions in highly unusual ways. Harnessing positive tensions and dualism.
Reduction Filters	Reduce to components? What are the commonalities? What if we eliminated aspects at random? Is it vital? Better?	Perfect Day	Bringing together the best of the best, from across companies, within the company, and over time/location.
Sacred Beliefs	What do you value and treasure? What does this enable and restrain? What if you adopted a new faith?	Creativity Techniques	Exploiting established creative tools such as lateral thinking, de Bono's hats, brainstorming, mindmaps, etc.
Disruptive Technologies	How could emerging technologies challenge, replace, change, or enhance how you currently do business?	Collective Genius	Harnessing the ideas of the best minds available to develop creative ideas interactively, e.g. realtime brain writing.
Thinking Dimensions	Changing the thinking tracks (the parameters, the blocks) in which you currently think, plan or work.	Extreme Sports	Applying your approach in to extreme situations, e.g. car brakes to space shuttle to stretch performance and application.
Corporate Fool	Asking the unaskable, challenging logic and assumptions, dismissing evidence, artistic, lateral, always asking 'why?'	Thriving on Paradox	Accepting what convention said was unacceptable – recognizing paradox, and how to 'have your cake and eat it'.

Most importantly, innovation needs both disruptive and creative catalysts to break the conventions as well as explore the possibilities. Creative thinker Edward de Bono might in some situations encourage a group to use his coloured 'thinking hats' through which they each take different perspectives on a problem, or might simply say 'take an object out of your pocket'. The team is then encouraged to generate as many solutions to a problem based on the attributes of the object. 'How would you solve the problems of retail stock-outs by comparing it to a matchstick?'

There are many other techniques to be selected and sometimes combined depending on the nature of the problem, the group of people who are seeking to solve it, and some of the broader objectives which people seek to achieve while solving it, such as team building or engaging decision-makers.

Inspiration 7.2 3M

In 1969 Neil Armstrong took man's first steps on the moon wearing space boots with soles made of synthetic material from 3M. In 2000 Michael Johnson sprinted to an Olympic 400 metre title wearing shoes made from 24 carat gold Scotchlite Reflective Fabric, developed by 3M.

3M describes itself as 'an innovation company'. Formerly known as the Minnesota Mining and Manufacturing Company, it is now a $18 billion global leader with an unrelenting focus on sustained profitable growth. Its 55,000 products are in areas as diverse as healthcare and safety equipment, electronics and industrial markets.

The company's 67,000 employees remain focused on creating 'practical and ingenious solutions that help customers succeed' and are encouraged to continuously seek innovation through a

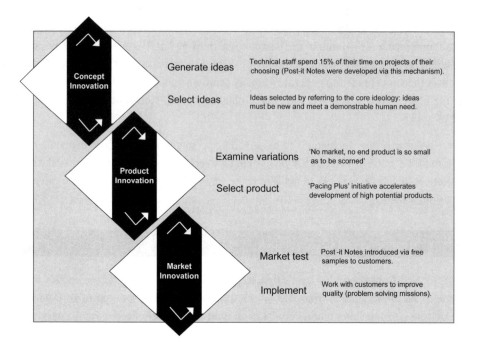

wide range of techniques. These include giving every employee 10% of their weekly time to 'bootleg' on crazy ideas, to insisting that at least 30% of revenues comes from new products.

3M has a long history of innovation – not only investing in new solutions, but also transforming markets and customer behaviours. In this way it ensures that its creations – everything from sandpaper to adhesive tape – become practical and profitable too. Its innovation process consists of an integrated and parallel approach to concept, product and market innovation.

Perhaps most famous is the story of the choirboy who dropped his hymn book during a church service, and with it all the loose bits of paper that marked the important pages for him. The observation led to the creation of the Post-it Note, now an essential part of any office desk and available in a bewildering range of colours, sizes and formats.

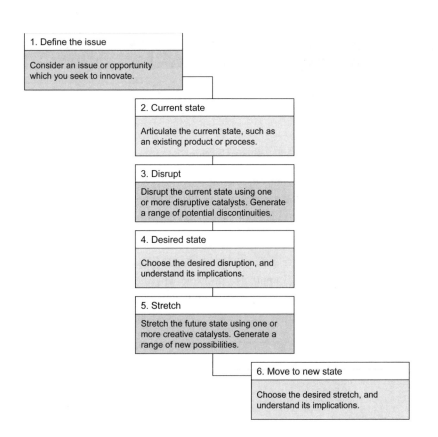

Application 7.2 CREATIVE CATALYSTS

How do you stimulate the radical thinking that can disrupt the conventions of markets, and stretch your mind to explore the radically creative ideas that can create a more innovative way of working?

Concept 7.2 INNOVATIVE DEVELOPMENT

Innovations most commonly address the product level. However, product innovation is increasingly difficult to sustain and, indeed, many new products become commodities before they even reach the market.

More radical innovation is typically achieved by thinking more holistically:

- Innovating not only the product, but also the process by which the innovation is delivered. For example, a beer company might create a radically different bottle or dispensing device that adds perceived value to the customer, as IMI Cornelius working with drinks companies have achieved.

- Innovating in a broader context than the product, rethinking the whole concept which the customer experiences, for example by rethinking why the customer is actually drinking the beer, transforming a bar into a restaurant, building a beer tap into the table so that

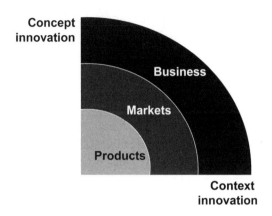

Concept innovation

Business

Markets

Products

Context innovation

drinkers can 'pull their own pints', or a café into a temporary working space as Reuters has done.

- Innovating the whole business model by which the company and the customer gain value, as Dell has so successfully achieved in the PC market, or Virgin Mobile has done by recognizing it doesn't need to invest huge sums in infrastructure, and can succeed more easily as a virtual operator on the back of somebody else.

Newcastle has emerged as a beacon of creativity in recent years – from the imposing Angel of the North to the ingenious Millennium Bridge. However, drive 20 miles north into the remote Northumbrian countryside and you come across Belsay Hall. This quiet neo-classical mansion is home to some of the most radical new works by designers like Alexander McQueen and Zandra Rhodes.

Stella McCartney is another. She chose the huge and romantic Great Hall to present her most ambitious creation never to hit the catwalk. Mottling the stonewalls with jewelled light is her astonishing 'Crystal Horse'.

This is English Heritage reaching out to people who didn't care for old buildings, applying the creative talent of design in a whole new way, and creating a visitor experience that disturbs, provokes and inspires.

Belsay demonstrates the potential for breaking new ground in the arts, to reach out to new audiences, to develop experiences that attract and inspire them, to keep the arts alive and relevant in today's fast-changing and time-impoverished world. It is a lesson for any type of organization.

So how can companies reach new audiences, develop new offerings, overcome inertia and avoid irrelevance? How can they tap into new and profitable revenue streams, whether they seek to make money for shareholders or raise funds to invest in doing better?

Newness occurs in the margins, not in the mainstream.

This goes not only for ourselves and how we innovate, but also for our audiences and how they think. If you evolve what you had, there is improvement but little inspiration. If you jump to a new place, there is discontinuity, not totally unrelated to what you do, but with breathing space to stand out.

Look at your toothbrush, or your shampoo. It is hardly innovative. If one brand angles the head, the others do. If another adds funky colours, everyone follows. If one has a special ingredient x, the others will soon add formula y. It doesn't break new ground; it merely levels the game. Moving forwards to stand still.

There are typically three levels of innovation:

1   **Cosmetic change** – the most basic level of innovation, typically involving some modifica-
    tion to the product or service. Cars, for example, constantly launch new versions – the new
    VW Golf, maybe 30 years in the making, but an evolution at best. Or consider Coke with
    lemon or Windows NT.

2   **Context change** – more genuine innovation on an existing theme – changing the market
    context, for example by taking an existing product to a new market. Gillette's Sensor for
    Women reached a new audience. Bacardi Breezer, a cool drink in clubs rather than big
    bottles in the supermarket.

3   **Concept change** – advanced innovation which rethinks the entire 'business model' in
    order to redefine how things happen. IKEA rethought DIY; easyJet fundamentally changed
    the airline model; Virgin Mobile rejected conventional thinking that you need to have a
    network to be a phone operator.

Of course they all start with an idea, and a need. Indeed, innovation is not just about creativity,
but about making ideas happen in a profitable way. However, conventional ideas are quickly
copied – Pepsi with lemon, Smirnoff Ice – it's about applying them in unusual ways that makes
the difference, is much harder to copy, and inspires you and your audiences.

Back up in the Northumbrian countryside, it is not just designers that are redefining heritage,
but also brands that are embracing the arts. Enter the manor house and you are drawn upstairs
by old confetti blowing on the staircase. The seven bedrooms each create illusions that are
intriguing and evocative. A glimpsed lovers' embrace, scorched on to a bed, vision and sound
that culminate in a very 'Agent Provocateur' moment. The lingerie may not be there, but the
suggestiveness is.

When breaking new ground, you are limited only by your imagination.

The development process by which radical ideas become innovations and then practical reality will differ depending on the challenge; however, a classic product development process

will most importantly have a series of stages, in which the concept is increasingly filtered, tested and shaped until it is right for the customer, and right commercially. Of course, these filters must be designed in a way that facilitates non-conventional solutions rather than only supporting the convention – that recognizes unarticulated customer needs or new sources of value creation.

Product development

New product development (NPD) should be one of the most energetic business activities, yet research by Consensus argues that NPD is often stifled by fear of the unknown, and the risk of failure. They found that 46% of all product development resources in US companies are focused on products that are canned before they reach the market, or fail when they get there. When they probed deeper, they found that most organizations addressed such failures with blame, rather than recognizing its inevitability if the other 54% are to be successful.

Einstein argued that 'it is impossible to solve a problem by using the same thinking that created it'. Similarly, Tom Kelley of IDEO, one of the world's leading product developers, argues that product development is 'part creativity, part logic and part golf swing'. New products need radical visions in order to break through convention, and to appeal to sponsors and customers. As Kelley argues, this vision will be part creative – the new idea – but also based on brand alignment, customer analysis and commercial logic. The vision then needs strong articulation.

One aspect of the dotcom hype was the rise of '90-day development cycles'. If you couldn't get ideas to market within 3 months, it would probably be too late. This encouraged new development processes. One was to apply more disciplined project management techniques, critical paths and parallel workstreams. Another was to reduce the number of products and focus on the diverse customization of a few. A third, as practised by innovative companies like Capital One, was to constantly evolve products through a rapid 'launch, test, learn' cycle of ideas.

Perhaps the biggest criticism of product developers is that they feel that a product launched is a project finished. In fast-changing markets, launch is often just the beginning of a successful development. First, the early adopters of a product are always the most challenging to satisfy, and can often provide lessons for improvement. Second, it is the applications of products that really matter to customers, and where a new product can often have the most impact, therefore requiring specific development. Third, markets themselves must be developed to embrace new products – in their knowledge and capabilities, distribution and support structures, with related products and service – if the product is to be successful.

Inspiration 7.3 CIRQUE DU SOLEIL

In 1987 Cirque du Soleil took the biggest risk of its brief life by putting on a show called *We Reinvent the Circus* at the Los Angeles Festival, and agreeing to underwrite the entire costs in return for the gate proceeds.

It gave the USA its first taste of Cirque's innovative approach to circus arts, a unique and awe-inspiring blend of acrobatics, theatre, dance and live music. It was the Canadian company's big attempt to break into the American market, and succeeded not only in doing that, but also in reinventing the whole concept of a circus.

In *Blue Ocean Strategy*, Renée Mauborgne argues that Cirque has completely redefined its market, and therefore its competitors and audiences too. Is it a show? Is it art? Is it entertainment? Mauborgne argues that Cirque has defined its own space by fusing the thrill of the circus with the intellectual sophistication of the theatre and ballet to create a new form of performing art.

From its Quebec origins of 1984, the accordion-playing, stilt-walking, fire-breathing CEO, Guy Laliberte, has turned a group of street performers calling themselves 'Le Club des Talons Hauts' (the high-heels club) into a world-leading act. Cirque is now a multi-million-dollar entertainment company, with over 50% brand awareness in the USA, and has produced 15 completely different shows that have been performed to around 40 million people worldwide.

Innovation has been a constant feature of Cirque's performances, and a driver of its rapid growth and global reputation. As one enthusiast describes it on the *Lovemarks* website:

> 'Cirque du Soleil's creative vision fills me with wonder and enchantment. I'm transported by their music, costumes, characters, and performances to a magical place, somewhere amazing. It feeds my soul and excites my senses. Whenever I see a show, I am inspired by what the human body can do and what the human mind can create. The highly imaginative performances enrich and transform me.'

In the early 1990s Cirque secured long-term partnerships for resident performances for MGM Mirage in Las Vegas and at World Disney World in Orlando. This gave it the financial platform to move internationally – into Europe, Japan and Australia. The shows continued to grow in their creativity and risk-taking too, always accompanied by their original music and handmade costumes that also drove a large licensing and merchandizing business.

In 2001 Cirque won an Emmy for the Outstanding Non-Fiction Program, a reality TV series called *Fire Within*. In 2003 it got even more adventurous with a sexy and provocative new show called *Zumanity* for adults only, while Cirque's website has won many awards too.

Marketing of the Cirque shows almost drives itself, such is the level of customer advocacy and media interest that it has built up.

In each location, the company selects media partners that then jointly fund and deliver the promotional messages. Over 15% of all tickets are sold to members of the Cirque Club, which you can join online and receive regular newsletters and invitations to exclusive events. There are now over 750,000 club members. This is upmarket entertainment, so attracting the sponsorship of prestige brands such as IBM, American Express or BMW is no problem, driving corporate hospitality and further enhancing Cirque's own premium brand credentials.

Like the high-wire artist, Cirque has to tread carefully to balance its need to generate profits with the significant investments required in an artistic and creative business. It is this balance that enables the brand to continually surprise and delight its audiences worldwide.

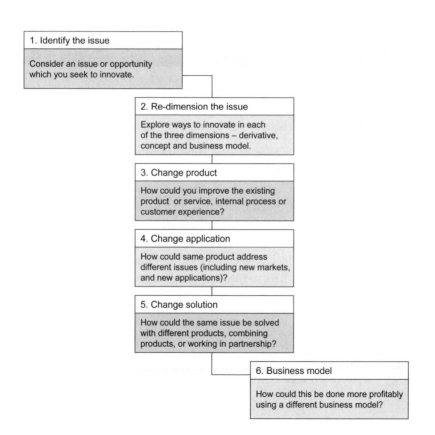

1. Identify the issue

Consider an issue or opportunity which you seek to innovate.

2. Re-dimension the issue

Explore ways to innovate in each of the three dimensions – derivative, concept and business model.

3. Change product

How could you improve the existing product or service, internal process or customer experience?

4. Change application

How could same product address different issues (including new markets, and new applications)?

5. Change solution

How could the same issue be solved with different products, combining products, or working in partnership?

6. Business model

How could this be done more profitably using a different business model?

Application 7.3 INNOVATION REFRAMING

How can you change the way you look at innovation? Change the context against which you can create change? What are the different dimensions in which you can rethink innovatively and create positive change?

Concept 7.3 BUSINESS MODELS

Business models have suddenly become an essential part of our business language, thrown randomly into conversations with nods around the table, but usually with little idea what the term actually means, or at least with very different interpretations.

Over the years business models have become more sophisticated, reflecting the changing nature of markets and competition, and the migration of value between industries and within the value chain. 'Bait and hook' models, for example, have been around for over a century, where a low-cost essential item (the bait) then requires regular, expensive refills, or associated products and services (the hook). The classic is the razor blade, where we buy the razor and then become locked into the unique blades that are regularly required to fit them. Similarly, printer manufacturers seek to lock people into their own branded ink cartridges, or mobile phone companies offer free handsets and are then subsidized many times over by the premium charges for airtime.

In the 1950s new business models emerged from McDonald's in the form of fast food, and Toyota through mass production. Hypermarkets emerged in the sixties thanks to Wal-Mart and others, while FedEx and Toys R Us transformed their categories through new models in the 1970s. The eighties saw greater convenience in the form of Blockbuster videos, as well as the consumer-marketed B2B brand, Intel. And the nineties saw the rise of low-cost airlines like Southwest, premium coffee from Starbucks and online models from the likes of Amazon and eBay.

Business models must fundamentally define how the business works, how goods and money flow between the various different constituents – customers, suppliers, partners, etc. – and how value is distinctively created and sustained. They are the ways you do business, the unique structures that bring people and finance together. We typically operate within them, yet, if we get it right, they can change to offer some of the best opportunities to make a real, sustainable difference.

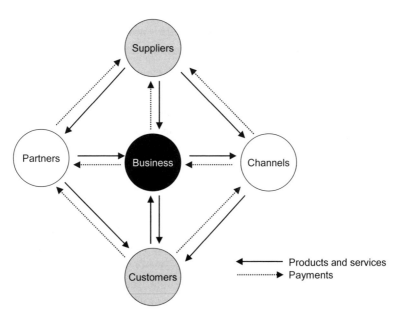

Of course, companies have always had business models; for example, Coca-Cola manufactures drinks based on the ingredients it buys from suppliers, then sells its product through distributors for revenue. The Internet's unique medium simply gave companies the opportunity and confidence to explore new ways of doing business, for example bringing together remote buyers and sellers in auctions like e-Bay, or enabling customers to offer their own price for available hotel rooms through Priceline.

A business model is essentially a blueprint for how an organization creates value. It typically involves some form of value exchange that requires the flow of goods and money between the business and customers, suppliers and partners. Conventional models typically offer goods in exchange for cash; however, it could take many other forms, for example the charging for information while the 'product' comes free, paying the customer to accept goods in return for a fee from elsewhere.

Regus, the leading business centre company, has captured a fast-growing market through an innovative model that helps it stand out from the traditional serviced office providers. The pay-as-you-use model enables business professionals to turn up, sit down and start work – anytime, anywhere in the world. This is compelling to the frequent-travelling project worker, where time and facilities are critical and price is far less important than convenience. Regus, meanwhile, grows at breakneck speed by acquiring further prime locations on short-term leases, places where there is untapped demand, from clients who deliver their significant margins.

ARM Holdings, unlike the rest of the semiconductor market, has been less affected by technology's rises and falls. It has a business model that sets it apart from competitors like Intel and Motorola, one that insulates it from the inevitable cycles in high-tech markets. ARM doesn't build chips; instead, it innovates, designs and licenses the 'chip's engine'. Announcing 2001 revenue growth of 58%, CEO Robin Saxby claims that 75% of the world's cellphones contain chips designed by ARM. Despite the downturn, manufacturers are desperate for cheaper, more powerful microprocessors that can help them stand out, and support the next generation of wireless services, which will repay the costs of 3G.

However, few business models last forever. Even the most stable of industries are not immune to the changing nature of business models. As customers and suppliers grow familiar with new models in other sectors, their expectations move across boundaries. Familiarity with free content on the web makes the price of a one-day conference unreasonably high. If they can lease rather than buy their new car, why can't they do this for household goods? However, admitting that the way your business makes money doesn't work any more is a sensitive issue. When Xerox's former CEO Paul Allaire suggested that 'we don't have a sustainable business model', a loss of stock market confidence meant that his shareholders ended up $38 billion poorer.

Inspiration 7.4 IKEA

IKEA, the Swedish home furnishing retailer, now has over 200 large stores in over 30 countries. The IKEA catalogue, containing about 12,000 IKEA products, is reputedly the second most widely distributed book after the Bible, with 100 million copies produced every year.

The brand is pronounced 'ee-kay-uh' by Swedes; however, in the English-speaking world it is pronounced 'eye-KEE-uh' rhyming with the word 'idea'.

IKEA was founded by Ingvar Kamprad at age 17. The name is a composite of the first letters of his own name, together with his house name in the village of Agunnaryd. Originally the company sold pens, wallets, picture frames, watches, jewellery and nylon stockings – practically anything Kamprad found a need for that he could fill with a product at a reduced price. The first furniture was introduced into the IKEA product range in 1947 and in 1955 IKEA began to design its own furniture. Initially IKEA was a mail order business, but eventually a store was opened in the nearby town of Älmhult.

Its furniture is well-known for its contemporary designs by young Swedish designers and its 'flat-pack' nature, allowing items to be assembled by the consumer rather than being sold pre-assembled. IKEA claims this permits it to reduce costs and use of packaging. IKEA has also pioneered the use of more sustainable approaches to mass consumer culture. Its founder calls it a 'democratic design', which leverages economies of scale, capturing material streams and creating manufacturing processes that hold costs and resource use down. The result is flexible, adaptable home furnishings, scaleable both to larger homes and the increasing, yet generally ignored, number of smaller dwellings.

IKEA prides itself on creating a new approach to consumption – recognizing that furniture can be changed often, and can be cheap while still well designed. It now even sells flat-pack houses, BoKloks, in an effort to cut prices involved in a first-time buyer's home.

Stores are usually very large blue boxes with few windows, designed around a mandatory 'one-way' layout which forces consumers to traverse nearly all parts of the store before reaching the cashier or check-out stands, although there are a few shortcuts for those in the know. The sequence involves going through homeware displays followed by the marketplace, before arriving at the warehouse to collect your own flat-packs and take to the checkout.

Application 7.4 NEW BUSINESS MODELS

What exactly do we mean by business model? How would you visualize your current model? What are alternative ways of doing business, and the innovative business models for ensuring that you still succeed through them?

1. Identify stakeholders

Identify all the stakeholders involved in doing business currently.

2. Map goods

Map the flow of goods between stakeholders (e.g. business to customer, supplier to business etc.).

3. Map payments

Map the flow of payments between stakeholders (e.g. customer to business, business to supplier etc.).

4. Consider redirections

Consider the impact of alternative flows of goods and payments (consider different connections, or reverse flows).

5. Consider eliminations

Consider the impact of eliminating one or more stakeholders (e.g. partners, distributors).

6. Evaluate options

Evaluate the optional models and which creates most economic value.

Competing: The touch of a marketing genius

PART 3

► Competing: The touch of a marketing genius

► What creates exceptional value for customers today? How can you cut through the noise and beat the intense competition? How do you really do business on their terms?

► How do you see your business through customers' eyes? How do you articulate the real benefits of what you offer to them in a way that is compelling, logical and memorable? And maximizes the perceived value?

► How do deliver a customer experience that truly engages customers emotionally, that is unique to them, that transforms how they think about your brand, and adds significant differentiation to your proposition?

► What does it mean to do business on customers terms – what, how, where and when they want? How do you reverse communications and distribution? How do you build an integrated network of connections?

► How do you build relationships that customers want to belong to? What actually makes a strong, two-way relationship? What would it take to engage customers more deeply, and even become partners?

'We need thinking in order to make even better use of information that is also available to our competitors.'

Edward de Bono

Seeing business through customers' eyes

'Customers must recognize that you stand for something important to them.'

Howard Schultz

'Problems cannot be solved by thinking within the framework in which the problems were created.'

Albert Einstein

Most purchase decisions are made in 2.6 seconds, according to the latest neurological studies. Indeed, Malcolm Gladwell, author of *Blink*, argues that the quicker we make decisions, the better they often are, arguing that more information often confuses rather than enhances our judgements. Rapid cognition is both intelligent and imaginative.

As you pause in the supermarket aisle, or sign-off purchase orders between meetings, when it comes to the moment of decision, does all that marketing science really work? Yes, most of it has an impact, but long before that moment of truth. The secret is to ensure that your brand is already lodged firmly in the decision-maker's mind, in their 'ROM' if you like. The challenge is to get it there, ensure that it is sticky enough to stay there, quick to recall and powerful to persuade when the moment comes.

More intelligent propositions	More imaginative propositions
Customers. Quantifying the value to each target customer or segment of your brand or specific solutions.	**Competitors.** Choosing the right context in which to position yourself, and how you seek to compare with others.
Propositions. Articulating this value in terms of distinctive benefits and price, and finding ways to deliver it profitably.	**Perceptions.** Defining the proposition on customer, not business, terms, priced relative to perceived benefits and peers.
Alignment. Aligning the business to deliver the proposition through relevant products, service and experiences.	**Narratives**. Capturing the proposition in structured and compelling language that is memorable and drives purchase.

'Customer value propositions' (CVPs) are the centrepiece of operational marketing that is focused, differentiated and engaging. While the format of a CVP may differ from company to company, every company should today be focused around propositions that align to meet the needs of their target audiences.

American Express, while having an overall corporate brand which is captured by the idea of helping their customers to 'do more', more specifically defines what its business is about by a series of value propositions, each with a target audience, each delivering a distinctive set of benefits. These value propositions become the guiding force of the business, and the way in which the inside aligns with the outside.

Propositions focus on what matters to customers: they are the high-level, benefit-driven themes or promises delivered by the products and services, functions and processes that enable the benefits to be realized.

Of course, unlike brands, propositions will change over time as customer audiences and needs change, as competitors catch up and markets evolve. They are therefore temporary – maybe for a number of years, as is the case of IBM's 'eBusiness on demand' – addressing the current issues of target customers, capturing the difference from today's competitors, and engaging the customer.

So what sticks in customers' minds?

Rarely is it the tech specs and geek-speak that lazy marketers rely upon – the processing power of the latest computer, the active ingredients inside your toothpaste, the meaningless serial numbers that define the latest mobile phone.

People remember what matters to them, language that they use, logical arguments that explain how the offer solves their specific problems and articulates the benefits to them in a way that makes sense and is memorable.

How do you win customers in 2.6 seconds?

- Propositions that articulate the value to the customer.

- Benefits that are relevant and distinctive.

- Pricing that is fair for the benefits attainable.

- Narratives that start with issues and describe solutions.

- Language that is simple and practical.

- Memes that are compelling and memorable.

- Dialogues that sense and respond at the right moment.

- Relationships that ensure you are in the picture when it matters.

Application 8.1 VALUE PERCEPTIONS

What is the perceived value of a solution to the customer? How much additional value does your offer create? Where should you pitch your price in order to capture most of this perceived value, while still offering some notional 'value for money'?

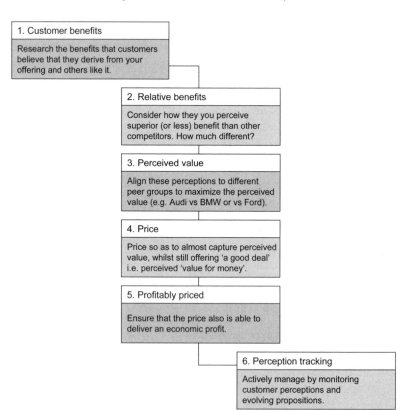

1. Customer benefits

Research the benefits that customers believe that they derive from your offering and others like it.

2. Relative benefits

Consider how they you perceive superior (or less) benefit than other competitors. How much different?

3. Perceived value

Align these perceptions to different peer groups to maximize the perceived value (e.g. Audi vs BMW or vs Ford).

4. Price

Price so as to almost capture perceived value, whilst still offering 'a good deal' i.e. perceived 'value for money'.

5. Profitably priced

Ensure that the price also is able to deliver an economic profit.

6. Perception tracking

Actively manage by monitoring customer perceptions and evolving propositions.

Concept 8.1 PERCEIVED VALUE

'Sex appeal is 50 per cent what you've got and 50 per cent what people think you've got', said Sophia Loren when explaining the power of perceptions alongside reality.

Customers perceive the value of a solution based on the relevance and applicability of the solution to them – the benefits that it creates, articulated in monetary gains or cost saving, time efficiency or what they wouldn't be able to do otherwise.

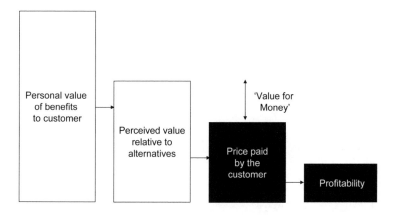

Consider an Apple PowerBook, the sleek and powerful laptop targeting graphic designers, agency creatives and other cool types:

- Absolute benefits to the customer include the ability to work anywhere and anytime, to work faster and more effectively, thanks to its software and functionality, and the incremental business that it enables you to do.

- Comparative benefits recognize that the customer actually has a choice, the Apple exists alongside similar solutions from Sony, Dell, IBM and many others. The benefits are therefore relative to those attainable elsewhere.

- Pricing should then reflect the marginal superior benefits attainable, but also recognize that 'value for money' requires a price that is more than justifiable for the additional benefits.

The superior price, if attainable with the some cost structure, then flows straight to the bottom line. Superior value to the customer should lead to superior value to the business too.

Customer value propositions articulate the value the business offers to a specific group of target customers, by understanding them better, and the competition, and focusing on what matters to them – their situation, issues and opportunities, needs and wants. If you can really solve a problem, the customer will care less about what it takes, and how much.

Products describe features (which may help solve the issue) As examples:	Propositions describe benefits (derived from solving key issues) As examples:
'24 hour home maintenance'	'Piece of mind at home'
'Wireless e-mails on your phone'	'Stay in touch anywhere'
'New running shoes'	'Achieve a personal best time'

While it is tempting to jump to a slogan, a value proposition should be built up internally through structured analysis. There are 6 steps:

1   Who is the target audience – who are they, defined by name or segment, and why they are interested? What are their needs and wants, issues and aspirations?

2   What kind of solution do they seek – the simple type of solution, e.g. a more refreshing drink, a more convenient IT solution?

3   Why should they choose this solution – what are the differentiators, how is it better or different from others, what are the few unique benefits being offered?

4   How will this difference be delivered – what are the unique products, services or processes that enable these benefits to be unique and deliverable?

5   How much would they pay – e.g. 10% more than market average, as much as market leaders, 5% of incremental revenues?

6   What do they not get which others provide – available in fewer stores, limited colour range, doesn't work on Macs, manual updating?

The template defines the structure of a value proposition, although it might be rearticulated in simpler and more creative ways externally.

Customer Value Proposition

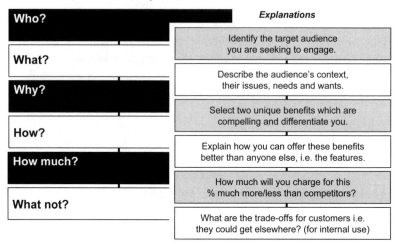

There may be one proposition for every market, segment, or even every customer in some cases. They can be rapidly tested, customized and continuously evolved. In this respect they are far more flexible and relevant than brands or products.

Most importantly, the same products and services might be delivered in support of a number of different propositions, but with different roles, benefits and pricing. Similarly, different products and services may be selected to deliver the same proposition, depending on the need and appropriateness.

Effective communication is a dynamic conversation, which spreads rapidly and sticks in your mind.

A conversation is distinctive in that it is mutual, progressive and desired. This requires communication which is on customers' rather than the company's terms, is interactive and two-way, interesting and memorable.

Disney's communication engages your imagination, creating the holiday of your dreams, or at least of your kids. Orange seeks to explore the future with you, where wireless communications will enable a better world. BMW wants to share their ultimate experience with you, in their showroom or in their cars.

Dynamic conversations are sparked by distinctive propositions designed to tap into the individual's agenda with carefully chosen media, packaged in compelling messages, and quite possibly delivered uniquely for each different customer. Few television adverts or direct mail campaigns genuinely fit this bill.

The Audi TT encourages driver dialogue on any lifestyle subject before and beyond purchase ... 'call us, mail us or even come in for a chat whenever you like, about whatever you want' goes their pitch.

Seth Godin argues that traditional 'interruptive' communication is typically pushed by the company, in their time and manner. Customers and data protection agencies are challenging this barrage and leading the drive for 'permission'-based approaches, on customer terms. Seeking such permission could actually become a positive opportunity to create 'terms of engagement'.

Conversations are typically stimulated by a compelling proposition that targets the crucial issues or motivations of the customer. This requires a deep understanding of the customer, perhaps built up over time, and also demands some relevant and new insights to stimulate their thinking and response.

Rolf Jensen, of the Copenhagen Institute of Future Studies, argues that in the future companies will thrive on the basis of their stories and myths, be they the antics of Southwest CEO Herb

Kelleher or Jack Welch's mission to destroy his own business before somebody else does. As intelligence is automated, people will place more value on emotions, imagination and ritual. Jensen believes that this will affect everything from purchasing decisions to customer loyalty, arguing that the most successful communicators will be storytellers, packaging their messages as great fables, stories which are retold time after time.

Inspiration 8.1 TESCO

Tesco is the UK's leading retailer. Originally specializing in food, it has moved into areas such as clothes, consumer electronics, financial services, Internet service and telecoms.

With profits of £2 billion on a turnover £24 billion, it has a 30% share of the UK grocery market. Across all categories, £1 in every £8 of UK retail sales goes to Tesco, which makes it much more dominant in its home market than Wal-Mart is in the USA. Tesco also operates overseas and non-UK sales for the year to 26 February 2005 were 20% of total sales.

Tesco was founded by Jack Cohen, who sold groceries in the markets of London's East End from 1919. The Tesco brand first appeared in 1924 after Cohen bought a large shipment of tea from T.E. Stockwell and made new labels by using the first three letters of the supplier's name and the first two letters of his surname, forming the word 'TESCO'.

The first Tesco store was opened in 1929, the first self-service store opened in 1948 in St Albans, and the first Tesco supermarket was opened in 1956 at a converted cinema in Maldon, Essex. It began to offer an own label range of products soon after by canning fruit from the nearby Goldhanger farm. Tesco's first 'superstore' was opened in 1968 in Crawley, West Sussex. It has also expanded through acquisition, particularly in overseas markets.

Tesco defines it core purpose as 'To create value for customers, to earn their lifetime loyalty'.

It seeks to deliver this through its values, defined as 'No-one tries harder for customers' and 'Treat people how we like to be treated'.

Tesco's UK stores are divided into five value propositions, each delivered through different sub-brands and formats, varying in size and range, addressing the different needs of consumers:

- *Tesco Extra* are larger, out-of-town hypermarkets which stock all of Tesco's product range. Around 100 stores, each with 6.6 million square feet of retail floor, account for 27% of Tesco's overall space.

- *Tesco* stores are standard large supermarkets stocking groceries plus a much smaller range of non-food goods. They are referred to as 'superstores' for convenience, but this word does not appear on the shops. They account for the majority of UK floorspace. Most are located in suburbs of cities, or on the edges of large and medium-sized towns.

- *Tesco Metro* stores stock mainly food, with an emphasis on higher margin products due to lack of economies of scale, alongside everyday essentials, mostly located in city centres and on the high streets of small towns.

- *Tesco Express* stores are neighbourhood convenience shops. They are found in busy city centres and small shopping precincts in residential areas, and on petrol station fore-courts.

- *One Stop* is the only category that does not include the word Tesco in its name. These are the smallest stores. They were part of the T&S Stores business and, unlike many which have been converted to *Tesco Express*, these will keep their old name.

Tesco's growth over the last three decades has involved a transformation of its strategy and image from the 'pile it high, sell it cheap' approach of its founder. In the late 1970s, Tesco's brand image was so negative that it was advised to change the name of its stores, but rejected the advice.

Instead Tesco claims its success has been achieved through:

- An 'inclusive offer', an aspiration to appeal to everyone – upper, medium and low income customers in the same stores.

- Use of its own brand products, including the premium 'Finest' range and the low price 'Value' range. This reversed consumers' earlier perceptions of own brands as being inferior in quality.

- 'Customer focus' as the only focus of the business, and the only route by which Tesco will achieve long-term value growth for shareholders.

- Diversification beyond its core UK grocery business into areas where it can deliver exceptional customer value, either in new sectors or in new geographical markets.

Source: tesco.com

Indeed, as the profits have piled higher by the year, CEO Sir Terry Leahy has stayed focused on his successful four-legged strategy, as described on their corporate website:

- 'Core UK business' – that is, grocery retailing in its home market. It has been innovative and energetic in finding ways to expand, such as making a large-scale move into the convenience store sector.

- 'Non-food business' – many UK supermarkets have attempted to diversify into other areas but Tesco has been exceptionally successful, rapidly moving towards leadership in categories as diverse as clothing, consumer electronics, health and beauty, and media products.

- 'Retailing services' – Tesco has taken the lead in its sector in expanding into areas like banking, telecoms and utilities. This is often through joint ventures with major players, where Tesco has succeeded through more effective and profitable implementation.

- 'International' – Tesco began to expand internationally in 1994, and this now accounts for over 20% of sales. It has focused on developing markets with weak incumbent retailers in Central Europe and the Far East. The medium-term aim is to have half of group sales outside the UK.

Source: tesco.com

Overall, Tesco's success is achieved by getting the basics of retailing right slightly more often than most of its rivals.

As it says in its marketing campaigns, *Every Little Helps*.

Application 8.2 VALUE PROPOSITIONS

How do you develop a customer value proposition (CVP) that turns the brand into a specific, relevant and tangible proposition for a specific audience? How do you articulate the components of customer value – the benefits of the general offer, the unique benefits you offer – and then recognize that the customer has to pay for it, and make some trade-offs by rejecting alternatives?

1. Target audience

Identify the target audience and their key issues (e.g. problem they seek to solve).

2. Benefits

Consider the benefits you offer these customers, and which are distinctive.

3. Differentiators

Articulate the two most important benefits which are superior to competitors.

4. Evidence

Provide evidence of these unique benefits (e.g. differentiated products).

5. Price

Identify the price positioning and trade-offs (i.e. what is not offered).

6. Articulate externally

Rearticulate the proposition externally so as to be distinctive and compelling.

Concept 8.2 CUSTOMER MESSAGES

It all tends to come out the wrong way.

We sit down in front of the customer, open our mouths and start talking about what we want to talk about. We describe the challenges and opportunities as we see them, rather than from the customer's perspective, and in language that makes sense to us, regardless of anyone else.

Yet we know that the starting point is to listen and understand, or at least to start by thinking about the audience and where they are, what's going through their minds, and what matters most to them.

Whether it's a 30-second TV commercial, a half-page press release with some exciting news, a roadside poster trying to catch a driver's eye, a four-page brochure to take home and dwell on, a 20-slide presentation to engage your sales prospect, or a 45-minute conference speech by the CEO ... they all have an audience to engage, all have a purpose to achieve, a key message to get across.

Audiences need to be engaged, by something that is meaningful to them, something that they can follow and understand, can empathize and agree with, something that takes them from where they are to a better place. They need structure, and a story.

A 'customer script' is used to convey the proposition to the customer in a relevant and compelling way. However, it doesn't jump into 'this is us, and this is what we do'. It starts, not surprisingly, with the customer, and takes them through a logic that will hopefully engage and inspire them to take the actions you seek.

A 'customer script' describes:

* Context – about the customer, the opportunities and challenges they face.

- Complexity – what is most difficult, or why their current solution to the context is inappropriate.

- Challenge – poses a key question relating to this complexity, and how to solve it.

- Core message – proposes a solution, a big idea that you would like to introduce them to.

The core message would typically incorporate the proposition that you want to deliver, the solution which you believe is right for them, the big idea that you want to stick in your audience's mind.

The narrative might then go on to explain 'why' the conclusion is appropriate, or 'how' it can be achieved in a sub-structure of messages, often with specific evidence to support the case or more detailed description as to how it will be achieved.

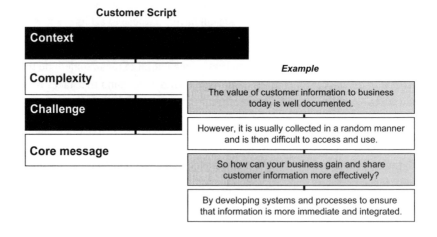

Customer Script

Context

Complexity

Challenge

Core message

Example

The value of customer information to business today is well documented.

However, it is usually collected in a random manner and is then difficult to access and use.

So how can your business gain and share customer information more effectively?

By developing systems and processes to ensure that information is more immediate and integrated.

The structure can be applied to anything from a script for a TV commercial to the copy for the brochure or the slides to support a sales pitch. And while it might run to many pages, it should also be possible to capture the essential narrative on one page.

Inspiration 8.2 CLUB WORLD

British Airways was one of the first service businesses to develop brands – to apply the brand management principles of consumer product companies to delivery of service experiences.

First Class, Club World, Club Europe, World Traveller, and Euro Traveller developed as a portfolio of sub-brands, all translating the high-level proposition of the master brand to specific audiences in more relevant ways.

The proposition captures the uniqueness, in terms of customer benefits, of the total customer experience. This can then be delivered in many different ways at each point of the journey – from initial booking to getting to the airport, check-in, lounges, departure, in-flight, arrivals, transfers and onwards.

Club World has set the pace in transatlantic business class travel for almost two decades now. The proposition could be articulated in more relevant and engaging ways, through a 'script' that might look something like the following:

- Context: Your business requires you to be in New York for an important meeting at 9 a.m. Tuesday morning, yet time is at a premium; you need to be in London all day Monday, and back on Wednesday.

- Complexity: The problem with business travel is that a night slumped in an airline seat is no way to prepare for a key meeting: you step off the plane and into the boardroom with tired eyes and crumpled suit.

- Challenge: How to travel overnight, and still perform at my best the next morning?

- Core message: Club World gets you there, rested and refreshed, looking and feeling your best.

- How?

- Evidence 1: British Airways offer the best schedules, enabling you to depart after a full day's work in the City, and arrive in plenty of time for the opening of Wall Street.

- Evidence 2: You can dine in our Supper Lounge before departure and, once on board, sleep undisturbed, with pillows and duvets, only waking up as we touch down.

- Evidence 3: On arrival, you can take a shower in our Arrivals Lounge while your clothes are pressed and, after a quick breakfast and checking of your e-mails, head straight for your meeting.

Application 8.3 CUSTOMER SCRIPTS

How do you articulate propositions in the customer's language, on their terms? What is the script, the logical argument or storyline that you can use to design a letter, a brochure, a slide presentation and a speech?

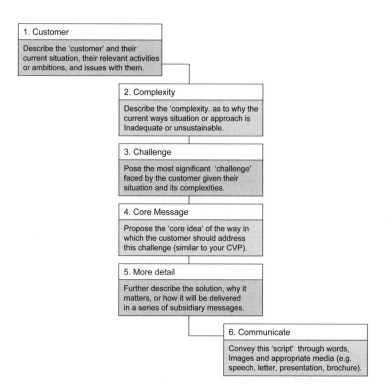

1. Customer

Describe the 'customer' and their current situation, their relevant activities or ambitions, and issues with them.

2. Complexity

Describe the 'complexity. as to why the current ways situation or approach is Inadequate or unsustainable.

3. Challenge

Pose the most significant 'challenge' faced by the customer given their situation and its complexities.

4. Core Message

Propose the 'core idea' of the way in which the customer should address this challenge (similar to your CVP).

5. More detail

Further describe the solution, why it matters, or how it will be delivered in a series of subsidiary messages.

6. Communicate

Convey this 'script' through words, Images and appropriate media (e.g. speech, letter, presentation, brochure).

Concept 8.3 NEURO MARKETING

Nike's Phil Knight, explaining his passion for the endorsement of sporting icons, said, 'You can't explain much in 60 seconds, but when you show Michael Jordan, you don't have to. It's that simple.'

Insightful propositions and carefully constructed narratives are only useful if they work in the 2.6 seconds when preferences are formed and purchases made. This is where memetics matters.

Richard Dawkins first coined the word 'meme' in his book *The Selfish Gene*, to describe 'a unit of cultural evolution analogous to the gene', arguing that replication and mutation happens within our culture – in the language we use, the symbols we use, the behaviours we adopt – in a similar way to way to genetic evolution. He considers memes as the units of information that reside in the brain.

Indeed, we see memes in everything from folk stories to pop songs, moral values to the latest fashions. Memes have patterns and forms that are easy to catch, to remember and to pass on. They are the basis of the songs that win the Eurovision Song Contest, or the e-mail jokes that spread rapidly over the Internet, or the latest fashions from the catwalks that everybody suddenly needs to have.

Memes are therefore important to marketers, to create brands and symbols, propositions and messages that catch people's attention, that stick in their minds, that quickly spread virally, by observation or experience, by word of mouth, e-mail or text. In order to reach out to target audiences, to leverage the power of virtual or physical networks, and to be there in people's minds at the point of purchase, value propositions and communications need to embrace memetics.

Memes stick in your mind and can be quickly accessed. They are constructs of memory that are more memorable, recognizable and contagious.

Examples of memes in the wider world are:

- Characters in children's stories, as so effectively exploited by Disney.

- Folk tales, memorable and with meaning, passed down through generations and evolved over time.

- Melodies sung by Kylie Minogue, which you just can't get 'out of your head'.

- Smells of freshly baked bread, or cut grass, or coffee, or strawberries.

In the marketing world, memes target each of our senses:

- Slogans, such as Nike's 'Just do it'.

- Colours, such as the FT's pink paper.

- Music, such as Intel's five-note jingle.

- The 'Nokia tune', as played by every Nokia phone.

- Designs, such as Apple's colourful iMacs.

- Numbers, such as Peugeot's trademarked central '0'.

- Packaging, such as Gateway's cow print boxes.

- Smell, such as Singapore Airlines, which bottle it.

- E-mail offers that are quickly forwarded to wide networks.

- Typography, such as the script of Coca-Cola's name.

- Endorsements, such as Tiger Woods and Nike.

A meme should:

- Be catchy, memorable, easy to say and recall.

- Include a key benefit, something to describe it by.

- Be different, original and easy to distinguish.

- Have emotional impact, imparting positive feelings.

- Be reflective, do something personal.

- Have shape, perhaps in terms of rhythm or rhyme.

- Be simple, short and easy to understand.

- Be contagious, so it spreads like a virus or fashion.

Some of the most ground-breaking work in recent years on how people think has come from Harvard professor Dr Howard Gardner and his 'Multiple Intelligence Theory' which has particularly focused on learning methods in schools, although it could equally be applied to consumers and marketing.

Gardner suggests that the traditional notions of intelligence – such as that measured by IQ, or as described in the simplified manner of left- and right-brain thinking – were insufficient to really describe the broader range of learning processes. In 1983 he proposed eight different types of intelligence – linguistic, logical, spatial, physical, musical, interpersonal, personal, and environmental.

He argued that society puts too much emphasis on structured, logical intelligence and not enough on the more artistic aspects. If we look back at the 'attributes of genius' we see a strong correlation with Gardner's eight categories, as when we consider the nature of memes.

Inspiration 8.3 MINI

The Mini was a classic of sixties culture, the car that defined a generation, the compact functionality, an ugly facia with poor suspension, squashed interior and a problem with rust, characterizing everything from the Sex Pistols to Mr Bean.

When BMW acquired its owners Rover in the late nineties, the Mini brand was little more than a subsidiary memory. However, the German motor giants were attracted to the tiny motor and reinvented it for the modern era, while disposing of the parent company. Today it outguns the revitalized VW Beetle and many of its more expensive rivals too. Today's Mini is hot and hip, with German reliability and a design echoing the past in a contemporary style.

The 2001 relaunch captured the spirit of the 1959 original, while delivering a small car that exceeds today's expectations for comfort, reliability, and style. The new version needed to capture the heritage of the old, while being a car for the future. The communications also set out to ensure that the Mini was completely different from any of its contemporaries, being quirky and cute, sporty and cool.

At the time of launch it targeted a 4.6% share of the UK small car sector, and has achieved almost double that penetration, despite an advertising budget of around £14 million in the first year, which was less than most of its direct rivals. Despite this it achieved the highest launch awareness in its sector, and has gone on to establish and sustain its position in the market, proving that, unlike the revived VW Beetle, it is no fad riding on a momentary burst of nostalgia.

Newspapers and magazines were targeted to feature the Mini Adventure as a regular comic strip; the adventures took the readers through suburban traffic, across deserts and around racetracks. It created a new character for the car that was captured with humour and creativity. It engaged audiences who knew the old cars, and others who didn't.

It quickly established the Mini as a modern day success, a cool car for today's youthful drivers, who would even pay a premium on standard prices to secure one. For BMW, it was a new venture, part of the group but a separate brand, strong and distinctive enough to stand on its own feet.

Application 8.4 CUSTOMER MEMETICS

How do you ensure that your messages are catchy, that they stick in people's minds and are contagious and so quickly passed on? How do you build memes, the building blocks of memory, into your messages, so that they can be quickly understood and remembered?

1. Core message

Seek to articulate your proposition,
Your core message, in your words,
eyes closed, in 20 seconds.

2. Find the key words

Imagine if you were highlighting
key words, which are unique or
most compelling, what would they be?

3. Imagine the headline

Imagine if it was a newspaper headline,
what would it say? Which issue would
It seize upon?

4. Picture the message

Imagine if you drew the message as a
picture, what would it focus on? What
style would it be in?

5. Rearticulate the message

Stand back and look at your outputs:
What do they tell you? Which words
and images capture it best?

6. Add rhythm

Put the key words together to a simple
familiar song like 'happy birthday' to
give simplicity, rhythm and even rhyme.

Walking in the customers' shoes

'Experiences are as distinct from services as services are from goods.'

Joseph Pine

'We see our customers as invited guests to a party, and we are the hosts. It's our job every day to make every important aspect of the customer experience a little bit better ...and if you do deliver a great experience, customers tell each other about it. Word of mouth is very powerful.'

Jeff Bezos

'It's one thing to have people buy your products, it's another for them to tattoo your name on their bodies', declared CEO Jeff Bleustein when explaining his business to shareholders.

'What we sell is the ability for a 43-year-old accountant to dress in black leather, ride through small towns and have people be afraid of him', he declared as he sought to capture the Harley Davidson experience in words.

More intelligent experiences	More imaginative experiences
Rational. Bringing together all the real and perceived interactions the customer has with the company or its brand.	**Emotional.** Redesign and rearticulate this to maximize the customer experience physically and emotionally.
Products. Embracing insight and technology to develop appropriate, distinctive and profitable new products.	**Services.** Enhancing service delivery by rising above process to deliver more intuitive and empathetic service.
Design. Appreciating both function and form, practical function and application, aesthetic feel and look.	**Theatre.** Creating rich and memorable experiences through scripted and impromptu interaction and immersion.

From local cafés to on-board planes, from Disneyland to the London Eye, companies are scripting and staging experiences for both consumers and business customers that they hope will transform the value of what they produce. Experiences go beyond traditional factors like products and services, support and accessories, and consider the transformation that an experience offers, the new opportunities that it opens up for customers, and how it can affect perceived value too.

A simple way of viewing experiences is to consider the function around which a product is developed, then consider the experience that a customer gains from the product by adding '-ing' to the function. BMW sell cars, but their customers buy driving experiences. Ikea sell furniture to customers who seek living experiences. Similarly, books become reading experiences, food becomes an eating experience, pans become cooking experiences.

	Make products	Deliver services	Stage experiences
	Tangible and standard	Intangible and customized	Personal and memorable
	Manufactured and in stock	Process ready on demand	Scripted, staged and revealed
	User buys features	Customer buys benefits	Guest buys sensation

Consider the value implications of this too: bake a cake for £2, buy a cake for £10, employ a catering company for £100. In this way, experiences deliver more perceived value, can charge more, and provide a significant opportunity for more sustainable differentiation and growth.

Customer experiences can be looked at from a number of perspectives. Most basic is the de facto experience that customers gain from a company or brand based on the totality of their interactions. Next comes the attempt by the company to make this set of interactions a more 'experiential' one, through additional services or theatrics. At the highest level comes the wider benefits-based experience that a customer realizes by fully exploiting the potential of their purchase. Most companies have embraced the buzzword but are still at base level in terms of delivery.

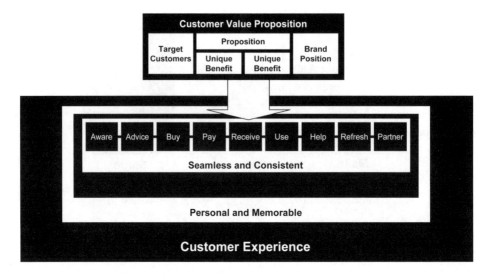

Mapping out a customer experience is like walking in the customer's shoes. The experience is likely to incorporate more than purchase and consumption, affecting the user more deeply. There are nine steps:

1   What is each of the contacts that the customer has with the brand, whether tangible or intangible, delivered by the company or its partners?

2   How do these steps connect into a sequential experience? There might typically be 30–40 steps from initial awareness through to next purchase

3   How are these described in the language of the customers rather than suppliers? For example, customers 'buy' while companies 'sell', 'need help' rather than 'support'.

4   Which steps are distinctive in some way, either unique or better compared with others?

5   Which steps add no value to the customer and are there for the supplier's convenience? How could you survive without them?

6   How can the sequence of events be improved – shortened, enhanced or re-ordered – to improve convenience, speed and flow?

7   How could individual steps be improved to make the most of the distinctive ones, and to personalize interactions?

8   How practical is the totality to deliver the proposition, to turn promise into reality, to engage the customer and bring the brand to life?

9   How can the profitability of the experience be enhanced, through pricing, efficiencies or additional revenue streams?

After this you really will start to 'walk in the customer's shoes' and, indeed, some companies formalize this approach through the way they measure customer and financial performance, and by appointing 'customer experience managers' who work across the business rather than focusing on individual functional contributions to it.

As Walt Disney once said, 'If you can dream it, you can do it.'

Inspiration 9.1 JONES SODA

'Run with the little guy,' says the tagline, yet Jones Soda has become a big story not only because of its soda. It has also become a cult brand with a revolutionary approach to marketing achieved through deep relationships with its customers.

If you want to take on global market leaders like Coca-Cola then imitation is unlikely to work. Jones has chosen a far more radical path.

Source: jonessoda.com

Founder and CEO Peter van Stolk is a former ski instructor who recognized that he was never going to make a fortune through his passion for the white stuff. He sold his beloved Chiraco car in return for 1440 cases of orange juice, from which he built up a business distributing 'New Age' soft drinks in Western Canada.

By 1995 he yearned for more: to make and sell his own drinks rather than those of other companies. He recognized that while the world perhaps didn't *need* yet another soda, there was an opportunity to offer something different, to entice customers in a more engaging way.

In a recent interview with *Fast Company* magazine, he recognizes the difference between customer needs and wants, admitting that 'the reality is that consumers don't need our s***'. But they might still *want* it, and even grow to love it.

He launched his own energy drink, WhoopAss, followed by Wazu spring water, then the first six flavours of Jones Juice. His target audience was Generation X, his generation, an audience who are more individual, sceptical, socially aware and media savvy than any other. They are 'moving downtown, rather than to the suburbs,' he observed. He realized that to reach them would require a brand with a very different attitude and approach.

In 2000 he renamed his business Jones Soda Co.

Van Stolk's ambition, he recently told the *European Marketing Conference,* was to 'create an incredible brand that is emotionally connected to customers'. He believes such a brand must be 'grounded, real, consistent, unpredictable and give something back'.

He also believes that a great brand will polarize people – some will love it, others will hate it. A great brand can't possibly please everybody, to be all things to all people, but the more focused it is on a target audience, the more special it can be.

And while he has created his company around the customer, saying in *Fast Company* that 'people get fired up about Jones because it's theirs,' he also reminds us that you still need to have ideas and judgement. It is not simply about doing whatever the customer says: 'the customer is not always right. F*** that. If you're always catering to everyone, you have no soul.'

At Jones Soda, that soul is captured in the line 'Sell soda, make money, make a difference, and have fun'.

The marketing of Jones Soda is different in its unconventional distribution channels and offbeat celebrity endorsements, its wide and wacky product range and revolutionary packaging, its deep customer involvement and social responsibility:

- Distribution channels include music stores, surfboarding shops and tattoo parlours, where the distinctive flame-designed coolers quickly gained attention. He wanted Jones to be discovered rather than be in your face. And while he reached people and places others did not, he has also embraced the mainstream and can now be found in the likes of Starbucks and Barnes & Noble.

- Endorsements come in the form of extreme sports and from the likes of surf legend Benji Weatherley, while the Jones team of BMX Pro Riders can be seen wearing the Jones colours around the country. Jones-branded vehicles also made their way to local communities, spreading the word and listening to people on the street. Listening 'from their perspective'.

- The soda gets more radical too: from Grape and Twisted Lime, to Fufu Berry and Blue Bubblegum, sold in stores and online. In 2004, Jones offered a whole Thanksgiving dinner – a box set of Turkey and Gravy, Green Bean Casserole, Cranberry, Mashed Potatoes and Butter, and Fruitcake sodas. They sold out in under an hour, and later reached over $100 on eBay.

- 'Fortunes' can be found underneath the cap of each soda bottle, submitted by customers to the myjones.com website. One, for example, reminds you that '76.4% of all statistics are meaningless'. Van Stolk is a thoughtful leader with a strong political agenda, supporting causes from the environment to the homeless, and an active charity fundraiser.

- Most eye-catching of all are the eccentric, black and white bottle labels. Jones encourages customers to submit their favourite photos. Thousands of cute babies deluged the website, and labels can be ordered as a customized 12-pack, as well as found at random in stores anywhere. The photo labels are clearly a talking point, and also form an online gallery.

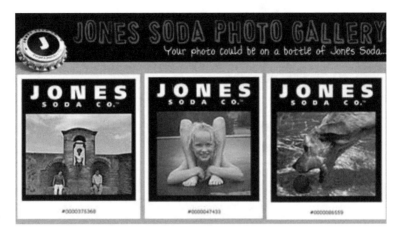

Source: jonessoda.com

Van Stolk is a business leader in tune with his generation. He is shaking up the North American drinks market on a shoestring, relative to the multi-million-dollar marketing budgets of Coke and Pepsi.

In less than a decade, Jones Soda has become a $30 million business, growing at around 30% per annum – largely because of its intimacy with customers and the alternative thinking of its maverick marketers.

Application 9.1 EXPERIENCE MAPPING

How do you map the customer experience, the way customers see our business, in their language? How can we improve the customer experience so that it brings the brand to life, more personally, efficiently and valuably?

1. Map the customer steps

Map each of the sequential interactions that a customer has with your brand - through their eyes, in their words.

2. Eliminate unnecessary steps

Eliminate steps that do not add value to customers and find ways to survive without it.

3. Design better interactions

Design new or improve existing steps to improve the customer experience.

4. Seek ways to differentiate

Explore ways to better differentiate and personalize each of the steps of the experience.

5. Bring the brand to life

Add theatre to key moments, through scripted or unscripted performance.

6. Define the experience

Define and deliver the branded experience, and measure the impact on customers.

Concept 9.1 COOL DESIGNS

Sir Harry Kroto has a passion for vintage cars and good wines. It made him stand out from the other university researchers or lecturers. Such an appreciation of aesthetic design and artistic style also helped him to identify a new carbon molecule, which had escaped more programmed, closed-thinking minds. He discovered C_{60} Buckminsterfullerene, a far more complex organic material than your typical diamond, and named it after the philosopher Buckminster Fuller who said, 'When I am working on a problem I never think about beauty. I only think about how to solve the problem. But when I have finished, if the solution is not beautiful, I know it is wrong.' In this simple thought is the essence of design.

Design starts with function and follows with form, addressing the practical needs of customers and their solutions, then adding the ergonomic desires of appearance and touch, creating differentiation and transforming its emotive possibilities.

Norio Ohga leads Sony's global innovation programme and explains, 'We assume that all products of our competitors have basically the same technology, price, performance and features. Design is the only thing that differentiates one product from another.' Indeed, Apple's Steve Jobs would go further by arguing, 'We don't have a good language to talk about this kind of thing. In most people's vocabularies, design means veneer ... but to me, nothing could be further from the meaning of design. Design is the fundamental reason why people love or hate man-made creations.'

Design creates differentiation and affinity. A great design makes a product stand out from competitors' – in appearance and performance. A great design is remembered and talked about. It touches emotions and inspires attachment. It can even help define who you are, or want to be – reflecting your own standards and style. Anita Roddick argues that 'What's imperative is the creation of a style that becomes a culture linking you to the community you serve. You can only do that through good design.'

Design goes far beyond the products. Design used to be the preserve of products – rather than service environment, communication materials, and even in-voice designs. Indeed the total experience for customers should be designed to ensure coherence and flow and that benefits are realized.

Designers are part architect and part artist. The Italian artist Ettore Sottsass is famous for seeing his work from the inside out. He is a humanist who seeks to touch people more deeply. He argues that humanist art, or design, cares about your quality of life, makes time for lunch, and seeks out a good beach. Design is experiential.

Design transforms our perceptions of what is possible. The Audi TT designer Freeman Thomas would be expected to have a passion for design, so what inspires his work? He explains, 'Car designers need to create a story. Indeed, every car provides the opportunity to create a new adventure.' He also co-designed the new VW Beetle, the retro car with the flower-pot in its dashboard. 'The Beetle makes you smile. Why? Because it's focused. It has a plot, a reason for being, and a passion.' Design is one of the most under-valued and least exploited disciplines within business, yet gives companies a rare opportunity to be and do much more.

There is no formula for great design, as much art as science; in fact, more social science than technical. For great design is about function and form, but starting with function – what is the item to be used for, and how can it optimize that performance?

Designers typically work alongside researchers, strategists and developers in order to shape solutions rather than provide input at any one point. They challenge thinking and champion customer applications. They consider what has not been done before, and how to make it pos-sible.

Indeed, designer Richard Seymour described design as 'making things better for people'.

He argues that 'scientists can invent technologies, manufacturers can make products, engi-neers can make them function, and marketers can sell them, but only designers can combine insight into all these things and turn a concept into something that's desirable and viable, commercially successful and adds value to people's lives.'

There are a number of valuable contributions to the design process:

- Insight – understanding social, economical and technological conditions in order to make the design relevant to the market.

- Provocation – challenging and shaping objectives and outcomes, matching business purpose with physical possibility.

- Ideas – design images can often stimulate and capture ideas as they evolve, through sketch and computer-aided design.

- Concepts – working the best ideas through in more detail, into card or foam models, or actual prototypes.

- Development – modelling and tooling can often coexist as the process to create the new product is also established.

While design might most typically be associated with products, it can equally apply to services or to the development of more compelling customer experiences. Retail interiors and coffee shops, hotels and airports can all be designed in a way which enhances their use by people, making them easier to navigate, more enriching to experience, and more commercially effective too.

Inspiration 9.2 PAUL SMITH

At 16, British fashion designer Paul Smith still wanted to become a professional racing cyclist; however, a bad accident put him in hospital and, by chance, in touch with a very different group of people. The local Nottingham arts students were more interested in Andy Warhol, David Bailey and the Rolling Stones than bike manufacturers and the Tour de France.

Within two years, Paul was hooked on the creative world and, with his fashion-addicted girl-friend (now wife) Pauline, opened his first boutique. Learning tailoring at evening classes enabled him to launch his first menswear collection at the age of 19 on the Paris catwalk under his own label.

Within 20 years, Paul Smith was established as the leading British designer, famous for mixing classic and contemporary and anticipating new trends with humour and imagination. Paul Smith extended to Paul Smith Woman, to the R. Newbold brand in Japan, and fields as diverse as shoes and watches, fragrances and furniture.

Paul Smith is now a global brand, with shops in all the typical fashion haunts of London, Paris, New York, Hong Kong and Singapore – plus an incredible 300 stores in Japan. Indeed, these stores reflect the brand too, full of quirky British furniture and features, often showcasing other British designs as well as those of the man himself.

Paul Smith loves to mix things up, to give conventions a twist.

Take, for example, his business suits, which bring together the classic European tailoring with vivid, flower-decorated patterns – not always just on the inside. He mixes colour and grey, heritage and contemporary, classic British and oriental, clothes and furniture.

He has also written books on fashion and art, including *You Can Find Inspiration in Everything*, and several museums have showcased his skills, including London's Design Museum, which held a 25-year Smith retrospective aptly entitled 'True Brit'.

Paul Smith continues to run the business as both chief designer and chairman, retaining his personal touch, and sense of mischief.

Application 9.2 FUNCTION AND FORM

How do you create more intelligent designs that meet customers' needs in a distinctive, aesthetic and memorable way? How do you combine the twin prerequisites of great design – function and form?

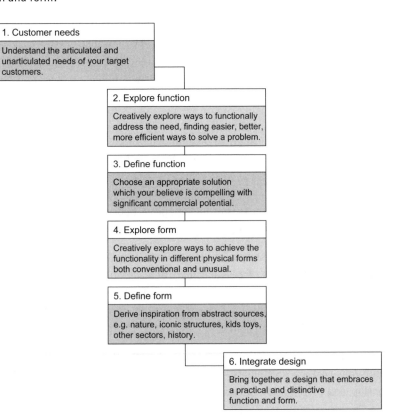

1. Customer needs

Understand the articulated and unarticulated needs of your target customers.

2. Explore function

Creatively explore ways to functionally address the need, finding easier, better, more efficient ways to solve a problem.

3. Define function

Choose an appropriate solution which your believe is compelling with significant commercial potential.

4. Explore form

Creatively explore ways to achieve the functionality in different physical forms both conventional and unusual.

5. Define form

Derive inspiration from abstract sources, e.g. nature, iconic structures, kids toys, other sectors, history.

6. Integrate design

Bring together a design that embraces a practical and distinctive function and form.

Concept 9.2 PERSONAL SERVICE

We know that customer service matters. Indeed, 'Have a nice day' is a welcome wish, particular when more sincerely combined with eye contact and a smile. But on other occasions, I'm just not in the mood for it.

The Starbucks Barista spends weeks learning how to serve a great coffee, and the philosophy of the brand. This is significant investment in an industry with short tenures, although not necessarily in the case of this coffee shop. Learning to make a great coffee matters because it lies at the heart of the proposition. It's like the technique training to be a great athlete; you have to learn to run efficiently before learning to run fast, or the tedious but essential grammar lessons when learning a language.

More important still is the philosophy of the brand. If Starbucks is to be 'the third place' for customers, it matters that they feel comfortable there, that there is space to meet people, that it feels like home, that they can stay as long as they want. This doesn't come in a training manual, it can't be taught. There is no right or wrong. It comes through Starbucks people understanding what it really means to be 'the third place' between home and work, making the right judgements for every customer on every occasion.

While customer service typically involves many people, doing operational roles, on relatively low salaries, it should never be a process and, in particular, it should never be one where standardization and efficiency are the measures of success. Customer service is not the result of a training course, a rulebook or process diagram. In a world of automation, it is important that people add even more value than before.

People create personal, emotional, memorable experiences – through the attitudes and behaviour of both employees and customers – that turn products into experiences, a transaction into a relationship, and person into a friend. Indeed, service across the experience can take many forms:

- Advising potential customers on what might be most appropriate to solve their problem or meet their need. Finding the right components to achieve a DIY challenge, or ingredients for a great meal.

- Guiding them to put together the right solution, addressing technical requirements such as the most appropriate spec for a new computer, and helping them make informed choices across a bewildering range of brands.

- Selling not only in terms of taking the money, but also in making available what they want when they need it, from the locations of stores and opening times to knowing what's in stock and how to get there.

- Delivering the solution, which might include installation or set-up, from home entertainment systems to wireless LANs and making sure all the software works.

- Supporting the customer in making the most of it, to enjoy their in-flight experience with their favourite magazine or video, to cater for their special needs and requests.

- Maintaining it as good as new, sustaining the positive experience of the car showroom into the workshop, keeping things going and continuing to deliver the promise day after day.

- Solving the specific problems that inevitably arise, dealing with complaints in a way that shows your true colours, suggesting routes when you hire a car. And making the most of the opportunity to really 'show what you can do'.

- Building relationships person to person, remembering people and seeking to enable people to build one-to-one relationships rather than just anonymously with the brand.

Customer service is a personal experience. But how can you possibly judge how to treat a customer in exactly the right way? One person ordering their coffee is there for a morning chat, the next is rushing to their next appointment, the next is grumpy after a big argument, and the next is trying to chat you up.

Nobody is predictable; everybody wants something slightly different, both from the product they are buying and from the wider experience they seek, and sensing this is the real skill of delivering great service.

How do you do the right thing?

There are three dimensions: from 'knowing' the standard processes, to 'doing' the job effectively, to 'being' with the customer more empathetically and personally, at that moment, in their shoes.

- *Knowing. What to do.* The standard procedures, what the book says, delivering the basic promise, the minimum service level. The right way to grind coffee, the temperature of the water, the frothiness of the milk.

- *Doing. How to do it.* This is more tailored to the stated or perceived needs and preference of the customer. It might be 'the regular' without having to ask, a special topping, or doing a little more than is actually required.

- *Being. Why do it?* This is the hard one. Unpredictable day by day. Sensing when to chat and when not. Getting inside the customer's head. An extra shot of espresso to cheer someone up. It could make their day. Or backfire.

Application 9.3 BEING INTUITIVE

How do you connect with customers more personally? How do you recognize the way each individual wants to be treated, each time you serve them? How can you make more of your own unique personality or talents, to deliver a more meaningful and memorable service experience?

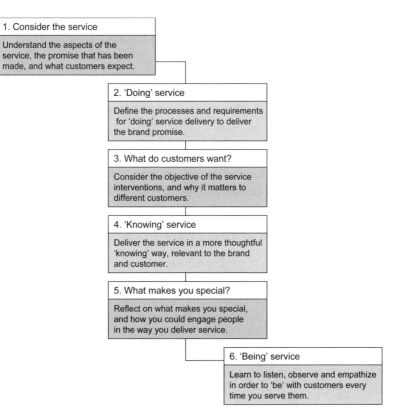

1. Consider the service

Understand the aspects of the service, the promise that has been made, and what customers expect.

2. 'Doing' service

Define the processes and requirements for 'doing' service delivery to deliver the brand promise.

3. What do customers want?

Consider the objective of the service interventions, and why it matters to different customers.

4. 'Knowing' service

Deliver the service in a more thoughtful 'knowing' way, relevant to the brand and customer.

5. What makes you special?

Reflect on what makes you special, and how you could engage people in the way you deliver service.

6. 'Being' service

Learn to listen, observe and empathize in order to 'be' with customers every time you serve them.

marketing
genius

Concept 9.3 CUSTOMER THEATRE

Niketown is not a usual store.

You can buy shoes there. But that's not really the point. It is also a commercial, with the whole store turning into an immersive advertising break every 15 minutes. It is the venue for five-a-side soccer competitions, and provides lockers to change and go for a run. It is a shrine to the brand, with showcases of the very first Nikes. It's a brand experience, a temple to sporting excellence, bringing to life the passion and personality of the brand, and the ambitions of those who wear the Swoosh.

Harley Davidson organizes the largest bikers rally in the world. It organizes the Harley Owners Club. It even offers Harley Holidays where you can live the dream for just a few days. How much would you pay to be Peter Fonda on his silver-chromed, low-riding bike, reliving the best moments of *Easy Rider*?

Nike and Harley Davidson create brand experiences through theatre.

However, the best theatre is rarely the scripted plays that are performed word and movement perfect and replicated time after time. You many as well buy the DVD if that is what you are after. Live audiences want something more, the unpredictable and impulsive, often leaving a performance remembering the occasional event that shouldn't have happened rather than what did.

Improvised or street theatre is far more compulsive viewing. It always offers something new and different, creative and inspiring. You don't know what's going to happen next, and maybe the actor doesn't either. Similarly with humour, the jokes that are planned and scripted have less power than what actually happens and how people uniquely respond to it. The most hilarious thing you ever saw is unlikely to have been a planned, scripted act.

Disneyland. The very name captures a certain kind of magic.

Why is it that kids are so captivated by the experience? 'Where your dreams come true' goes the line, yet for many they really do. For years children will have read the stories and watched the cartoons of Winnie the Pooh, Mickey Mouse or Cinderella, and here they are in the real Magic Kingdom. But its not the buildings that make the fantasy reality, it's the people, the cast who come up to you, hug you and want to be your friend for the day.

The Baloo Bear who squeezes your three-year-old daughter so tight that she won't ever forget. The Tinkerbell who really does fly though the sky, sprinkling magic dust on your shoulders. The Cinderella, in her trademark yellow ball gown (a stroke of marketing genius by Disney to 'own' the look of characters in fairy tales which they don't otherwise own), is on her way to a magical ball, and really does wear glass slippers that fit perfectly.

It's not just the characters. It's the music that greets you at the entrance gates. It's the food on the menu in the many different restaurants, sometimes even served by Mickey Mouse himself. It's the excitement and enthusiasm in every 'cast member' who works there day in day out, but makes dreams come to life, every hour of every day. It's the signposts that are thoughtfully designed on the back as well as the front. And it's the enormous amount of merchandising, allowing you to take a little bit of the magic home with you.

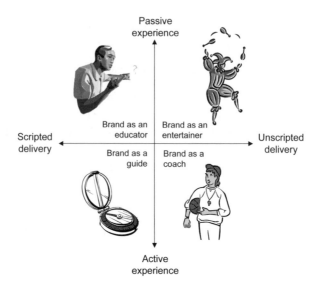

Experiences can take many forms, some where you are part of the experience yourself, and others where you can just observe:

- Entertaining experiences, from sporting events to rock concerts, far more dramatic than when edited and viewed remotely.

- Educational experiences, from historic monuments brought to life through re-enactments to training courses based on role-play and interaction.

- Guiding experiences, from art galleries that embrace all the senses, to health spas that stimulate and pamper them.

- Coaching experiences, from adventure sports to video games that take participants into extreme or imaginary worlds.

Any brand could embrace any of these types of experiences, and to engage customers like never before, to bring the brand to life uniquely at that moment for that person.

Inspiration 9.3 AGENT PROVOCATEUR

Joseph Corre and Serena Rees opened their first boutique in London in 1994, and launched a social revolution in attitudes towards lingerie, and sexuality more broadly.

Their vision is to create lingerie that stimulates, enchants and arouses those who wear it, and their partners. Their approach is the very antithesis of the conventional and rather prudish attitude that anything to do with sex must be unspoken or sleazy. In a world where our tolerance and expectation is stretched ever further, Agent Provocateur is ever more radical to keep one step ahead.

This is upmarket fantasy for some, and functional underwear for others. However, for all, Agent Provocateur is an experience. Partly through the product designs, partly through the thrill and excitement the brand builds into everything it does.

Visit one of their stores in London, New York or LA, and you will be greeted by a stunning female in short pink dress, slightly unbuttoned to hint at more, stilettos and black stockings – eye-catching if not a little intimidating, a boudoir of exotic lingerie and escapism.

> A woman wearing a scrumptious pair of turquoise tulle knickers promotes in herself a
> sexy superhero feeling which exudes itself as a confident and positive sexuality.

Source: agentprovocateur.com

Agent Provocateur seeks to create an intensely private and personal experience for customers, both when choosing and wearing its products. Mass advertising is rejected in favour of highly seductive window displays, art and photographic exhibitions, and cinema advertising. Browse through the brochure and it is more akin to a nineteenth century peep show. Visit the website and you can voyeuristically tour the whole house – the bedroom and bathroom, the lounge and kitchen. Most of the action is in the latter.

The brand has more recently extended into accessories such as shoes and jewellery, fragrances and music. A diffusion range, Salon Rose, was also developed and sold through the far more conventional retailer Marks & Spencer. While in 2004, their first album, 'Peep Show', brought together 14 eclectic tracks that together created a journey of sexual discovery.

Agent Provocateur will undoubtedly continue to provoke and excite, to rattle the cage of inhibitions and reject the superficial trends of fashion, and to celebrate and help people enjoy their sensuality and sexuality.

Application 9.4 THEATRICAL PERFORMANCE

How do you bring the experience to life in more unusual and unpredictable ways, to truly catch people's attention and do something for them that has never happened before?

1. Moments of theatre

Identify points during the experience that could be delivered in more dramatic and engaging ways.

2. How could you do this?

Discuss with your people how they believe they could best achieve this. What could they do or use?

3. Script or improvise?

Consider scripting the activities, or how to encourage and enable people to improvise in their delivery.

4. Passive or interactive?

Consider whether customers would prefer to be involved, or just observe Passively.

5. Planning the experience

Consider designing unique environments, or whether theatre could be delivered anywhere.

6. The performance

Design the appropriate theatrics, and ensure you capture this added value in the price too.

Doing business on customers' terms

We	We
don't see	see
things	things
as	as
they	we
are	are

Anaïs Nin

'I roamed the countryside searching for the answers to things I did not understand. Why shells existed on the tops of mountains along with the imprints of coral and plant and seaweed usually found in the sea. Why the thunder lasts a longer time than that which causes it and why immediately on its creation the lightning becomes visible to the eye while thunder requires time to travel. How the various circles of water form around the spot that has been struck by a stone and why a bird sustains itself in the air. These questions and other strange phenomena engaged my thought throughout my life.'

Leonardo da Vinci

Companies physically connect with customers through distribution channels and communications media. While communications – and certainly the impatience of a marketing manager to leap into bed with his or her advertising agency – has long dominated the role of the marketer, distribution has been perhaps the least attractive part of the marketing mix, more associated with warehouses and haulage companies than the sexy new technologies that capture the imagination of marketers today.

More intelligent connections	More imaginative connections
Media. Communicating with more impact, progression and efficiency by bringing together media impartially.	**Inversion.** Reversing connections to give customers control, to do business when, how and where they want.
Channels. Developing distribution channels to reach target customers to serve and sell more profitably.	**Fusion.** Connecting the best ingredients within existing media and channels to connect with customers better.
Networks. Building physical and virtual networks that are able to replicate brand experiences, and scale efficiently.	**Connectivity**. Unlocking the power of networks for customers, peer-to-peer, leveraging knowledge and connections.

The rise of digital media, in the form of websites and e-mail-based marketing, SMS and interactive TV is well hyped; however, some of the other changes to the traditional ways we connect with customers include:

• Recognition that advertising is not always the most effective way to drive sales and build brands, or even a prerequisite.

- Shift to direct marketing, most typically direct mail and telemarketing, but increasingly resisted as intrusive and requiring permission.

- PR and sponsorship, events and personal selling offering a greater ability to connect with people, their aspirations, and bring brands to life.

- Increased power of the big supermarkets which dictate terms to suppliers, build strong own-label products and loyalty schemes.

- Acceptance that direct channels are inevitable and, while some traditional channels have disappeared, other types of intermediaries have emerged.

- Globalization of markets, particularly driven by online sales, eroding the previous price and product differences by market or segment.

- Media integration that brings together everything from ads to events in a more balanced and symbiotic way, that fuses with distribution channels too.

- Fusion of communication media, and distribution channels, creating many more ways for customers to interact with brands.

However this is not enough.

They are moves in the direction, but insufficient to deal with the growing power of the customer, and the need to fundamentally re-engineer the ways in which suppliers connect with them to do business when, how and where they want.

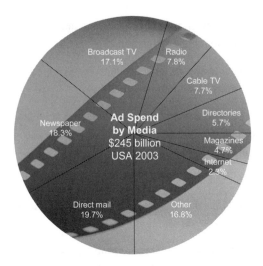

Source: *Advertising Age*

'Reverse marketing' requires:

- Communication that is initiated by the customer, saying what they want to know and how they want to receive the information.

- The end of blanket 'campaigns' where companies choose to tell everybody, in the same way and at the same time, that they need a new car, now.

- Market research driven by individual preferences rather than average statistics that represent nobody effectively.

- Channels that act on behalf of customers rather than suppliers, understanding their individual needs, then going out to source them.

- Pricing driven by customers and their perceived value, where the lowest prices anywhere in the world can be checked within seconds.

- Products customized to the individual needs of customers, brought together from various suppliers to form the most appropriate solutions.

Indeed, the 'Google' has in many cases transformed communication and distribution processes, making them genuinely customer initiated, although a click is rarely the starting point on most marketing process diagrams.

Inspiration 10.1 DELL

Michael Dell created Dell in a fanfare of high-tech revolution in the late nineties. At first its direct model suggested a lower-quality product. However, this was quickly dispelled, and the brand is now a leader in consumer and corporate markets. How has Dell achieved this? In the company's own words, 'Everything we do starts and ends with our customers.'

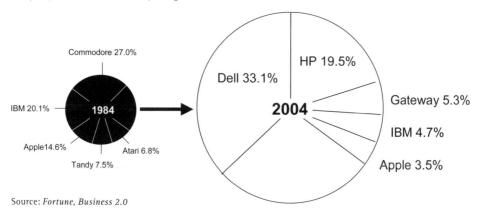

Source: *Fortune, Business 2.0*

Dell's customer-focused direct business model is a leading example of how companies are gradually moving to these new dynamics, to embrace all of the 'value disciplines' at a higher level than ever before, to do business on customers' terms and still be hugely profitable.

Michael is an entrepreneurial marketer. Born in 1965, he attended the University of Texas intending to study medicine. However, his real interest was in computers, and within a year Michael was in his college room assembling PCs from component parts and selling them to students and staff, and calling it PCs Limited. His staggering first month's revenues of $180,000 quickly signalled an end to his medical ambitions.

He started to manufacture personal computers, but with a difference: he held no stocks of finished goods or components, instead building the PCs to order, selling and delivering them directly to customers. This was mass customization, but it was also highly efficient, receiving orders and payments from customers before needing to order and pay his suppliers.

'I realized that the computer market was very inefficient. The mark-ups were incredibly high over the cost of materials and the service was very poor,' he said at the time.

His 'take-away pizza' mentality, where you could order by phone and choose your 'toppings' was an immediate hit. His low-cost, direct approach also meant that he could undercut even far less sophisticated PCs by 15% or more.

The company became successful enough that he dropped out of college at the age of 19 to run the business full time. In 1987, the company became Dell Computer Corporation, and later, simply Dell. It became the most profitable PC manufacturer in the world, with sales of $35 billion and profits of $2 billion in 2002.

In 2004, Michael stepped down as CEO but stayed as chairman, while Kevin Rollins, then president and COO, became CEO. 'I was CEO for 20 years, now I'll be chairman for 20 years,' Dell says. 'Then we'll see,' he explained.

He says he feels as entrepreneurial now as when he started. 'There are plenty of markets to discover,' he says, 'and each new venture requires tenacity and a willingness to take risks.'

'The Soul of Dell' is a philosophy with five elements:

1   'Customers', gaining their loyalty through the best products and services at great prices, and a superior customer experience.

2   The 'Dell Team' believing that continued success lies in teamwork and the opportunity each team member has to learn, develop and grow.

3   'Direct Relationships', being direct in all we do, with customers, partners, and suppliers without inefficient hierarchy and bureaucracy.

4   'Global Citizenship' embracing responsibility and sensitivity to global cultures and local communities.

5   'Winning' with a passion for winning in everything we do.

Source: dell.com

This translates into a business model built around customers and the direct connections with them. Among it obvious financial benefits are the dynamics of 'built to order', which results in minimal stock and a negative working capital, given that customer payments are typically received before suppliers are paid.

Dell | Direct Model

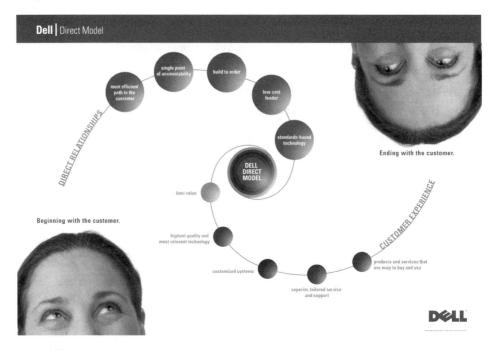

Source: dell.com

Dell's Direct Model

Dell's Direct Model starts and ends with our customers – focused on superb value; high-quality, relevant technology; customized systems; superior service and support; and products and services that are easy to buy and use. With its singular focus on the customer, it creates a unique way of buying and selling technology.

The five tenets to the model are:

1 Most efficient path to the customer

We believe that the most efficient path to the customer is through a direct relationship, with no intermediaries to add confusion and cost. We are organized around groups of customers with similar needs. This allows our teams to understand the specific needs of specific customers – without customer needs being 'translated' by inefficient resellers and middlemen.

2 Single point of accountability

We recognize that technology can be complex, so we work to keep things easy for our customers. We make Dell the single point of accountability so that resources necessary to meet customer needs can be easily marshalled in support of complex challenges. Our customers tell us they want streamlined and fast access to the right resources; direct provides just that.

3 Build-to-order

We provide customers with exactly what they want in their computer systems through easy custom configuration and ordering. Build-to-order means that we don't maintain months of aging and expensive inventory. As a result, we typically provide our customers with the best pricing and latest technology for features they really want.

4 Low-cost leader

We focus resources on what matters to our customers. With a highly efficient supply chain and manufacturing organization, a concentration on standards-based technology developed collaboratively with our industry partners, and a dedication to reducing costs through business process improvements, we consistently provide our customers with superior value.

5   Standards-based technology

We believe that standard technology is key to providing our customers with relevant, high-value products and services. Focusing on standards gives customers the benefit of extensive research and development from Dell and an entire industry – not from just a single company. Unlike proprietary technologies, standards give customers flexibility and choice.

Source: dell.com

Application 10.1 CONNECTIONS MAPPING

How do you connect with customers? How effectively do you use distribution channels and communications media to build these connections? What is the purpose and effectiveness of each connection?

1. Identify the contact points

Map all the interactions between the supplier and customer, e.g. advice, purchase, delivery, complaints etc.

2. Channels and media

Identify the platforms, distribution channels and media which support these connections.

3. Partners and mechanisms

Identify all intermediary partners and processes, systems and devices, that facilitate these.

4. Role and objectives

Evaluate the role(s) and objectives of each connection, e.g. communication, distribution, selling, support.

5. Costs and revenues

Estimate the revenue contribution of each connection, and the costs of enabling it, and compare effectiveness.

6. Prioritize connections

Identify the most important connections, ranking media and channels separately to focus resources and performance.

Concept 10.1 INTEGRATED COMMUNICATION

Customer power challenges the very fundamentals of marketing communications. While new technologies have enabled customers to do more – for example, to make their booking online from anywhere, anytime – the majority of communications is still done with suppliers rather than customers.

In *The New Bottom Line*, Alan Mitchell argues that we should not term customers as such, but rather as buyers – people out there with a problem to solve, a need to satisfy, or a desire to fulfil. In markets of surplus supply rather than surplus demand, not only does being different matter, but the whole way in which we do business matters too.

The notion of 'campaigns' still dominates the marketing department. Advertising as one of many possible media for conveying messages still dominates the campaign. And marketers over-rely on their agencies, far more than financers do on accountants, or company secretaries on lawyers.

There is incredible noise in markets due to the tripling in the intensity of competition and the far more aggressive, desperate actions of marketers. While customers resent intrusion into their privacy, most of this noise, clutter and confusion is largely a problem for marketers.

- Campaigns don't work because they expect customers to conform to their terms – 'you will watch this ad, at this time and on this channel, and you will consider buying this car' even if you aren't looking for a new car.

- Advertising still dominates the media mix because we feel good about big messages with emotive visuals, our bosses expect it, it's great fun to make, a tangible outcome line for the CV, and it is still seen as a brave step to take.

- Agencies are too often used as the surrogate brains for marketers who, once they've written their short brief (the shorter the better, to maximize creative interpretation, goes the argument), surrender the consequences to agency planners and creatives.

Communication must today start with the customer, or rather 'the buyer', who is seeking to achieve something with all sorts of purchase and product requirements or preferences. It requires:

- Customer-initiated communication where he or she can request information, explore options, get advice.

- Communication that is flexible and personalized to specific needs, so that one person's interest in engine specs can be balanced by another's passion for aesthetic design.

- Communication that is more relevant and engaging, linking to what matters to the customers, for example through sponsorship or affinity branding.

- Communication that is human and empathetic, intelligent in that it anticipates questions and suggests appropriate alternatives.

- Communications with better ROI, for example PR, is cheap and fast at connecting a brand with key issues in accessible and relevant ways.

- Communication that is connected, so that the messages are consistent and the knowledge of the customer is shared.

- Communication that complements and enhances other aspects of the marketing mix – brands, propositions, distribution channels and pricing, products and services, to provide an aligned, intelligent approach to customers.

Conventional models for communication are one way, sender to receiver, seeking a response that leads to a transaction. The majority of communications media were constructed for such purposes – advertising and direct mail most prominently – and these single-dimensional, push mechanisms still dominate most companies' marketing.

Integrated communication is about:

- Communication that starts with the strategic context – the brand, the proposition, the objective, and the fit within the marketing mix.

- Communication without prejudice, and an open-minded choice of the most appropriate media and messages for each objective.

- Communication that uses messages and media that progress and interact, that play off each other, and progress.

- Communication that integrates with the customer, enabling them to initiate a dialogue, when, where and how they want.

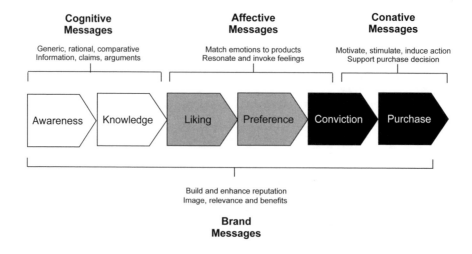

- Communication that is radically creative, differentiated in style and content, embracing unusual media, and new messages.

- Communication that in its style and activities reinforces the brand and is itself part of the customer experience.

Integrated communications must have customers at its centre and neutrality as a philosophy. It must be rigorously measured and effectively project-managed by the client, not the agency.

Inspiration 10.2 AMAZON

In 1994 Jeff Bezos was working on Wall Street, watching Internet use grow by 2300% every year. Deciding it was time to catch the dotcom wave, Bezos jumped into his Chevy and headed west on Interstate 90. On arrival in Seattle he launched 'the Earth's largest bookstore'. Based in his garage, he started by selling books to friends, who then referred others.

Amazon.com was founded in July 1995. In the early days, every time an order arrived a beeper would sound. The beeper started to drive staff crazy. Within three months it was beeping 100 times every day, within a year it was beeping 100 times every hour and, more recently, 100 times every minute.

Amazon's IPO came in May 1997, and soon after the millionth customer had signed up for its innovative 'One-Click' process. Indeed, this small innovation has been a key to success, holding a customer's personal and payment details so that a new purchase can be made literally within one click of finding the book.

This knowledge of the customer has enabled Amazon to build up a detailed profile of the customer's interests and tastes, so that it can start to recommend other or complementary items (a process known as collaborative filtering). Sometimes its assumptions of your favourite music or novels can be accurate as well as spooky. Regular customers are then e-mailed, if requested, letting them know when a new book or music CD has been released which they might be interested in.

1999 was 'Get Big Fast' year for Bezos, with growth in Europe, and developing new distribution centres to ensure fastest possible delivery times. This enabled Amazon to offer its 10 million users everything from toys to videos, electronics to DIY tools. Indeed, it has continued to attract 10 million more visitors every year, and once customers overcome their initial concerns about buying online, their individual purchases start to mushroom too.

Amazon seeks to be the world's most customer-centric company, a place where people can find and discover anything they might want to buy online. Bezos describes the challenge 'to constantly think like customers and shareholders, to both innovate and focus on delivering an unparalleled online experience, all at the same time'.

Bezos was determined it would succeed. In the late nineties Amazon rode high through the dotcom boom, held up as the reason why high streets would become desolate and every middleman in every industry is facing a certain, imminent death. Yet as soon as the bubble burst, people were quick to write off the online books and music retailer too.

Not so, and in 2004, Bezos finally broke through into profitability. Amazon has quietly moved forwards, adding to its range and hooking in customers who initially visited for the novelty but were eventually persuaded that this really was a better way.

Application 10.2 MEDIA INTEGRATION

How do you integrate the many different communications opportunities at your disposal? How do you resist the temptation to turn straight to advertising as your natural solution? Do other media actually achieve the goal better? How do the different media collaborate, work off one another, to create a distinctive dialogue that customers want?

1. Define communication goals

Define the objectives of communication, e.g. target audiences, proposition and script, desired outcomes and measures.

2. What do customers want?

Research how customers want to interact – what, how, where and how – by segment and individual.

3. Engage the right partners

Articulate the specific brief to potential internal and external partners to achieve this (media/agency neutral).

4. Design the communication

Bring together all the likely partners to gain their perspectives on how they could add value cohesively.

5. Define an integrated plan

Define an integrated comms plan as part of the wider marketing plan, business case and implementation.

6. Manage effective dialogues

Project manage the who activity, measuring impact, cost and responses, adjusting and evolving over time.

Concept 10.2 CHANNEL INVERSION

Distribution channels, from shops to telephone, websites to mail order, connect us with companies and facilitate our transactions in the way we prefer. They might be direct, in that they belong to the supplier, or indirect, in that a third party gets involved. These middlemen, from food retailers to travel agents, insurance brokers to car showrooms, define our high streets.

Distribution channels were traditionally an extended arm of suppliers, their representatives locally, so that they could reach more people, make more sales.

Channels have increasingly added more value through advice, personalization and offering complementary products and services, for example:

- Online aggregation portals.

- Interactive TV and wireless services.

- Employers and associations, such as unions and professional bodies.

- Local corner shops.

- Personal concierge services, like Quintessential.

Channels are now more on the customers' 'side' than the suppliers'; they represent the buyer first in finding the right product at the right price.

Reverse channels typically have a strong affinity with the customer – building up a detailed understanding of their needs and then searching around for solutions. They would typically be more local, more convenient, more trusted.

Imagine the corner shop where you only buy milk, confectionery and newspapers, and which now sells everything from travel tickets to lottery tickets, dry cleaning to fresh flowers, photocopying to cash machines. Imagine the professional association where you can now buy anything from Caribbean holidays to car hire, mobile phones and credit cards, jewellery and accessories.

Channels must work together – so that the experience of customers across different channels is connective as well as consistent. Consider Next, the clothing retailer. View their new range in their catalogue, check availability online, order it by phone, and receive it by mail, try it on but don't like it, take it back to the store. In this scenario five different channels are used for different elements of the purchase. The connections between channels enables each customer to interact in a way most convenient for them.

One step beyond multi-channel management is channel innovation.

One approach to this is to deconstruct the attributes of each channel – for example, the ability to customize solutions, the selection available, the amount of advice given, the complementary products available, the method of delivery, the speed of delivery, the payment options, etc. and then reassemble them in a new format more appropriate to target customer groups.

- Imagine a self-service supermarket on your high street where you can buy milk or bread 24 hours a day.

- Imagine getting the expert advice of a financial adviser at minimum convenience, online anytime.

- Imagine sitting at a table in a restaurant and serving yourself as much beer as you like from a tap on the table, then paying on account.

- Imagine doing your weekly shop at a supermarket, and then just giving it to someone to go through checkout and take it home for you.

They all exist today as examples of fusing the best bits of different channels together to improve the convenience and experience of customers, to drive incremental sales and reduce costs.

The travel market illustrates how the channel landscape has changed.

Ten years ago an airline, hotel or package holiday company hardly dare tell its customers that they could buy tickets directly, rather than through a conventional travel agent. The suppliers feared the backlash of the intermediary, and in particular the large travel agency chains. They paid these agents enormous commissions and incentives too, typically giving them around 15% of the ticket price, leaving little room for the business to make a profit margin.

How times have changed. Driven by the disruption of the online players such as Expedia and Priceline, the entry of low-cost carriers such as Jet Blue and Ryanair, and also by the dire economics of the industry, the airlines were forced to take radical action. Direct channels became the norm, heavily promoted and with the best fares, while agency commissions and kickbacks were massively cut back. Many of the traditional intermediaries struggled to survive – Amex refocused on its credit card businesses, Thomas Cook became a charter airline. The airlines went high-tech, driving online sales and ticketless travel.

Inspiration 10.3 MTV

Still the rebellious teenager of the media world, MTV is now in its mid-twenties and the world's most widely distributed television network, reaching almost 400 million households in more than 140 countries around the globe.

MTV, now part of the Viacom group, has achieved much in its short life, largely due to its intelligent use of satellite, cable and online channels to reach many customers in more relevant and interactive ways. MTV completely transformed the nature of popular music during the eighties and nineties, as influential on that sector as the introduction of the compact disc was to music sales, and is one of only a handful of media companies that have managed to become a lifestyle brand. Yet MTV began as simply a cheap way of filling a dead slot in a regional US cable system.

MTV is built on 94 locally managed and operated channels and a brand portfolio that includes MTV itself, plus VH1, TMF and Game One, and MTV Networks International. In a digital world, MTV is also able to provide many diverse tribal points of view through its different channels, be it MTV, its R&B channel, or dance channel, alternative rock channel or pop channel, enabling them to better engage specific audiences while meeting many more people at the same time.

The network is headquartered in London and counts 80% of its audience from outside the US (although this 80% reportedly generates only 20% of total revenues).

The online presence is as important as on screen. MTV.com features deep, original content including music premieres and exclusives, multi-media shows like *TRL* and *Control Freak*, original programming for specials like music awards, community games and messaging. The website is consistently ranked the No. 1 music content site by teenagers.

MTV is not just a network targeting youth audiences. From Nickelodeon to VH1 Classics, the company can now take its audience from cradle to grave. Juggling regions and cultures, combining a global and local feel, while constantly innovating to stay ahead.

Finding new and innovative content is not easy when you are already on the cutting edge. MTV deploys a wide range of research techniques, yet it can still miss the real winners. *Jackass* is a good example, a concept that tested poorly, perhaps not surprisingly. At other times, it uncovers unexpected trends, for example the changing child-to-parent relationship that refines family life and led to programmes like *The Osbournes*.

Application 10.3 CHANNEL INTEGRATION

How do you make the most of your distribution channels? How do they connect with each other? How can you create more innovative 'hybrid' channels that connect your customers and products more effectively? How do you achieve multi-channel management?

1. Define your distribution goals

Who are you seeking to reach, how it delivers the brand experience, and what value does the channel add?

2. Understand how customers buy

Understand what customers seek from channels – what additional services they seek – when, where and how?

3. Develop channel framework

Construct a framework of direct and indirect channels that reaches target audiences and meets purchase needs.

4. Explore innovative hybrids

Develop unique customized channels to meet specific needs, selecting the best components of other channels.

5. Integrate multi-channels

Define the role of each channel, and how they complement – audiences, role, added value, and effectiveness.

6. Manage effective distribution

Manage the integrated channel mix, working with channels to deliver the band experience and personal service.

Concept 10.3 MARKET NETWORKS

In giving us the 'World Wide Web', Tim Berners-Lee, a British physicist, defined a networked model of the world, where everything is connected to everything else, where the power is in combining global knowledge, and the more connections increases the power. It was democratic in that there were no rules or hierarchies; once you are online it is free and instant, what you make of it.

The marketing opportunities are well documented, although we are probably still in the embryonic stages of recognizing its full potential:

- Global reach – a one-man business in Brazil can do business with a large company in China, or the small English butcher who is now the world's leading source of Cumberland sausages.

- Personalization – knowledge can be leveraged to offer personalized solutions, e.g. design your own car, through to Nike ID individually designed shoes and apparel; which, of course, is a great source of understanding what customers really want.

- E-mail messaging – we can interact with enormous numbers of customers frequently at no cost. Witness the 40–50 news alerts, most of which you've requested, which arrive in your mailbox every morning.

- Online communities – we can bring together customers to share their passions for our products and their applications. Consider the rapid emergence of blogging.

- Viral communication – where ideas and messages can spread freely like wildfire, like the 100 million people who signed up to Hotmail, which has never spent a cent on conventional marketing.

- New business models – new ways of making money emerge, from eBay's success in facilitating peer-to-peer transactions to Kelkoo and many others that scan the world for the best-priced goods.

However, network thinking can be applied to the physical world too and, while networks could easily exist, their connectivity is largely unexploited. If you are a retail chain, how do you turn your network into an advantage over single stores? If you are a consumer goods company, how can you make more out of your huge network of stockists?

The main consumer benefit of one bank over another is largely a question of which has the best network of cash machines, so that you can access your money wherever you are. Although as soon as they all accept each other's cards, the advantage is lost.

Mobile phone companies leverage their network of subscribers by offering lower rates, or even free calls to people on the same network. Coffee shops offer their 'loyalty' cards where every tenth drink from any of their outlets is free. However, these are still fairly primitive benefits.

Franchising is a more radical example whereby companies can leverage networks to quickly grow without high capital investment and effort. The number of franchising magazines on the shelves of bookstalls today is testament to the legion of individuals who would love to run their own businesses but lack the know-how, the brand or the confidence.

Subway sandwich bars, 7 Eleven convenience stores, Krispy Kreme doughnut stalls, Marriott hotels, Hertz car rental, Ford showrooms and KFC restaurants are franchise models which have come to dominate high streets from Auckland to Alma Mata in just a few years.

Inspiration 10.4 KRISPY KREME

The licensing of a brand to be used by a third party in return for a royalty fee on their sales is a compelling but risky business, particularly when retail is such a people business, and one shabby store or poor service experience could damage the whole brand. Yet for Krispy Kreme it has been phenomenally successful.

Krispy Kreme is the world's leading brand of doughnuts, made throughout the day in its vast network of largely franchised stores. Yet they regularly have 3000 customers waiting for the opening of a new store. From the production line within every store, visible to whet the appetite, to the neon signs outside that proclaim that a new batch has just come out the ovens with the words 'Hot' illuminated, to the smell of fresh baking pumped out to the street, Krispy Kreme creates an experience made of 'magic moments' well beyond the simple doughnut.

Vernon Rudolph won a secret recipe from a New Orleans baker in a poker game for yeast-raised doughnuts and began selling them to local grocery stores in North Carolina in 1937. Because of customer demand, he began selling them directly from his bakery to customers. The first Krispy Kreme store was in Winston-Salem. In 1976, Krispy Kreme Donut Corporation became a wholly owned subsidiary of Beatrice Foods Company; however, a group of franchisees repurchased it in 1982. Krispy Kreme began another phase of rapid expansion in the 1990s through franchising.

It is run largely as a virtual business, a small head office team and a global network of stores. Individuals attracted to seek a brand franchise are given the power of the brand and reputation of the product. They recognize that there is far more money to be made using somebody else's brand, rather than trying to set up a new business as a nobody.

The franchise agreement specifies in detail the look, feel and performance requirements of the third party. To the customer, it must be Krispy Kreme – in terms of retail design, visual identity, product range, service style, price structure, complaints process, everything. Training and manuals are provided, with regular reporting and the occasional visit. Otherwise it's the individual's business, and it's up to them to make the most of it.

Krispy Kreme sits back and watches their slice of revenues roll in from outlets around the world. Once the model is defined, and control processes are in place, scalability is easy, limited only by how much Krispy Kreme the world can eat.

Application 10.4 NETWORK MARKETING

How do you leverage the effect of networks to reach many people rapidly and efficiently? To carry your memetic messages with the impact of Metcalfe's Law? How do you make networks work for you and customers?

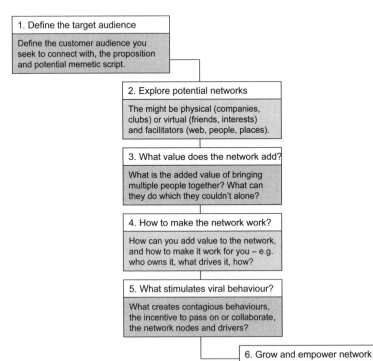

1. Define the target audience

Define the customer audience you seek to connect with, the proposition and potential memetic script.

2. Explore potential networks

The might be physical (companies, clubs) or virtual (friends, interests) and facilitators (web, people, places).

3. What value does the network add?

What is the added value of bringing multiple people together? What can they do which they couldn't alone?

4. How to make the network work?

How can you add value to the network, and how to make it work for you – e.g. who owns it, what drives it, how?

5. What stimulates viral behaviour?

What creates contagious behaviours, the incentive to pass on or collaborate, the network nodes and drivers?

6. Grow and empower network

Enable the network to better achieve their goals in a way that promotes, endorses and sells your brand.

Who do you want a one-to-one with?

'Strange is our situation here upon earth. Each of us comes for a short visit, not knowing why, yet sometimes seeming to divine a purpose. From the standpoint of daily life, however, there is one thing we do know: that man is here for the sake of other men.'

Albert Einstein

'Creativity is the ability to see relationships when none exist.'

Thomas Disch

Do customers really want relationships with companies? Who is it that they would have the relationship with – the company or brand, product or person? While every company seeks to build them, it would be foolish to kid ourselves that customers want relationships with a business in the way they would a friend or lover. Not only this, but do companies really want relationships with customers, or to be honest, aren't they more interested in selling, and then being there for the repeat sell?

Are they really after a relationship, or just sex?

More intelligent relationships	More imaginative relationships
Friends. Knowing customers as individuals in order to personalize communication, products and service.	**Lovers.** Knowing customers more deeply, committing to them, doing more and being special for them.
Affinity. Tapping into the deep passions and interests of customers, with more effective affinity-based marketing.	**Advocacy.** Encouraging customers to be ambassadors for you, to positively endorse you to more people like them.
Partners. Building strong partnerships, through customer (e.g. key accounts) and partner (e.g. agency) management.	**Communities.** Building relationships with whole customer communities, and enhancing their own relationships.

'Who do you want to have a one-to-one with?' went the advertising line.

Of course, what it meant was which of your colleagues or friends should you call more often, rather than promoting the one-to-one mission of relationship marketers such as Don Peppers and Martha Rogers.

Companies have long sought to build relationships with their customers.

Relationship marketing really took off in the early nineties with the increasing sophistication of customer databases, and technology-enabled communications approaches. Of course, B2B companies have long had personal relationships with each of their customers, and some of the largest companies in the world only have a handful of customers.

The one-to-one approach seeks to treat each chosen customer individually, uniquely understanding their needs, building genuinely personal dialogues with them, and creating highly personalized solutions for them; then you can charge a premium, and gain their loyalty. The returns are then measured in lifetime value rather than short-term sales. Of course, it is difficult to do this in mass markets, and so you have to start small, with the best customers and then gradually increase the number, provided it still makes sense economically.

But do customers actually want relationships with companies?

For starters, it is rare, certainly in consumer markets, that a customer is able to have a relationship with any person; rather, it is with the brand, which is why it is so important that the brand is about the customer rather than the business. However, human relationships are not naturally based only on transactions – they also require understanding, patience and tolerance, support and participation, seeking to achieve common goals and realizing mutual benefits.

As we will explore later, customers are more likely to build relationships with other customers that are actually like them rather than with companies that are not. If brands can become facilitators of groups of people with similar interests or goals – let's call them communities – then the brand becomes essential and more valued by that group of customers. The whole community recognizes that the real value that the brand offers is in enabling the relationships they seek – perhaps by bringing unknown people together with an unusual hobby, or a group of workers with a common problem – as well the value it offers through products and services.

Customer relationship management (CRM) was overtaken by the pursuit of targeting customers and selling more to them, rather than being the basis of more enlightened relationships with those customers that want them.

The original concepts were excellent, driven by the folk stories of Southwest Airlines (how Herb Kelleher created levels of impassioned service) and Feargal Quinn (the Irish retailer who, on spotting a dissatisfied customer, would refer to their lost lifetime value as 'There goes another £2000 walking out the store').

Yet CRM was gobbled up by software monoliths whose systems claimed to recreate the relationships that we all thought were largely based on people, emotions and empathy. CRM got a bad name by struggling to integrate effectively with company practices, and the cost of the systems quickly became enormous relative to the benefits. In reality such systems do have a real purpose, effective in managing customer data and enabling precision-based direct marketing and contact strategies, but that's not quite a relationship.

Some have argued that CMR – where customers manage the relationships – is a far more empowering approach, more likely to succeed if customers are able to define the way in which they would like to build relationships, and the value they seek from them.

Relationships, of course, can be emotional as well as physical. We can love brands without ever interacting with a person from the company; indeed, some of the consumer brands with incredibly high loyalty never actually touch their customers. Instead, relationships are more about how the customer engages with the brand, identifies with its aspirations and values, and what it then says about them to other people.

This is the basis of affinity marketing, where one brand leverages the customer's love of another brand, as well as more tangibly through increasing benefits of customer loyalty. At the highest level it becomes a genuine partnership with customers, which is often achieved in the largest business transactions, for example between a retailer and its major suppliers, or between a marketing team and its creative agencies.

So what actually does build a strong relationship?

There are many slightly removed models to learn from – from the theories of transactional analysis to personal relationship counsellors, through to experts in organization collaboration. A number of themes come through.

Relationships require:

- A sense of equality and humility.
- Mutual attraction.

- A strong commitment.

- Tolerance.

- Something special for each side.

- Achievement.

It is unlikely that many companies will ever be able to build relationships that people want as much as the relationships with each other – more likely that a new Mum will have a better relationship with other new Mums who live locally than she would with Huggies or Pampers.

Marketing would do better to help people build relationships between themselves rather than with a business. The brand then acts to bring people together who have a common purpose or passion, but who struggle to find each other. The brand is recognized as the facilitator of the group, and as a consequence has a tangible relationship with the community rather than its individuals. Look at garden.com's success in bringing together people with a passion for plants through online communities. While it doesn't directly drive sales, it gives them a place to connect, so they come to the website, they feel positive to the brand for enabling this, and are far more likely to reward it with purchases, and far more likely to keep doing so too.

Inspiration 11.1 PANERA BREADS

Panera is the bread shop from St Louis that has driven an American obsession for speciality breads, and now has more than 800 bakery cafés in 36 states, with the highest level of retail brand loyalty of any company in the USA.

CEO and chairman Ron Shaich tries to spend as much time as he can in Panera's stores, talking to customers, finding out what makes them tick. He describes the company in a very human way:

> 'Listening to what our customers have to say is important to us at Panera. We strive to
> provide them with something worth going out of their way for – an experience that
> allows them to enjoy our tradition of fresh-baked artisan bread.'

Indeed, Panera is more than a bread shop, more than a coffee shop, but not quite a restaurant, with good food and atmosphere. Its huge range of speciality breads, bagels and muffins can, of course, be washed down with a Jones Soda, if not a speciality tea or coffee.

Each Panera store is spacious and contemporary, in warm colours, often with fire burning during the colder months. Near the entrance to each store are the takeaway menus, featuring the bread of the day, with free samples, and during the holiday season copies of *The Panera Bread Cookbook*. Customer service is key, generating huge consumer engagement.

Speciality breads were a relatively new phenomenon in the US, so Panera was quickly able to make its mark, recognizing that people want food 'they can trust', which is not heavily processed and full of artificial ingredients – 'breads are offered with whole grain; sandwiches and salads are made with anti-biotic free, humanely raised chickens.'

Panera builds its loyal customer following by placing itself at the heart of local communities. Shaich, who originally founded the Au Bon Pain chain of bakers in 1981, has built on the 'third place' concept of Starbucks to do more. The food as well as the coffee is exceptional, and the free Wi-Fi network is highly attractive too.

While two-thirds of the Panera network is franchised, there is no set formula – no two stores look the same, no store offers quite the same range as the next. It is all about the local community, and the people who come back day after day.

Since changing its name to Panera in 1999 the share price has grown thirteen-fold, creating over $1 billion of shareholder value. In 2003, Panera received the *Wall Street Journal*'s

'Highest Customer Loyalty' award, and earned the title of one of *Business Week*'s 'Hot Growth Companies'. Maverick marketer Peter van Stolk identifies Panera as one of the coolest brands around.

Panera even puts its brand promise into verse:

> We are bakers of bread.
> We are fresh from the oven.
> We are a symbol of warmth and welcome.
> We are a simple pleasure, honest and genuine.
> We are a life story told over dinner.
> We are a long lunch with an old friend.
> We are your weekday morning ritual.
> We are the soft doughy insides and the crunchy crust.
> We are the kindest gesture of neighbours.
> We are home. We are family. We are friends.
> We are Panera.

Source: panerabread.com

Application 11.1 RELATIONSHIP MAPPING

How do you build effective relationships? What are the building blocks of your mutually valuable and long-term relationship with your customers? What does it take from both sides, and what do they get from it? Are you up for it?

1. What does success look like?

Map out what each side would like to achieve from the relationship, what is essential and desirable from it.

2. Define your relative values

Understand the principles, ethics and emotional values which you have in common and what is different.

3. Compare your mutual ambitions

Compare your end states – in a perfect world what would success look like for each side – what is same and different.

4. What does each offer the other?

Explore what each side could bring to the relationship, and how this enables the achievement of mutual ambitions.

5. What are the benefits to each?

Articulate the benefits of the relationship in functional, emotional and financial terms – what is the 'added value'?

6. How committed to it are you?

How strong is the commitment to the relationship on each side – it is essential or just a nice to have?

Concept 11.1 CUSTOMER AFFINITY

Affinity marketing works when a brand leverages the strong emotional bond that customers have with it, and adds value to the customer in some new way. This might be some initiative in which the company seeks to engage its 'fans' more intimately, beyond the sale of products, or it may be where another company works with that brand to add value in some new way, and to benefit itself too.

Examples of brands leveraging the emotional affinity of customers to engage them more deeply, and connect with their passions would include:

- Hewlett Packard seeking to engage the niche but crucial audience of graphic designers by creating the 'HyPe Gallery' where new as well as established designers can exhibit their work and discuss issues and ideas.

- Illy, the Italian coffee company, creating a number of coffee ambassadors who cycle round Europe, engaging people in conversations about what makes great coffee, and what Illy does to achieve this.

- Land Rover inviting its existing customers on an all-expenses trip to Paris to celebrate the launch of a new model, making them feel part of the brand's achievement, and encouraging them to become brand ambassadors.

Other brands might seek to leverage these affinities too and, indeed, collaborating with partners in other categories to reach new audiences and make people think differently about their own brands is one of the easiest and cheapest ways to build a brand.

Of course, there needs to be transparency and partnerships must work hard to find the complementary emotional – as well as tangible – connections, ensuring that there is value for both partners, as well as for the customer through new products and services.

Examples of affinity brand partnering would include:

- Philips working with Nike to offer a range of entertainment devices tailored to the needs of active lifestyles. Philips reaches a new market, gaining some of the adrenalin of the Nike brand, while Nike gets a brand extension.

- Intel working with its customers to promote its microprocessors (through 'Intel Inside') at the same time as promoting individual brands of computers; indeed, customers often seek the Intel brand before the hardware brand.

- Shell sponsoring the Ferrari motor racing team, providing funding to create faster cars, while gaining the prestige of speed and leadership which it then uses in its broader advertising of its own products, as well as around racetracks.

In each of these cases the brands are doing more for the customer, as well as the partnered companies doing things for each other that they couldn't do otherwise.

Application 11.2 AFFINITY BRANDING

How can you make use of the affinities customers have for another brand, in order to attract those customers to your brand? How does affinity branding actually work for you and your partner?

1. Map your brand audience

Map out your target audience, and which of these customers you manage to reach and engage today.

2. How is it perceived?

How do your customer perceive you, what is it that you do or offer that attracts and engages them?

3. Who do you struggle to engage?

Which of these customers do you fail to attract, and would like to? Which new audiences would be desirable too?

4. What would engage them?

How would you need to be different functionally or emotionally in order to engage these elusive audiences?

5. Which brand do this for them?

Which brands already engage these customers? What are the values that they have which you don't?

6. Develop a brand partnership

Consider with which of these brands you could develop an affinity marketing relationship to reach new people.

marketing
genius

Inspiration 11.2 CENTRICA

Centrica, with its subsidiary, British Gas, has a vision 'to be the leading provider of essential home services' in the UK. It recognized that a more customer-centric organization and approach to marketing is the best way to achieve the goal.

In early 2001, Centrica had a poorly connected range of products – from gas and electricity to financial and breakdown services. Customer satisfaction and loyalty among their 15 million customers was in decline.

The first step towards a more consistent and less confusing customer experience was to create and deliver a single, unified brand experience out of what had been three separate business divisions.

In particular, they chose their online channel as the focus of customer and culture change, and retention initiatives. An online development team was set up with the role of ensuring that the channel worked effectively.

They worked with third-party affinity partners to improve the online proposition, adding more engaging content and investing in software to enable more personalized content and newsletters. They also created an integrated 24-hour contact centre to support the online channel.

The website was launched as 'house.co.uk'.

It was supported by an annual marketing spend of £80 million and registrations have increased by 500%, and some automated transactions by more than 375%. More than 700,000 customers have registered to use house.co.uk since its launch, with the customer base rising by about 2,000 registrations every day.

According to their winning entry to the 2004 Marketing Society Awards, the new approach has delivered a 5% reduction in defection within the high-value/high-risk customer segments, while online customer satisfaction rose by 4–8% above that achieved for offline customers.

The web channel now accounts for 9% of sales across all channels for certain products, with house.co.uk contributing a 50% improvement in terms of sales. Cross-selling online has achieved more than 3% conversions against a forecast of 2% and 55% of customer contacts for British Gas are now fully automated.

Perhaps most impressively, 64% of all utility-related web traffic now goes to house.co.uk, reaching well beyond British Gas's current 43% share of the energy market.

Concept 11.2 CUSTOMER LOYALTY

Customer loyalty is rare and difficult to achieve. Choice, convenience and cheap prices mean that it is now incredibly easy not to be loyal. And, indeed, the initiatives that were supposed to drive loyalty – loyalty cards and their points schemes – have deeply marginalized the pursuit from business mainstream to marketing gimmick.

Customer loyalty has become associated with cards, points and rewards. Yet gaining a person's loyalty – so that they will drive an extra ten minutes to their preferred supermarket, or pay a premium for their preferred brand, or dress themselves from top to toe in the same label, or forgive a company when something goes wrong – is a much more involved and represents a long-term challenge.

The economics are important too. In *The Loyalty Effect*, Fred Reicheld defined the financial logic for building customer loyalty, arguing that loyal customers will:

- Stay longer – renew their purchases over time.

- Buy more – adding other products or services.

- Pay more – prepared to tolerate a premium, or no discount.

- Cost less – cheaper to serve, requiring less selling and support.

- Tell others – become advocates, telling their best friends too.

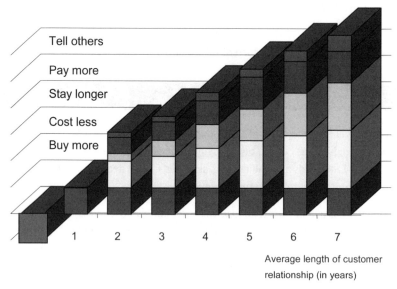

Source: Adapted from *The Loyalty Effect* by Frederick Reicheld

Indeed, Reicheld's most recent work considers the last point in detail and demonstrates how advocates are the most important source of improved long-term value, and a key indicator of future profitability. He calls these customers 'net promoters', as on balance they positively go out and recommend your brand to others like them, who of course are likely to become loyalists too.

The 'loyalty ladder' is a simple device that demonstrates each level of customer loyalty, and how each step reflects a greater level of engagement and more profitable purchase behaviours.

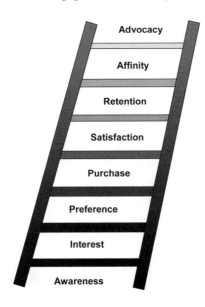

However, in language at least, we have grown tired of the mechanisms that have become associated with loyalty. 'Loyalty cards' came to our attention initially through the frequent flyer schemes of airlines, AAdvantage of American Airlines, followed by the Executive Club of British Airways, and everybody else who then had to have one. More recently everything from luxury goods to bagel stores offer loyalty cards too.

While there are many fantastic aspects to the best programmes, the basic principle of collect-ing points for the more you buy is tired. The monetary value of such programmes is usually 1–2% and, while it might seem like you are getting something for nothing, there are far easier and quicker ways to save more money.

Martin Lindstrom, author of *BrandSense*, considered how to ultimately measure brand loyalty. Inspired by Christof Koch, one of the world's leading neuroscientists and also the owner of an Apple tattoo, he researched which brands people would be most willing to have tattooed on their bodies. He found that the world's leading 'tattoo brands' were:

1	Harley Davidson	18.9%
2	Disney	14.8%
3	Coca-Cola	7.7%
4	Google	6.6%
5	Pepsi	6.1%
6	Rolex	5.6%
7	Nike	4.6%
8	Adidas	3.1%

Inspiration 11.3 MERCEDES

When Daimler Motoren Gesellschaft (DMG) delivered its first Mercedes in 1900 it started the development of a quality car brand that has stood out over the decades for its technical perfec-tion, quality and innovation. Classics such as the 300 SL Gullwing captured the imagination of motorists who either sought the premium brand or aspired to the state of the art.

DaimlerChrysler emerged as a new corporate structure in 1981, the result of bringing together two of the most historic companies in automotive industry – Daimler-Benz and Chrysler Corporation. The merger task has been to combine the economies of scale, through sharing design platforms and production, but to preserve the unique cultures that sit behind some of the world's leading car and truck brands, including Mercedes Benz, Chrysler, smart, Dodge, Plymouth, Jeep and many more.

Other non-core business still contributes around 10% of the overall revenue and includes the manufacture of diesel engines, aircraft and helicopters, space and defence systems, and financing services and insurance brokerage.

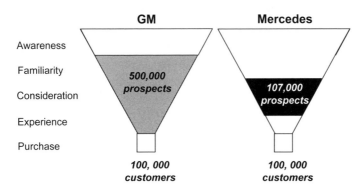

Source: CNW *Marketing/Research & McKinsey Quarterly*

Mercedes has achieved substantial brand awareness and established strong customer relationships that the company leverages more effectively than competitors in order to optimize the return on their marketing spend.

The established brand and customer relationships have allowed Mercedes to reallocate marketing spend further down the purchasing funnel, thereby achieving the industry's most effective conversion rate of prospects to sales.

In the scenario, Mercedes has to attract just 107,000 prospects for every 100,000 cars sold. By contrast, for every 100,000 people who buy a GM car, more than 500,000 people have to be persuaded to consider the car.

Application 11.3 LOYALTY LADDERS

How can you map each of your customers on the loyalty ladder to understand their current level of affinity to you? How can you use the ladder to identify potential strength of relationships with individual customers, and build it through customized relationship programmes?

1. Profile the loyalty of customers

Profile your customer database in terms of attitudes (e.g. preference) and their behaviours (e.g. purchase, referrals).

2. How do they differ in affinity?

Segment the customers by the strength of their affinity to you, and current value of their purchase behaviours.

3. Where is each on the ladder?

Map each customer (or segment) on the 'loyalty ladder' identifying the step which best describes each.

4. What level could they go to?

What is the potential to take each customer higher up the ladder? To the top or the most realistic level?

5. What would grow this loyalty?

How would you grow their affinity? What actions or incentives would move each up the loyalty ladder?

6. Develop loyalty action plans

Develop a one-to-one relationship programme to better engage the most potentially valuable customers.

Concept 11.3 CUSTOMER PARTNERING

Boeing recently invited anybody to become part of their 'World Team' by submitting designs for their next generation of aircraft – the 787 series – recognizing that there are more ideas outside their organization than inside, and people who have the pure enthusiasm and personal interest to share them.

While this may seem like design on the cheap, it recognizes the need to think more openly, from a customer perspective and, of course, to reward any individual who does come up with the most innovative and right commercial solution for Boeing's future.

Indeed, co-creation with customers – the rise of customized products is just one example, such as designing your own cosmetics from P&G's reflect.com, or your own shoes at Nike ID – as well as other aspects of partnering has long been the way in business markets, and is increasingly being embraced in consumer markets.

Customer partnering is fundamentally about working together for mutual success. Of course, the nature of that success might be more than just financial; a partnership is typically based on a collective vision of what each is trying to achieve, and then the sharing of resources and knowledge, investment and time in order to create a better solution.

B2B marketing often feels like the poor relation compared to the glamour and focus on B2C. Yet there are many aspects of business marketing that is way ahead of the thinking of their consumer cousins. Not least in the area of managing relationships.

Clearly, if there are fewer customers it is easier to build stronger relationships. Intel's primary customers, the electronics manufacturers, can be listed on one page, as could the major retailers targeted by P&G. Indeed, some might argue that this is organizationally the domain of the sales team. It is still key to the marketing process.

There are a number of principles:

- Focus on a few key accounts rather than many.

- Seek to build relationships over time rather than one-off sales.

- Build a team of people dedicated to supporting the client.

- Understand the client's business, strategy and priorities intimately.

- Map the key activities, key people and key opportunities.

- Allocate specific people to build relationships with their opposite numbers.

- Engage senior management on both sides to collaborate strategically.

- Develop a relationship plan, identifying key projects and ways of working.

- Coordinated and managed by an overall relationship manager.

Indeed, this becomes more than a customer–supplier relationship; it becomes a business partnership. This must become a win–win relationship if both sides are to commit to it, and this can only be achieved by openness, patience and commitment on both sides. Examples of the level of commitment might include:

- Supplier having an office and staff full-time within the client building.

- Mention of the relationship in the annual report as a strategic 'asset'.

- Regular meetings of CEOs on both sides on wider business opportunities.

- Secondment of staff on either side, for personal and business learning.

- Reward based on sharing in the success, e.g. as a percentage of profits or shares.

- Talent attracted to the supplier, specifically because of the relationship.

Look at many ad agencies and their large clients. The office of London agency St Luke's is a series of client rooms – where you step into a client experience and meet the agency's dedicated account team, often complemented by client people too. Conversely, the agency's team often also has a desk in the client's office so that they become part of the extended team.

Application 11.4 PARTNER DEVELOPMENT

In the B2B world how do you form business partnerships? What are the elements in building this partnership, and what could the B2C world learn from it too?

1. Identify potential partners

Map all the interactions between the supplier and customer (e.g. advice, purchase, delivery, complaints etc.).

2. Compare strategic goals

Identify the platforms, distribution channels and media which support these connections.

3. Define partnership plans

Identify all intermediary partners and processes, systems and devices, that facilitate these.

4. Align partnership teams

Evaluate the role(s) and objectives of each connection, (e.g. communication, distribution, selling, support).

5. Work openly and collaboratively

Estimate the revenue contribution of each connection, and the costs of enabling it, and compare effectiveness.

6. Manage partnership for success

Identify the most important connections, ranking media and channels separately to focus resources and performance.

Leading:
The impact of
a marketing
genius

PART 4

Leading:
The impact of a
marketing genius

▶ What is the real measure of marketing success? How do you lead and manage marketing activities in a more powerful and profitable way? How do you articulate the real value of marketing to boardrooms and investors?

▶ How do you measure marketing performance? How do you reconcile the short and long-term impact? How do you get more out of your budgets? And how do you articulate your value to the business and shareholders?

▶ What is the role of today's marketer? How can marketers become more strategic, innovative and commercial? How do they market for maximum impact and ensure that their promises become reality?

▶ How do you lead marketing and marketers? What does it take to be a Chief Marketing Officer (CMO)? What are the different roles functionally and across the business? And how do you become the next CEO?

▶ What is the emerging world of marketing? Indeed how are markets, customers and business changing, and how should we anticipate and respond? And what is it that really inspires extraordinary results?

'The people who get on in this world are the people who get up and look for the circum-stances they want, and, if they can't find them, make them.'

George Bernard Shaw

Unlocking the real value of marketing

'Whenever you see a successful business, someone once made a courageous decision.'

Peter Drucker

'Of the five business deadly sins, the first and easily the most common is the worship of high profit margins.'

Peter Drucker

Marketing is the most important driver of economic value creation. It is also often the largest discretionary spend in business, so how do you ensure that it really delivers? For too long, marketing has been perceived to be unaccountable, unfocused and indisciplined in connecting its creative executions with business performance.

More intelligent performance	More imaginative performance
Measuring. Developing the metrics and scorecards to measure what matters most to deliver business performance.	**Managing**. Connecting people and teams, activities and resources to the performance metrics.
Optimizing. Allocating marketing budgets and capital investments for the best short- and long-term results.	**Improving**. Identifying where and how to improve performance, the quick wins and strategic priorities.
Articulating. Quantifying the value of brands, relationships and innovation as your 'customer capital'.	**Reporting**. Capturing the real value of marketing in boardroom reporting, annual reports and investor relations.

While the outcome of marketing may seem obvious – increased sales – many a marketing director has survived and thrived on the wave of advertising that is beautiful and emotive, even if nobody has any idea whether it actually delivers incremental sales, or any other improved results.

Even if you do know that it has a financial impact, there is no guarantee that consumer preference will convert ultimately into stock market performance. Taking great rivals Coca-Cola and Pepsi, for example, numerous research studies have shown that while more people like the taste of Pepsi, they prefer to buy the Coke brand. Similarly, despite the higher sales revenues of Pepsi worldwide, analysts and investors have more confidence in the future cash flows of Coke (or, more precisely, The Coca-Cola Company over Pepsico). Brands therefore have a significant impact on investors as well as consumers.

	Coke	Pepsi
Consumer preference (blind)	44%	51%
Consumer preference (named)	65%	23%
Estimated revenues (2004)	$22bn	$29bn
Average share price (2004)	$54	$47
Average market value (2004)	$111bn	$87bn

Source: Data from Bloomberg and Leslie de Chateney

Measuring marketing performance through a focus on the most significant 'metrics' enables you to:

- demonstrate the ROI on the business's largest discretionary spend;

- distinguish short- and long-term impacts of marketing;

- improve activities through adjustment as initial results come in;

- focus the efforts of creative and ill-disciplined marketers;

- provide a useful lead indicator of future business performance;

- improve the respect for and influence of marketers across the business; and

- engage business leaders in marketing and its business impact.

Most marketers realize this, although many still do not appreciate the financial significance of getting it right. While marketers might be tempted to focus on the creativity and see measurement as a bolt-on at the end, measurement itself can make a significant and rapid impact on performance by influencing the upfront decisions – targeting, designing and prioritizing actions.

> 'CEOs are understandably growing impatient with marketing. They feel that they get accountability for their investments in finance, production, IT, even purchasing, but they don't know what their marketing spending is achieving.'

> *Marketing and the CEO: Why CEOs are fed up with Marketing*, Philip Kotler

Indeed, according to an ANA/Booz Allen Hamilton study, clearly entitled 'Marketing Department Priorities Often Differ from CEOs' Agenda', marketing is considered a critical business function but the lack of actionable metrics has removed it from the CEO's agenda. Their research indicates that 75% of senior executives agree that marketing is far more important than it was five years ago; however, most see it as increasingly disconnected from the business agenda.

Measurement and accountability again come out as critical. CEOs expect marketing to provide measurable outcomes like ROI, but see current metrics as detached and not up to the task: 66% of executives say that true ROI analytics are marketing's greatest need, rather than relying on surrogate metrics like awareness and preference. Research by the CMO Council supports this, with 90% of respondents saying measuring marketing performance is a key priority, particularly in larger companies, and 80% saying they have no formal marketing performance measurement system – even when marketing spends 25% of the company's revenues in some cases.

Some marketers have already spent much time addressing these challenges and recognize that they are not administrative distractions cramping the creative process but significant opportunities to improve the bottom line, and the credibility of marketing within the business.

'Over the last two to three years, the value we have created for the company via our marketing accountability work is the equivalent of launching a new global brand the size of Tide.'

Jim Stengel, Global Marketing Officer, P&G

ANA Marketing Accountability Summit, 9 September 2004

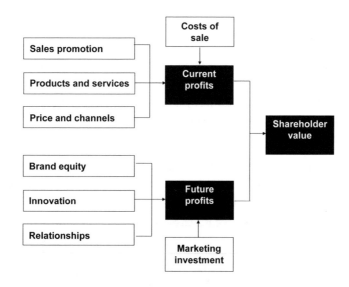

Even when marketing takes measurement seriously, it is still not easy to quantify the full impact of marketing's efforts. The impact is diverse, affecting both current and future sales, and also other behaviours such as the propensity to pay more, buy more or tell others. All of these factors contribute to the real return on marketing investment.

Accounting does not help. Accounting statements are flawed at the best of times, but particularly in companies with high growth, where brand building and innovation are key. Such statements treat these strategic investments as expenses to be deducted from current profits, rather than considering the future profits which they will drive.

Such accountancy-driven behaviours discourage managers from investing in brands and innovation, despite them driving the future potential in which shareholders are most interested. This is why a value-based approach, one that considers cash, current and future, is so useful to marketing and marketers.

'Marketing ROI' has become the fashion that every marketer now feels they should be focused on, and every consulting firm wants to sell. Yet the majority of proponents are notoriously short sighted and, in a not dissimilar way from the hijacking of CRM, they see it as a piece of analytical software to plug in and somehow connect marketing spend as inputs and sales results as the outputs.

Of course, this might well be a step forwards, compared with no measures at all. However, if focused just on the short term, it is likely to reflect less than half of the true picture and, as a result, refocus marketing on short-term tactical sales promotions. This is both damaging to marketing, as it seeks to position itself as the strategic driver of business, and to the performance of business.

We should therefore consider marketing performance, including marketing ROI, more thoughtfully – the metrics that are most sensible to measure performance, the appropriate ways to optimize the outcomes, and how to articulate the results as part of internal and external business reporting to boardrooms and investors.

Inspiration 12.1 CADBURY SCHWEPPES

Cadbury Schweppes sets a clear framework of strategic intent, and how it will conduct business. Its core purpose is 'working together to create brands people love', while its objective is 'to consistently deliver superior shareowner returns'.

While this goal is quite single-minded, it recognizes that it cannot be achieved in isolation – that the business also has obligations to consumers and customers, employees and society, communities and the environment. Indeed, the statements seek to capture the heritage and future of the business.

Two men, quite separately, provide the roots to the confectionery and drinks giant. In 1783, Swiss inventor Jacob Schweppe perfected a process for carbonating mineral water that was sourced from near his Geneva home. In 1824 John Cadbury opened a shop in Birmingham, England, selling cocoa and chocolate. The great names merged in 1969, and the business has grown ever since.

Acquisitions have been key to the growth over the last two decades – bringing together over 50 iconic brands such as Trebor, Bassett, Halls, Trident, 7 Up, Snapple, Orangina, Dr Pepper, Canada Dry and many more. The more recent purchase of Adams – bringing its large portfolio of US-based brands, and distribution network – makes Cadbury Schweppes the leader in the confectionery world, and the third largest soft drinks company.

In 1997 'Managing for Value' was introduced by CEO John Sutherland, to focus the entire organization on the delivery of 'superior shareowner returns'. As well as a far more rigorous approach to portfolio analysis, focusing on the markets and brands that delivered the best future cash flows, this also required a significant education process so that every person in the business understands the drivers of success. Production line workers, for example, were helped to understand the real meaning of economic profitability, and why returns needed to exceed the cost of capital.

In 2003, a new set of goals and performance measures were added, recognizing that acquisition is only a stepping stone to success and that the real challenge was now to grow this consolidated portfolio of brands more profitably and sustainably. This also recognized the importance of people and capabilities, not only to deliver what they currently do, but also the need to grow the strategic and innovative capabilities.

'Smart Variety' growth, for example, recognizes that the business model is based on a wide variety of local and global brands, and puts in place a number of new management and commercial disciplines to get the right focus on geographical markets, the best channels to market in each, and the optimal balance between global and local brands.

Application 12.1 VALUE-BASED MARKETING

How do you do marketing in a more value-based way? What would be different about the criteria you use to make decisions, and the way you measure performance? Where should you start?

1. Understand the concept of value

Understand the concept of economic value and how it is different from the way you evaluate your business today.

2. Evaluate your portfolio

Start strategically with portfolio analysis of markets, brands, and products to identify value creators and destroyers.

3. Evaluate your resources

Also consider operationally how well your current resources and investment drive value, and could do better.

4. Focus on what really matters

Focus your effort on the best value opportunities strategically, typically 'doing fewer things better'.

5. Allocate resources better

Allocate your marketing budget and resources on the activities which unlock the most value.

6. Measure your real performance

Articulate the real value of marketing, its contribution to long-term value as well as short-term profitability.

marketing
genius

Concept 12.1 MARKETING METRICS

Marketing measurement to date has largely been driven by the need of marketers to demonstrate the return they get on their advertising budgets and for agencies to quantify their contribution to their clients. It has therefore typically focused on tactical outcomes unrelated to financial results.

Examples would include:

- Brand awareness – how many people recognize a brand or its advertising campaign when prompted?

- Response rates – how many people responded to a direct mail incentive, or a telemarketing campaign?

- Conversion rates – how many of these people then went on to choose to buy the product?

And, indeed, each business sector has developed measures that they believe to be crucial, and have therefore become the imperatives for sector marketers. For example:

- Average revenue per user (ARPU) in telecoms.

- Number of subscribers in Pay TV.

- Sales per square foot in retail.

- Percentage of revenue from new products in an FMCG company.

- Number of products sold per customer in financial services.

- Products in the development pipeline in a pharma company.

Prof. Tim Ambler's research *What should we tell the shareholders?* mapped out the current use of metrics in marketing, and how good the marketers themselves thought they were.

Source: *Marketing and the Bottom Line*, Prof. Tim Ambler, London Business School

In business generally, the balanced scorecard is still the most popular measurement tool, despite the vast majority of companies not using it effectively. Kaplan and Norten's model proposed that organizations measure their effectiveness on four dimensions, with goals and measures for each:

- Financial – how do we want shareholders to see us?

- Customers – how do we want customers to see us?

- Internal – what must we excel at ourselves?

- Innovation and learning – how should we continue to improve?

The balanced scorecard has merit in bringing a more rounded perspective to business previously blinkered by finance. However, the value is largely lost as managers scrabble around to find any measures to populate each dimension, and with very little idea of their relative importance or how they connect.

The objective is clearly to develop a scorecard that focuses on the most important outcomes for the business, and the most important inputs to achieve this.

We have already considered how marketing drives shareholder value and, indeed, this is the starting point for choosing the right metrics. It first requires us to link:

- Marketing spend to marketing activities – how much you spend on advertising, PR, product development, etc.

- Marketing activities to purchase drivers – how advertising addresses the priorities of customers, e.g. quality, price, image, etc.

- Marketing activities to customer attitudes – how advertising drives increased brand preference, perceived value, etc.

- Customer attitudes to purchase behaviours – how perceived value translates into price premium, multi-purchases, etc.

- Sales results to financial results – how sales and margins translate into operating profits and growth.

- Financial results to shareholder value – how profits and growth translate into future cash flows, investor confidence and share price.

Of course, customer preference might drive immediate behaviour, or be stored in the customer's head for some future moment (for example, you go a motor show, love a car, but it may be some years before you are ready, or can afford, to buy one).

A marketing scorecard would typically capture these dynamics and flow. Building on the balanced scorecard framework it might have dimensions of:

- Customer engagement.

- Market impact.

- Financial performance.

- Marketing improvement.

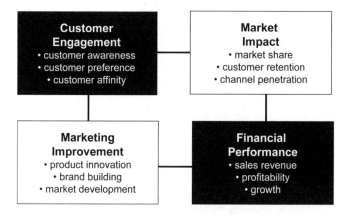

We need to capture these potential revenues that have been achieved but not yet realized. This is often referred to as 'brand equity', the sum of future cash flows driven by the investments of today. Similarly, new market development, product innovation or relationship building account for a significant proportion of the marketing budget, but may not influence current sales. Some of these additional unrealized revenues go beyond 'brand equity' as customers may not know about them, but they are still important to quantifying the value of marketing, and to shareholders.

Inspiration 12.2 DIAGEO

Diageo is quite clear on what it is, what it wants to achieve and how it will get there. While many corporate missions and strategies are reduced to generic phrases that are so undecipherable as to be irrelevant, or so bland as to be a commodity, Diageo has worked hard to articulate itself.

Source: diageo.com

There are seven components to defining Diageo:

• Diageo is clear on what it is today, *'the world's leading premium drinks business'* with the broadest and most recognized collection of premium drinks brands globally.

- There is a compelling customer-oriented vision, *'celebrating life, every day, everywhere.'* Indeed the word Diageo comes for the Latin for 'day' and Greek for 'world'.

- Diageo has a single-minded goal, similar to a mission statement in other companies, that *'every adult adores at least one of our brands.'*

- It has a clear strategy too, represented in its 'Strategic Triangle' defining the imperatives that will achieve the goal, recognizing the needs of all its stakeholders, from employees to customers, investors and society.

- Diageo recognizes that it is made of many parts, and leaves the bottom two layers of the triangle – initiatives and enablers – to be defined by each business in the most relevant way.

- It articulates the four underpinning values that will make this happen – being *'passionate about customers'*, giving people *'freedom to succeed'*, being *'proud of what we do'*, and *'we will be the best.'*

- Finally, Diageo reminds us of what it wants to be famous for:

  People. Releasing the potential of every employee.

  Brands. Using great consumer insight to power our brands

  Performance. Winning where we compete.

Diageo began a strategic realignment behind its premium drinks brands in 2000, which included the uncoupling of its previous interests in non-drinks activities such as a partnership with General Mills. Organic growth of core premium brands is seen as key to success, while the company recognizes that it has to take a lead in responsible marketing, particularly with regard to health and the youth market.

> 'Our brands help people mark big events and brighten small ones. Enjoyed responsibly, they enable people to celebrate life, every day, everywhere.'

As well as being the home of Guinness, Diageo also manages 17 of the top 100 premium spirit brands in the world – from Smirnoff, the world's number one premium vodka, to Johnnie Walker, the leading Scotch whisky. Baileys is the worlds top-selling liquor while Jose Cervo is the global leader in tequila.

Innovation has also been key, focusing on the specific opportunities to do more in high-value-creating markets, and with high-value-creating brands. These have typically been a combination of new drinks formats, particularly reflecting the shift to lighter, smoother drinks. Baileys Glide, Guinness Extra Smooth, Smirnoff Cranberry Twist would be examples.

Packaging can equally be important, not just in enhancing the visual appeal, but also in introducing more effective materials, or smaller, multiple formats where margins are even greater. Baileys Miniatures, Smirnoff Icon and Johnnie Walker Red Label would be good examples.

Indeed, the financial benefits of such moves are obvious. Mixer drinks contain far less alcohol, and when promoted as a funky drink to be seen with in lifestyle bars, can quickly command a price ten times more than the same quantity of drink could be purchased for off-trade. Spirits can also become dated, associated with an older generation – the difference an ice cube and more youthful context can make to advertising representation can have enormous impact.

However, market leadership is not Diageo's measure of success. It very publicly ranks itself (annually in its report and on its website) against a broader peer group, against a more meaningful measure of shareowner return: the total return through capital growth and dividends delivered to them over recent years. The table is far more insightful into the true performance of the business, and others, rather than looking at any more transient or narrow-focused metric.

TSR ranking within Diageo's defined peer group (total shareowner return in period 1 July 2000 to 30 July 2004):

1	Yum! Brands	95%
2	P&G	58%
3	Kellogg	56%
4	Altria	46%
5	Allied Domecq	40%
6	Diageo	39%
7	Unilever	38%
8	Anheuser Busch	27%
9	Nestlé	22%
10	Gillette	22%

Diageo's marketing team have been successful in responding to the focus on performance that pervades every organization today. They have successfully influenced the business to recognize brands and marketing as the driving force of profitable, sustainable growth. The result is efficient cost control and maximization of shareholder value. Led by Rob Malcolm, their president of marketing, sales and innovation, they have achieved this through fact-based analysis,articulating the ROI of brands, and being completely transparent in their reporting of what is good and what is not.

Malcolm's view is that marketing has changed little, in perception or reality, since the days of Lord Leverhulme who argued that 'half of what marketing spends is wasted, we just don't know which half'. Indeed, for all they know, it may have got worse for many companies, given their lack of ability to measure it. He realized that if brands and marketing were to drive the business, things needed to be different. They needed much more than 50% success. He set out in pursuit of what he called '100% marketing'.

In seeking to establish marketing with at least the same prestige and influence as the finance department, he recognized three challenges:

> **Our journey; from 50 to 100% marketing**
>
> **How do we motivate our stakeholders to understand the importance of brand building, and buy-in to marketing as a professional function and discipline?**
>
> > understand and be ready to articulate difference between book value of your assets (brands) and the share price
>
> > garner the evidence that a consistent brand building ethos and capability improves shareholder return
>
> > research or develop case histories where strong brands saved the day
>
> > brand continuity through change – evolution, not revolution
>
> > understand growth as a value driver, relative to cost savings and efficiencies
>
> > lobby for the CEO to be a marketeer?

Source: diageo.com

- To articulate how much value marketing contributes to the business.

- To build true professionalism into the function everywhere.

- To establish clear accountability and measurement of this contribution.

While this could easily have thrown his marketers into the deep end of complex economics, creating spreadsheet models that were impossibly difficult to calibrate, to engage financial people in an endless debate about how to allocate costs, he chose a different route: 'Keep metrics and measurement simple, if you want any chance of them being delivered and embraced.'

Diageo's marketers now use a small number of simple tools to evaluate marketing investments, with a bit of rigour behind them.

First, there is the the 'Dogs and Stars Chart', a simple two-by-two matrix that measures the financial performance against consumer impact. Ideally he wants to see everything in the top right-hand corner; therefore, things bottom-right need attention to improve their efficiency, things top-left need attention to improve their consumer attractiveness, and things bottom-left are eliminated. 'It's a simple tool that every marketer understands, and the finance director loves.'

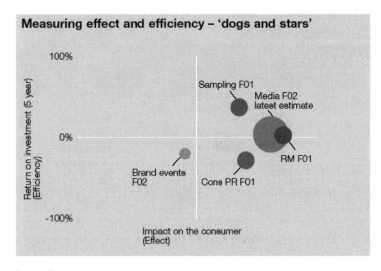

Source: diageo.com

Second, there is a tracking chart that is reviewed by the executive committee every quarter. It identifies the effectiveness of advertising by brand, medium and market. Colours identify where he can demonstrate effectiveness, and where he cannot, while arrows show whether things are getting better or worse. Indeed, he recognized that senior management weren't so much interested in the numbers, more in terms of gaining confidence that things are under control.

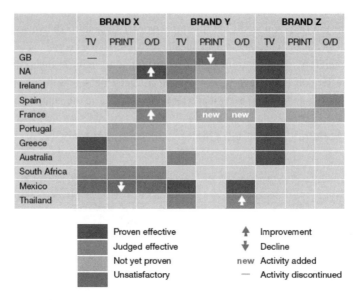

	BRAND X			BRAND Y			BRAND Z		
	TV	PRINT	O/D	TV	PRINT	O/D	TV	PRINT	O/D
GB	—				↓				
NA			↑						
Ireland									
Spain									
France			↑		new	new			
Portugal									
Greece									
Australia									
South Africa									
Mexico		↓							
Thailand						↑			

Proven effective
Judged effective
Not yet proven
Unsatisfactory

↑ Improvement
↓ Decline
new Activity added
— Activity discontinued

Source: diageo.com

At first Malcolm felt nervous showing his CEO the true picture of his domain, warts and all. The response was revealing: 'This is the most honest and transparent picture of marketing I have ever seen'. It built trust and confidence, it demonstrated that the marketing department understood what matters to business, and immediately improved the credibility of perceived professionalism of the whole function in the business.

Application 12.2 MARKETING SCORECARDS

What is your marketing ultimately trying to achieve for the business? How do you measure marketing performance? What are the right metrics, and which ones matter most? How do you target and reward performance at each level?

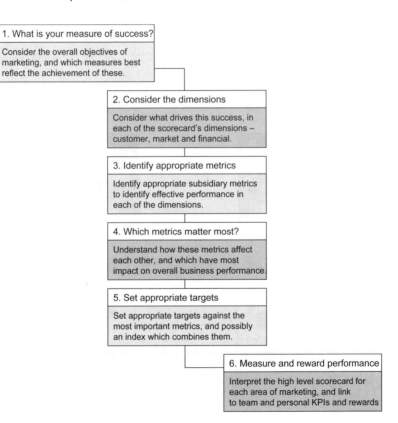

1. What is your measure of success?

Consider the overall objectives of marketing, and which measures best reflect the achievement of these.

2. Consider the dimensions

Consider what drives this success, in each of the scorecard's dimensions – customer, market and financial.

3. Identify appropriate metrics

Identify appropriate subsidiary metrics to identify effective performance in each of the dimensions.

4. Which metrics matter most?

Understand how these metrics affect each other, and which have most impact on overall business performance.

5. Set appropriate targets

Set appropriate targets against the most important metrics, and possibly an index which combines them.

6. Measure and reward performance

Interpret the high level scorecard for each area of marketing, and link to team and personal KPIs and rewards

Concept 12.2 MARKETING OPTIMIZATION

Optimizing marketing performance must be considered at both strategic and operational levels as there is little point in seeking to optimize activities if they are focused on an area that is never likely to be significantly profitable.

Indeed, seeking to market 'value-destroying' brands or products only results in even more value being destroyed. You might have a brand that has strong sales and market share, and even operating profits look good, yet because the cost of capital is greater, every additional sale will destroy value.

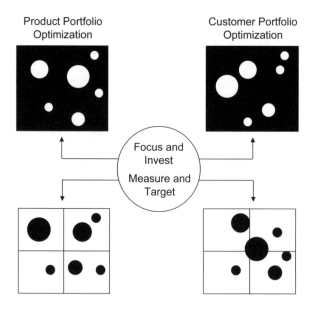

It is therefore important to optimize marketing performance:

- Strategically – focusing on the right markets and customers, brands and products (i.e. portfolio optimization).

- Operationally – most effective allocation of budgets of people and partners (i.e. resource optimization).

- Tactically – tracking impact of marketing, identifying the right moments to act to target customers, or incentivize behaviours (i.e. sales optimization).

Marketing ROI can be used as a framework to optimize performance at each of these levels, taking into account the short- and long-term impact on financial results. However, given that companies will seek to align expenditure with revenues using conventional accounting practices, it is useful to sometimes distinguish the short- and long-term impacts.

A new product developed and launched this year may deliver some revenues this year, but much more in the next three, while all of the development costs must be borne this year. The present value of these future revenues can be calculated, and the ROI based on (i) this year's revenue, (ii) present value of future years, and (iii) net present value of this year and future years.

Marketing is not short of theories and terminology for how to measure the contribution to long-term business performance, i.e. the likely future cash flows and the intrinsic value of the business. Of course there is no avoidance of clear financial analysis, but there are many ways to capture the 'stuff' that drives it.

Inspiration 12.3 STELLA ARTOIS

In a highly competitive world where so many products are marketed on the cheapest price, Stella Artois has stood apart as a brand that is never afraid to promote itself as *'reassuringly expensive'.*

Few brands can trace their roots as far back as 1366, when Den Horen brewery was first established in Leuven, Belgium. Centuries later, in 1717, it was acquired by its then master brewer Sebastian Artois. 'Stella Artois' was originally produced as a festive beer, named after the Christmas star which remains part of the brand identity, alongside the horn of the original brewery.

Stella Artois is now one of the best-selling beers in the world, sold in over 80 countries. It is brewed traditionally with malted barley and the finest hops, and famed for its quality and flavour. Advertising, in particular, has always been important to the brand – breaking the mould of beer marketing with its upmarket style and evocative imagery.

'Reassuringly expensive' as a theme proved highly successful. However, in the early nineties the brand began to lose market share in an increasingly crowded premium market. With more quality choices, a premium price alone seemed a risky differentiator to rely upon.

However, Stella Artois refused to abandon its position, instead opting to support it with an even stronger investment in product quality. Still using the line, but with more justification, Stella Artois has fought back from decline and is now re-established as the UK's biggest premium lager brand.

Design is a primary communication tool for this approach. Packaging initiatives such as embossing the can and re-designing the crate box in the style of champagne reinforce the brand's quality and prestige. A Stella Artois pint glass was introduced in 2001 and, within 12 months of launch, 66% of UK households possessed at least one glass.

Driven by a strong rise in draught sales, distribution growth has remained strong, with Stella Artois now being the most widely circulated lager in the on-trade. Marketing communications has focused on TV advertising, sponsorship and price promotion in the off-trade markets, while using point of sale presence and new drinks delivery technologies on-trade.

Between 1996 and 2003, Stella Artois has seen its volumes grow by over 200% in the UK compared with category growth of around 60%. This rise has made it the third-biggest lager brand and the biggest premium lager brand, selling 3495 million barrels in 2003. Stella Artois now holds an 8.9% share of the total beer market, more than triple its 1996 share of 2.2%.

Application 12.3 MARKETING ROI

How do you measure the return on investment in marketing, particularly when the majority of revenues driven by the investments you make do not happen in the same year?

1. Quantify your marketing spend

Understand how your marketing budget is currently spent, how much of it is sales incentives vs strategic investment.

2. Calculate initial impact

Research the impact on customer behaviours, and how these drive short- and long-term revenues.

3. Add your brand equity

Quantify the future long-term revenues that are driven by today's marketing and define as 'brand equity'.

4. Calculate your ROI

Calculate the total spend relative to its impact on current and future revenue and profit streams.

5. Quantify economic value impact

Interpret the net present value of future profit streams, i.e. how much value marketing has added to the business.

6. Relate to intangible assets

Relate these to the recognized and potential intangible assets of the business (brands, relationships, etc.).

Concept 12.3 MARKETING REPORTING

One of the most perverse attributes of boardrooms is that directors typically spend less than 10% of their time focusing on where 90% of their success comes from. Little time is spent on discussing where the revenues come from, and how they could be improved, before the conversation quickly progresses to operational performance and cost management.

Marketing performance should be included and ideally lead the agendas of:

- Board meetings for executive and non-executive directors.

- Quarterly business reviews for managers and staff.

- Investor relations briefings to analysts and media.

- Annual reports available to all stakeholders.

Imagine the CEO standing up at the next board meeting, or the first page of the annual report, and brands and marketing being the focus of commentary, their current performance, and the investments that are currently being made to secure and enhance future results.

This might seem an obvious place to start in reviewing a business, yet the vast majority will start with costs, processes and supply chains.

Why are business leaders so reluctant to focus on marketing, or at least the customers it focuses on, and the revenues it drives? While supply chains can be measured in all sorts of units, and the costs of them are real and influenceable, understanding the dynamics of brands and innovation, communication or distribution is much harder without numbers.

One retailer was amazed at the impression it made at an investor briefing when it described the financial impact of getting new fashion from catwalk to clothes rail in two weeks less than anybody else on the high street, and the incremental sales and margins that this drives.

Consider also the value of in-store merchandizing, or the value of being able to manage three store brands to better target different segments of high street shoppers, rather than just having one store for everyone.

Marketing reporting complements the traditional internally biased, financially dominant information by being:

- *Strategic.* Marketing drives success in future markets and innovation, building brands and relationships to ensure their success.

- *Outward-facing.* Marketing relates to the external environment, seizing the best opportunities, responding to the changing world.

- *Forward looking.* The majority of marketing investment is geared to future success, rather than current performance.

- *Non-financial.* Providing a richer, qualitative analysis of current performance and future prospects, supported by quantified metrics.

Such information would offer investors, analysts and, indeed, all stakeholders a much more insightful and useful view of the current and future prospects of the company. This paper defines marketing and explains why it must, and how it should, be incorporated as an essential component of future reporting.

Marketing performance, short and long term, should be a key part of all business reporting and, while conventional accounting principles may not do it justice, there are increasingly more opportunities for directors to articulate non-financial, forward-looking information to investors (and indeed all stakeholders) in a way that helps them to make a more informed judgement about the future prospects of the business.

Sarbanes Oxley is a set of more strict reporting requirements of directors introduced following the corporate mis-reporting scandals of recent years, where a number of companies were found to have artificially boosted revenues in the short-term, with resulting improvement in share price. These were extreme, and illegal, examples of where 'shareholder value' has got a bad name, perceived negatively as associated with one-sided shareholder greed, driven by short-term performance incentives for senior managers, rather than the long-term pursuit of economic value that can only be achieved through customers.

In Europe, the EU's Modernisation Directive changes the way companies are required to report performance. In the UK, for example, the Accounting Standards Board encourages every director to report information about the future prospects of the business. In particular, it encourages the reporting of marketing information, alongside HR (or human capital) and CSR (environmental and socially responsible practices). This is a significant opportunity for marketers to raise the profile of their longer-term effects, and for companies to better demonstrate that it will deliver future success.

In particular, marketing should ensure that internally and externally the performance and value contribution of the following is fully articulated:

- Return on marketing investment, i.e. both short- and long-term.

- Key differentiating activities, e.g. time to market, store interior.

- Strategic initiatives, e.g. new market entry, new innovations.

- Intangible assets, e.g. brands, customer relationships.

Even more significantly for marketers are the new international financial reporting standards (IFRS) for the accounting of intangible assets.

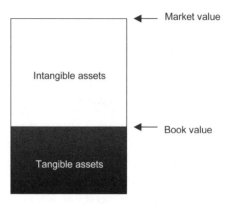

The new international standards now enable companies to articulate and retain acquired intangible assets on their balance sheets as specific categorized items, rather than just grouping them under the fairly meaningless phrase 'goodwill' and requiring them to be written off over time.

The new categories are:

- Market-related intangible assets (including trade names, trademarks, domain names and mastheads).

- Customer-related intangible assets (including customer lists, customer contracts and relationships).

- Artistic-related intangible assets (including white papers, pictures and video, and advertising jingles).

- Contract-related intangible assets (including licensing agreements, advertising contracts, operating and broadcast rights).

- Technology-based intangible assets (including patented technology, computer software, trade secrets, e.g. recipes).

Indeed, provided that the company can prove that the acquired brand has retained its worth, it can stay on the balance sheet over time. Brands would appear as a trademark, but would typically bring together a number of different assets in a more holistic way.

However, and somewhat perversely, brands that have been developed organically, and by definition are often the more important to the business, are not permissible on the balance sheet at any time, causing confusion and further brand transactions that are not necessarily in its interest.

Examples of marketing performance within annual reports include:

'In a challenging year for the retail energy industry in Britain with the impacts of warm weather unusually coupled with rises in commodity costs, British Gas increased its turnover by 2.4% to £6.2 billion (2002: £6.0 billion). This was due to an increase in our electricity market share, higher energy pricing and continued growth in our home services business.'

Centrica plc (first paragraph of their OFR, 2003)

'Total marketing expenditure in 2003 was £702 million, an increase of 28% [on 2002] and an increase of 30% at constant exchange rates. This represents a spend to turnover ratio of 10.9% compared to 10.3% last year. Much of the increase being due to the acquisition of [brand].'

Cadbury Schweppes plc (final paragraph of their OFR, 2003)

'Marketing investment for premium drinks increased 5% organically to £1,185 million, with investment in the global priority brands up 4% to £769 million. The major drivers of the increase were higher spend on [named brands] and the launch of [brand].'

Diageo plc (final paragraph of their OFR, 2003)

Marketers should rise up to the opportunities of new accounting standards, to better explain the value that they create and their own value to the business.

Marketing reporting should therefore be both quantified data and qualitative statements:

- *Current performance* should be measured and audited, and compared with previous years. For example, 'Sales in product x continued to grow by 7% to £2.5 billion, at a gross margin of 26%, largely due to an increased retail penetration of 92% of large retailers, and a price premium of 42% relative to competitors. As a result product x delivered an economic profit of £625m last year.'

- *Future prospects* should be described qualitatively, with some quantification. For example, 'In the x market, our brand awareness has now reached over 90% and customer retention is close to 50%, positioning us to grow our share to around 60% in three years Simultaneously, we will invest £570m in product development to secure 30% of the y market.'

There are many marketing metrics in use, depending on the sophistication of the company and the nature of the market. The definition and quality of measures varies but is improving. They could be:

- *Short or long term:* sales revenue is short term while brand valuation is long term; customer satisfaction is short term while customer loyalty is long term.

- *Inputs or outputs:* marketing expenditure is an input, whereas customer preference is an output; retail penetration is an input, while market share is an output.

- *Strategic or operational:* brand equity is strategic, while brand awareness is operational; number of patents is strategic, while price discounting is operational.

Ideally, a balanced scorecard of metrics would be used to drive marketing decision-making and performance measurement. Best practice would then calibrate the appropriate marketing activities to financial performance, based on an understanding of their relative importance and the linkage between them.

In this way the activities or measures that can be most influenced, and have most impact on business performance, can be focused on and reported. For example, customer satisfaction is culturally regarded as very important in companies but there is little evidence of a strong correlation with value creation. Similarly, average customer revenue is crucial in one industry, but far less significant in another.

Inspiration 12.4 CUSTOMER CAPITAL

Customers are the scarcest resource in business today, yet the majority of management, boardroom and investment analysts' time goes into counting the cash, rather than understanding how effectively this is being created.

Not only this, but also the source of future cash flows – marketing – struggles to articulate itself to non-marketing audiences. This is not just because it hasn't been able to quantify its impact in financial terms, or even that it is still misinterpreted as peripherally 'a bit of advertising', but because the language it wraps this up in can often create even more resistance from financial or operational people.

Marketers themselves struggle to articulate what they mean by the likes of advertising salience or brand equity, while the mere mention of it to a finance person has them confused.

Marketing needs to articulate its performance in a simpler language, and go back to where we started: boardroom directors spend less than 10% of their time talking about customers and the revenues that come from them, whereas this accounts for around 90% of the business's performance.

'Customer capital', developed in partnership with the IPA and the Marketing Society, while a new phrase that doesn't particularly want to add further complexity to a crowded language, is simply about articulating the value created by a business from its customer activities – 'the value of a customer focus', you could say.

Customer capital can be expressed as:

- A 'basket' of customer-based measures tracked over time.

- A weighted index of the most important customer-based metrics.

- Sum of likely future cash flows due to customer-related activities.

This basket of customer measures might well differ by company depending on what has most impact on business results in their business model. However, imagine a company where these were the core targets:

- Customer preference (% of people who like us).

- Customer volume (% of people who buy from us).

- Customer retention (% of people who stay with us).

- Customer referral (% of people who tell others about us).

Everybody in the business can feel motivated to come to work to create customer capital, more than stark financials, and to understand what behaviours helped to deliver each. No boardroom director can argue that these factors are worthy of regular review, and every analyst could directly use these to help understand whether this company is more or less likely to outperform its peers in the future.

Customer Reach We currently reach 90% of the UK population. This is more than our nearest competitor at 79%. **Customer Preference** 45% of our customers say they prefer us. 60% of existing customers intend to use us next time. **Customer Satisfaction** 27% of our customers say that they are very satisfied. 45% say they are satisfied to some extent.	**Customer Contracts** 40% of customers are on long-term contracts of > 2 years. **Customer Retention** 67% of our customers have stayed for over one year. We seek to increase this retention rate to 80% in the next 3 years. **Customer Loyalty** 60% of existing customers intend to use us next time . 12% of customers say they would recommend us.
Customer Volume We currently have 12.2m customers. This has grown by 12% over the last year. **Customer Share** We currently have 33% of the UK market. **Customer Yield** We generate £365 per customers. This is 45% higher than the market average.	**Customer Growth** We expect to grow customer numbers by 15% for next 3 years. The UK market will grow at 7% for next 3 years. **Customer Innovation** 26% of our revenues come for services released in last year. We expect 12% of next years revenues to come from new products.
Tactical marketing costs We spent £120m on sales promotions and discounts. **Revenues** We generated £2.1b in revenues. This is 12% increase on the previous year. **Operating Profit** We generated £254m operating profit. This is 45% increase on the previous year.	**Strategic marketing investments** We spent £180m on marketing costs relating to brand and relationships. **Intangible Assets** We calculate that its brand, consumer and distributive relationships are worth £4.2bn. **Business Value** We project that profits will grow at 12-15% each year over the next five years (producing an intrinsic value of £xbn).

Indeed, the recent Tomorrow's Company report *'Restoring Trust: Investment in the Twenty-First Century'* concludes that 'the trust and confidence of investors has been damaged recently' and believes that 'the current system is not serving customers well – a failure to align with customer needs and timescales, and a lack of transparency and accountability is eroding trust in the system.'

Not only do these measures appeal to more people, and cut through the complexity of business to what matters, but they also present marketing's contribution in a much more collaborative and positive manner.

Application 12.4 INVESTOR RELATIONS

What should you tell the shareholders about marketing? How do you make marketing essential to these strategic audiences? How does it become the number one item on the board-room agenda, analysts' briefing or annual report?

1. Articulate real value of marketing

Make marketing essential by articulating it's added economic value in terms of customer, innovation and growth.

2. Get on the boardroom agenda

Ensure that these issues are top of the board agenda. Target market-thinking directors to champion the cause.

3. Get on the analyst's agenda

Make the issues a priority item for investor relations meeting, helping analysts to understand their significance

4. Get into the annual report

Make these issues a front page aspect of annual reports, both historic and future plans, using the new OFR.

5. Build investor dialogue

Build an ongoing dialogue by which analysts request marketing information and shareholders make decisions on it.

6. Positively influence share price

Demonstrate how marketing can make a tangible and immediate difference to the market value of the business.

Time for marketing to take centre stage

'Do you want to sell fizzy water for the rest of your life, or do you want a chance to change the world?'

John Sculley

'A brand for a company is like a reputation for a person. You earn reputation by trying to do hard things well.'

Jeff Bezos

Marketers should be the most important, influential and inspiring professionals within the business community. Yet for too long their talents have been restrained to functional delivery, a support function, and their contributions marginal to the core challenges of business. Businesses cannot survive in today's markets like this.

Business needs marketers and marketing more than ever, to step up to the challenges of market complexity and intense competition, to be the creative and commercial driving force of business, and to embrace real customer orientation, innovation and profitable growth.

There is an open door for marketing to take 'centre stage', to drive strategic direction and aligned delivery, to be a stronger function and a holistic mindset for business. However, this requires marketers to change. While there are undoubtedly good examples of those who are already there, others must become more strategic, innovative and commercial. There has never been a more exciting time to be a marketer.

More intelligent marketers	More imaginative marketers
Customer. Harnessing customers as the 'power base' of marketing, from insights to propositions and experiences.	**Champions.** Working across the business to inspire and ensure effective delivery to customers every time.
Business. Seeing business as a whole and how it must align, focus and evolve to seize the opportunities of markets.	**Innovators.** Encouraging more creative thinking across the business, leading innovation as a core discipline.
Growth. Driving profitable growth through strategic focus on markets and brands, innovation and relationships.	**Drivers.** Becoming the driving force of business strategy and decision-making, investments and priorities.

Yet marketers need to do more, to be more commercially focused in the way they approach their markets, more competitive and creative, and more future focused in where their organization is going next. Indeed, it is perhaps not surprising that the most successful marketers today are often not even called marketers any more. Marketing leaders today often come in the guises of commercial directors, managing directors of business units, business managers of market segment, or even customer managers.

A recent survey by McKinsey for the Marketing Society reveals that CEOs need marketers to do much more. The research indicated the business priorities, all of which have close relevance to marketing:

- Achieving sustainable, organic top line growth – through investing in brands, with better customer understanding, more innovation and an improved balance between strategy and implementation.

- Coping with increasing regulation – needing to build better relationships with regulators, to positively influence the direction of markets, to be better corporate citizens rather than challenging everything as a threat.

- Cost management – finding smarter ways to work, to do things better and more effectively rather than doing things the same way and slashing the costs by which they are done.

- Speed and responsiveness of the organization – the need for agility to respond to fast-changing markets, being less tied to certain products and skills, being more culturally attuned to the present and future rather than the past.

There are clearly significant challenges and opportunities for marketing and marketers. In particular, CEOs are keen to foster a marketing mentality in all parts of the business, not just functionally:

'From having great marketers in places, to having great marketing capabilities every-where.'

CEO, FMCG company

They entirely support the need for marketing to be a driving force across the business, bringing a greater orientation towards customers and aligning it with the drivers of business success. They argue that this requires a new or at least a broader role for marketing, as well as a market-ing mindset for the whole business:

'Marketing is about having a point of view about the future.'

CEO, FMCG company

'Marketing leads, operations works out how, and finance assesses.'

CEO, Financial services

'Effective marketing is the key driver of future cash and shareholder value.'

CMO, FMCG company

The research found that while marketers are recognized for their unique contribution to the business, this is not without frustrations:

- The energy that goes into marketing tactics needs to embrace more commercial thinking, better measurement and greater accountability.

- If marketers are to lead strategy development, they need to be more business aware, have broader business skills and more commercial vocabulary.

- Marketers must work more collaboratively across the business to improve the customer focus of the whole business.

- Marketing can only take the lead in a company if it gains significantly higher status by delivery of results, and their commercial articulation.

- Marketers need to collectively build a better understanding of these issues and roles, both within their community and across business.

However, marketers are not currently perceived by CEOs to be up to the challenge of delivering this. While they are recognized for their creativity and energy, they are perceived to lack discipline and the right capabilities, as well as being inflexible and arrogant.

How do CEOs perceive marketers?

At best	**At worst**
Creative	Indisciplined
Committed	Not value-orientated
Hard working	Inconsistent
Inspiring	Self-important
Essential	Not commercial
Passionate	Narrow
Talented	Not accountable

Source: The *Marketing Society*

While CEOs recognize the need for marketing, they don't want functional marketers who are not aligned to their own priorities, who are remote from customers, resistant to change, obsessed with the short term, and are some of the least accountable people in business.

Also interesting was the widely differing definitions of marketing within companies, meaning that language internally and externally can often be misinterpreted. Defining marketing by functional activities, marketing was variously viewed thus:

- 'Commercial' marketing teams as corporate image and reputation, communications, research, development, pricing, distribution, sales, CSR and integration.

- 'Functional' marketing teams as communications, research and development, pricing, marketing integration, CSR.

- 'Creative' marketing teams as communications, research and development.

- 'Corporate' marketing teams as corporate image and reputation, investor relations, internal communications and CSR.

While marketers, as one would expect of such creative professionals, are constantly seeking new ideas, new models, new solutions, it is the greater strategic thinking, innovation and commercial implementation that CEOs want to see.

Indeed, a marketing genius is unlikely to talk about concepts that are all that groundbreaking. It is more about the way we implement them, how effectively they are aligned to the business, how they combine both radical creativity and rigorous discipline to engage customers and deliver exceptional results.

The Marketing Society then worked with its members, and other professional bodies, to create 'A Manifesto for Marketing'. It defines a new role for marketing and the imperatives for marketers if they are to effectively embrace this new role.

A MANIFESTO FOR MARKETING

Marketing must realign itself to the priorities of business, and to create exceptional value for both customers and shareholders. Marketers must adopt a new role in the organization, exhibiting new behaviours and acquiring new capabilities.

The new role of marketers

- **Customer Champions** – building on marketing's insight into the real needs and concerns of customers, both consumers and intermediaries, ensuring that brand promises become efficient and compelling reality.

- **Business Innovators** – seizing the best opportunities to innovate across the business, providing clarity of vision and radical creativity to turn the best ideas into distinctive products and services.

- **Growth Drivers** – leading the business in driving profitable growth, ensuring that the business focuses on the best opportunities to create, accelerate and sustain future cash flows, and thereby superior returns to shareholders.

If marketers cannot change, then they will become an increasingly isolated and irrelevant function, whilst the business will look to other disciplines more willing to accept the challenge and accountability for business success.

The imperatives for change

Marketing has a unique opportunity to drive the business, to move to the heart of strategy formulation, to understand and engage customers more deeply, to provide the fuel and focus for business colleagues, and reposition itself as the engine of value creation.

However, in assuming these new roles, marketers will also need to behave in new ways and develop new capabilities. Most importantly, they require marketers to:

- **Be accountable** – marketers must be accountable for the profitable growth of business, driving decisions and priorities, balancing short- and long-term goals, measuring and articulating the value created.

- **Act collaboratively** – marketers are ideally positioned take a lead in working across the business, balancing strategy and implementation, driven by customer insight, delivering compelling experiences.

- **Develop new capabilities** – marketers must become more strategic, innovative and commercial, embracing new marketing processes and models, and translating the language of customers into that of finance.

Marketers must take personal responsibility for their own behaviour and capabilities, but also work as a professional community to change the perceptions and impact of marketing overall.

Source: The Marketing Society

Inspiration 13.1 NESTLÉ

'Nestlé feeds the world.'

Bite into a piece of chocolate, drink a glass of water, prepare an evening meal, feed your dog, or enjoy an ice cream. In each case, the chances are that you have chosen a Nestlé product, and while the corporate brand was in the past hidden behind one of its many product brands – Nescafé, KitKat, Maggi, Buitoni, Häagen Dazs and many more – its corporate brand is increasingly being used to endorse its wide portfolio, an additional stamp of quality.

Nestlé, with its headquarters in Vevey, Switzerland, was founded in 1866 by Henri Nestlé and is today the world's largest food and drinks company. The company's strategy is guided by growth through 'innovation and renovation'. Long-term potential is never sacrificed for short-term performance, with the priority being to bring the best and most relevant products to people, 'wherever they are, whatever their needs, throughout their lives'.

When Nestlé's top marketer was off sick for a long period, the job was delegated upwards to Peter Brabeck rather than downwards. Brabeck, who is a CEO with a marketing background, now takes day-to-day responsibility for Nestlé's 8000 products, with 20,000 variants and a marketing budget of $2.5 billion generating revenues of over $65 billion.

'We are a branded consumer goods company,' says Brabeck. Marketing is recognized as the engine of growth, and brands are primary to this. Key to this success is its partnership with retailers, recognizing that rather than getting into a costly fight with them, Nestlé's biggest challenge is finding ways to work better with the key distributors for mutual success. He argues that some of its competitors have capitulated by agreeing to develop more own-label items for the retailers. 'This is the ultimate expression of an FMCG manufacturer's failure to create value,' he argues.

In order to address this challenge, he has focused his marketers on being the 'demand generators' through consumer insight, communication, promotions, sales and retailer management; while also being 'brand guardians', protecting and developing the core brands through research, innovation and brand development.

Indeed, Nestlé has clustered its huge portfolio under six umbrella brands – Nestlé, which accounts for 40% of the business, Purina pet foods, Maggi, Nescafé, Nestea and Buitoni. Nestlé, for example, has grown visibly as an endorsement brand on products ranging from milk and spreads to chocolate and ice cream.

Brabeck has put marketing centre stage, partly due his frustration with previous organizational structures. Marketing was previously a peripheral and largely unaccountable function in a 'matrix organization' where marketing was able to drive some aspects of innovation, but not all, and, importantly, would seek to measure ROI on advertising, instead of ROI for the business.

The head of marketing is now responsible for the company's seven strategic business units – each a different category of food, each responsible for developing its global business strategy, which drives R&D, leads to production, and regional and local performance. This leads to localization of brands and products, and stronger relationships with retailers. There is a clear approach to the customer, with the marketer in control and fully accountable for business performance.

marketing
  genius

Application 13.1 MANAGING MARKETS

How do you manage markets effectively, shape them in your vision, drive change within them, and influence their structures and regulation? How do you ensure that this thinking drives the business too?

1. Understand market dynamics

Understand the space-time dynamics of existing and adjacent markets, the sources and drivers of long-term value.

2. Create future market scenarios

Consider possible future scenarios, relative to market shape, customer needs, and competitive positions.

3. Define your market strategy

Define where and how you will compete and how you will create value, as the foundation of wider business strategy.

4. Create your own market vortex

Identify the market positions which you seek to 'own' and how you can define and shape the market in your vision.

5. Influence standards and regulation

Proactively take a lead role in arguing for, and defining standards and regulation, and influence appropriately.

6. Create an 'outside in' culture

Use the customer, the market strategy and marketing mindset to define an outside-in orientation and prioritization.

Concept 13.1 CUSTOMER CHAMPIONS

Marketers must be the 'customer champions', ensuring that customer insight is available throughout the organization, driving decisions and focusing action. As a result, decisions are more insightful, balanced and effective, and the experience for customers is more satisfying, aligned, consistent and delivered efficiently.

This requires marketers to:

- articulate prioritized, actionable customer insights;

- take responsibility for customer issues (e.g. health, environment);

- ensure that the organization understands and acts on them;

- lead the organization in delivering customer promises effectively;

- build brands that reflect and engage the priorities of customers; and

- ensure that the business builds successful customer relationships.

Marketers have sometimes retained knowledge of customers, and sought to build relationships with them within their own functional areas. This is clearly not possible or desirable. They must be the guiding force for all parts of the business in making customer focus meaningful and ensuring that promises really do become reality.

This will require marketers to actively champion all customer information as a key part of their role, to work harder to analyse market research and find real insights, and make research and insights more accessible and comprehensible. In order to ensure that the insight is relevant and practical, marketers must listen and understand the issues of business and other functions, apply these insights to key business issues and opportunities, and get more involved in decision-making in all functions and at all levels.

Marketers have the responsibility for ensuring that customer issues are higher on the business agenda. They must take a lead in the development and delivery of customer propositions, and articulate more clearly how propositions are delivered operationally.

A customer orientation cannot be mandated; it is for marketers to work with their colleagues to influence and persuade them to orientate more around customers, to deliver in a more personalized and brand-relevant way. This requires a more open and collaborative way of working non-functionally and in non-hierarchical teams, leading cross-functionally to be guided by customers.

In some organizations this is encouraged by establishing leaders who champion the experience of a customer within a particular sector, or for a specific brand. In some organizations they are customer experience managers, or segment managers, while in others it is core to the role of brand management.

Inspiration 13.2 BRITISH AIRWAYS

British Airways was formed in 1973 from the merger of the state-owned British Overseas Airways Corporation and British European Airways. Lord King was appointed chairman in 1981 with the mission of preparing the airline for privatization, and he hired Colin Marshall as CEO in 1983. The flag carrier was privatized and floated in 1987.

Between them, King and Marshall turned a badly run, bureaucratic and operational company into a leader in customer service. The early culture change focused on the importance of employees delivering great customer service as the route to profitability, led through a programme called 'Putting People First'.

Marketing and customer service became the focus of the business. Indeed, BA became one of the first service businesses to introduce the idea of brands, packaging and labelling the different propositions to different customers, bringing together the many different product and service elements as seamless journey experiences.

Advertising was key in changing perceptions, promoting 'The World's Favourite Airline' through memorable images of people from around the world coming together. Executive Club became one of the pioneers of customer loyalty. And, of course, there was Concorde – the timeless state of the art in travel – enabling travellers to arrive in JFK before they took off in London – according to their watches.

For some years, as the global travel market grew, British Airways thrived on this approach, despite no longer having the state hand-outs still subsidizing many of their competitors. However, the outbreak of the first Gulf War, the rise in oil prices, the increasing challenge of competition, and the inefficiencies caused by an inability to change operational working practices soon brought the customer champion into problems.

First came, the rise of Richard Branson's Virgin Atlantic, targeting some of BA's most lucrative routes, and the so-called 'dirty tricks' as the two airlines came to terms with what was acceptable competitiveness. At the same time, management and trade unions clashed and the resulting disruption cost the company hundreds of millions of pounds.

In 1997, the airline took the bold branding step of replacing its traditional Union Flag tailfin livery with a range of globally diverse tailfin designs.

It wanted to show the world that it was no longer British and aloof, but global and cosmopolitan and caring. While the concept of depicting a brand idea in multiple ways has great merit, the designs received a strong backlash from some of the older, vociferous British travellers, who clearly still had influence in the boardroom, and the new tailfins gradually faded away.

The airline market was evolving rapidly, and BA recognized that it needed to shape its destiny rather than be shaped by others. Alliances became hugely important, sharing flight codes, sychronizing schedules, combining frequent-flyer programmes, and franchising its brand to a number of regional airlines that operated in smaller markets which were uneconomical for the main business to serve.

However, mergers and acquisitions were seen to be key. After initially failing to capture USAir, BA devoted huge amounts of time trying to create a merger with American Airlines, which was ultimately unsuccessful due to the conditions placed on its precious Heathrow landing slots by regulators.

At the same time BA's marketing, under commercial director Martin George, has continued to set the industry standard, leading the development of the One World alliance of airlines, continually seeking new ways to upgrade its brands, to enhance its customer experiences and improve the efficiency of its sales, marketing and customer service through a huge investment in ba.com, and re-establishing the airline's reputation and leadership.

Brand management has remained a core discipline across the business. Indeed, brand management in a service business has more diverse challenges than in marketing a brand that is centred on a physical, tangible product. Service brands have an infinite number of interactions with customers, are reliant upon many operational processes, many provided by third parties, and, most significantly, services are delivered by people.

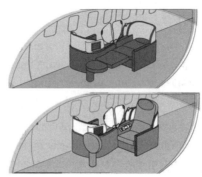

Source: thetravelinsider.com

Unlike the can of Heinz Baked Beans, where the food is good and the packaging consistent, even if it is delivered by a grumpy sales assistant in a grubby retail store, a service brand is everything. In a travel experience, one grump or grub can affect the entire perception of the brand and the customer's experience. BA recognized that brand management was paramount, and couldn't simply exist in an ivory tower. It had to embrace every part of the business.

While British Airways is the master brand that sits above everything, defining the broad promises to customers of being a safe and secure airline with the best schedules and punctuality, its sub-brands – including Club World and Club Europe, World Traveller and Euro Traveller – define the more specific and relevant propositions to customers, and the products and services that make up the experience.

A brand manager in British Airways thinks customer, not product; horizontal, not vertical. The Club World brand manager thinks about the entire experience of the business traveller leaving home, parking, checking-in, flying, arriving, and doing what they need to do at their destination. These, and around 20 other aspects, make up the Club World experience.

The brand manager's task is more about coordinating an incredibly complex set of interactions – working with sales, check-in, airport authorities, lounges, cabin interiors, catering suppliers, cabin crew, car and hotel partners, and many more to ensure that they can deliver a total, consistent and seamless branded experience. Indeed, the brand manager had little direct budget, which instead is held by functional teams. This requires a collaborative, influencing approach, working across the business to cajole, support, connect and encourage the delivering of a seamless and distinctive brand experience for each customer.

This is brand management as a whole business discipline.

Application 13.2 MANAGING BRANDS

How do you manage brands beyond the traditional discipline of product-based FMCG brands? How do you manage the corporate brand that goes far beyond the marketing role? How do you manage delivery of the brand that involves everybody in the company, and partners too? How do you ensure that the brand aligns with the business and market, and stays alive?

1. Clearly define your brand
Define your corporate brand, its core idea and explain its meaning and implications for everyone internally.

2. Align brand to stakeholders
Ensure that the brand aligns to the needs of customer, employee and shareholder, and related groups.

3. Reflect brand in the business
Connect the brand with the core purpose of the business, driven by the CEO, and delivered through strategy.

4. Interpret brand into propositions
Develop sets of customer and employee value propositions that make the brand relevant and meaningful to people.

5. Deliver brand as experiences
Manage the 'operationalization' of the brand promise into an coherent brand experience for each customer

6. Manage intangible brand assets
Manage and nurture the brand as a valuable intangible assets, defining and growing its equity and value.

Concept 13.2 BUSINESS INNOVATORS

Marketers must be the 'business innovators', responding to fast-changing market conditions, identifying the best opportunities and driving innovation to creatively and commercially exploit them.

Innovation, although loudly trumpeted as a business prerequisite today, rarely has a home in organizations, which is good in that it can be embraced by everyone, but can also get lost as it's nobody's specific responsibility. A dedicated innovation role enables faster and better response to market trends and regulation, competition and technology, where the best opportunities drive strategy, differentiation and growth.

Marketers can embrace this role effectively, requiring them to:

• articulate the changing nature and future of their markets;

• be more active in positively addressing changes in regulation;

• creatively explore new market applications of emergent technologies;

• lead the development of product and business innovation;

• focus their efforts on the best markets, customers and products; and

• ensure that innovation is faster and more successful.

Like the customer champion role, marketers will not magically become anointed; rather, they must have the foresight and energy to embrace the role, its challenges and opportunities, and earn the title by doing it better than anyone else.

Business innovators must be more strategic as well as focused on implementation, take a lead in understanding how markets will evolve in future, and better understand macroeconomic and social trends. This positions them to develop market strategies that become the core of business strategy. Such strategies are more strategic and holistic than the activity-driven, functional marketing plans.

Marketers must take a lead in understanding and responding to change in regulation, gaining a better understanding of new technologies and applications; indeed, they should be the leaders in considering how network technologies or changing social patterns could transform their markets and propositions.

Innovation is much more than product development, in that its creative and commercial approach can be applied to any facet of the business – from supply chains to payroll systems, complaint handling to knowledge management. Indeed, marketers must learn to innovate entire functions, experiences or business models too.

Marketers must do marketing in more creative ways – so much of our distribution, pricing and communication thinking has changed little in the last 40 years. While new technologies and media have emerged, we have largely continued to do things in similar ways.

Inspiration 13.3 PHILIPS

Koninklijke Philips Electronics N.V. (Royal Philips Electronics) is one of the world's largest consumer electronics manufacturers with worldwide sales of around €30 billion. These are delivered through Philips Consumer Electronics, Philips Semiconductors, Philips Lighting, Philips Medical Systems and Philips Domestic Appliances and Personal Care.

Philips was founded in 1891 by the brothers Gerard and Anton Philips in Eindhoven, The Netherlands. Its first products were light bulbs, and it was almost 50 years before it started to diversify – first with electric razors, the Philishave, and then with the compact audio cassette tape, which was wildly successful.

Philips is Europe's largest electronics company. Its impact is everywhere, if not always recognized. For example, every year Philips produces over 2.4 billion incandescent lamps and 30 million picture tubes; 60% of the world's televisions contain Philips products, 30% of the world's offices are lit by Philips lights, and 2.5 million heart procedures are carried out each year using Philips technology.

While Philips has long been recognized for its technical excellence, and its inventions, it could have often fallen at the last hurdle of innovation. It has failed to create products that engage people – with the empathetic design, and compelling attraction that makes a great product stand out. As a result, it often failed to consolidate its new approaches, standards and inventions. It failed to lead the market when it should have done.

Perhaps the most influential driver of marketing in Philips was not the customer, or the product, but the 'technology roadmap'. This culturally drove the business, every manager responding to the macho timelines of when a new technology would be available, and subsequently when a new product derivative would be ready for market.

The market and customer were an afterthought. This was product push at its worst. Some of the younger marketers, who had grown up in non-tech, consumer-based companies, recognized this failing and started to challenge the technology roadmap. They created a 'customer roadmap' to rival it, understanding market and customer trends, maturity of competition and when they are likely to be ready for the technology.

The product and customer roadmaps, while travelling in different directions, created a positive reinforcement of what to develop, when to launch it, and how most effectively to position and market it.

Application 13.3 MANAGING INNOVATION

How do you manage innovation, the strategy and process, the major business-wide initiatives alongside the product derivatives? How do you ensure that markets are ready for innovations? And that they achieve commercial results?

---

1. Encourage innovation mindset

Build the desire, attitude and capability to think and act innovatively in every area and aspect of business.

2. Develop innovation strategy

Develop a specific innovation strategy that identifies and prioritizes strategic, product and process innovation.

3. Manage portfolio of innovations

Manage a portfolio of 'big bets' and derivative innovations so as to balance risk and reward.

4. Connect to market strategy

Ensure that markets are ready for innovations, by innovating their needs and structure to accommodate them.

5. Manage innovation process

Manage the formal innovation process, creative and commercial, so that it aan be applied to any aspect.

6. Commercialize market innovations

Ensure that innovations balance market opportunity with technical possibility, and are commercialized effectively.

Concept 13.3 GROWTH DRIVERS

Marketers must be the 'growth drivers', exploiting the best opportunities for revenue growth and ensuring that growth is profitable and has a positive impact on shareholder value.

Business has a thousand people managing costs, constantly discussing and reporting on their cost performance at every level of the organization. And, indeed, the relentless drive for efficiency means that they and their teams spend much of that time thinking about how they can further reduce costs.

Yet few people champion growth; while sales managers seek to grow their individual accounts, and brand managers their brands, few people other than business leaders take a business-wide perspective on the best places and focus on driving top-line growth.

Like customers, and innovation, growth is another 'imperative' for business, which everybody recognizes and nobody directly champions. Marketers can make themselves essential to the business and actively influence its direction by demonstrating leadership here too.

What will marketers need to do differently?

- Identify the best market opportunities to drive profitable growth.

- Contribute more to strategy and planning through insight and analysis.

- Stimulate demand by focusing on priorities and effective marketing.

- Leverage brands and relationships to sustain long-term growth.

- Be accountable for performance through a clear set of metrics.

- Articulate the value of these initiatives internally and to investors.

While many will call for marketers to be more commercial, in order to understand business and articulate their own value, being a growth driver requires more: to be strategic and innovative, as well as commercial. It builds on the customer insight, and innovation focus, to provide business-wide, non-functional leadership.

It requires that marketers must improve their knowledge of business processes and issues, apply more rigorous analysis to identify profitable opportunities and spend more time on the strategic analysis of their markets. Obviously, marketers must work particularly closely with strategy and finance to do this, and find ways to get fully involved in business strategy and planning processes.

Marketers must educate business on the role of customers and marketing in growth, take a lead in defining and delivering growth-based initiatives, work across the whole business in order to champion growth, and understand how to leverage their brands in more dynamic and virtual ways to drive growth.

In order to gain business acceptance, marketers must articulate the short- and long-term value of activities, define and communicate a clear set of growth-based metrics that achieve both customer and business objectives, and ultimately articulate their initiatives in economic value terms for boardrooms and investors.

Inspiration 13.4 DISNEY

Since 1923 the Walt Disney Company has remained faithful in its commitment to delivering the best entertainment based on its rich legacy of creative content and storytelling.

Today Disney is divided into four major business areas, each bringing together a range of famous and integrated brands and activities, but linking together across the group in order to maximize their exposure, engagement and impact.

Indeed, Disney as a brand has been so consistent and successful in its marketing over the years that it has gained 'ownership' of a handful of emotive words that perhaps define its brand better than any slogan. Disney words (where over 80% of people associate the word with Disney, according to Martin Lindstom's *BrandSense*) include:

- Fantasy

- Dreams

- Magic

- Creativity

- Smile

The four businesses that make these words come to life are as follows.

Disney Studio Entertainment

The studios are the foundation of the company. From Mickey Mouse to *Snow White and the Seven Dwarfs*, the world's first full-length animated film, they entertain the whole family. The productions are distributed in the form of movies and music, recorded and for hire through well-known subsidiary brands such as Touchstone Pictures, Miramax and Buena Vista.

Disney Parks and Resorts

This is where the magic lives, home to Disney's beloved characters. In 1952 Disneyland first started to develop in Arnheim, California, and has since spread across the world with 11 parks, 35 hotels and 2 luxury cruise ships. From the Magic Kingdom to the Epcot Centre, Disney creates a series of fantasy environments that build on its studio productions and sell yet more of its consumer products.

Disney Consumer Products

The brand extends into every form of merchandising – including toys and clothing, interactive games and fine arts, home décor, food and drink. Indeed, Disney is one of the largest licensors in the world. Its publishing arm is the world's largest children's publisher, and Baby Einstein is the leader in developmental toys, while Disney Stores and its online and direct marketing are never far away.

Disney Media Networks

Disney has brought together a vast array of television, cable, radio and Internet brands. ABC brings together a broad portfolio of TV stations, while ESPN, Disney Channel and Fox Kids are some of its cable properties. Also in the media networks business are Buena Vista television, a leader in syndicated programming, and Disney Internet Group, which brings together the online activities of all its businesses.

The timeline of growth in Disney's portfolio demonstrates the gradual acquisition of multiple content sources and their integration, and the ways in which subsidiary brands have evolved to stand alongside the Disney master brand.

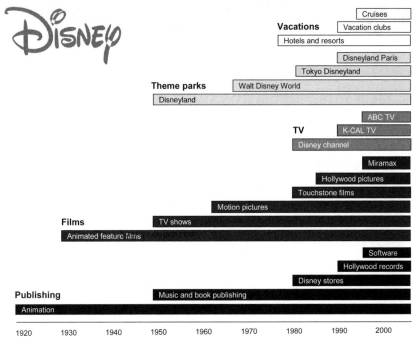

Source: Data sourced from disney.com

Application 13.4 MANAGING GROWTH

How do you manage growth, which is clearly a whole-business discipline? How do you identify the best opportunities and approaches to achieving that growth? How do you ensure that the growth is profitable and creates maximum value for the business?

1. Identify high growth markets

Prioritize profitable growth above all else as the long-term driver of value, riding on the high-growth markets.

2. Evaluate options to grow in them

Evaluate the best options (i.e. customer, products) and ways (organic, partners, acquisitions) to achieve growth.

3. Ensure growth is profitable

Manage growth so that it delivers economic profitability longer-term, not revenue growth at any price.

4. Make core to business strategy

The 'growth strategy' should be the key action of the business strategy, building on markets and innovation.

5. Persist with best opportunities

The best growth opportunities may not deliver the fastest returns, therefore persistence and patience is needed.

6. Balance today and tomorrow

Maintain stakeholder confidence by ensuring that you continue to deliver the promise profitably in the short term.

Why marketers make better CEOs

'Obviously everyone wants to be successful, but I want to be looked back on as being very innovative, very trusted and ethical and ultimately making a big difference in the world.'

Sergey Brin

'Theories of management don't matter much. Endeavours succeed or fail because of the people involved. Too often, people are assumed to be emotional chess pieces to be moved around by grand viziers, which may explain why many top managers immerse their calendar time in deal making, restructuring and the latest management fad. How many immerse themselves in the goal of creating an environment where the best, the brightest, the most creative are attracted, retained and, most importantly, unleashed?'

Gen. Colin Powell

Marketing leaders are ideally positioned to become the next CEO in today's complex market-driven environments. They offer more insight into the best opportunities for business, they are the guardians of the firm's most valuable intangible assets, and they should be able to better combine the creative and commercial, collaborative and directional skills required of business leaders.

Indeed, research by PA Consulting Group shows that 21% of the FTSE 100 CEOs have a marketing background, and that their companies' output is greater than others', delivering more than 5% superior returns to shareholders.

Yet getting there is probably the hardest job, out of the functional silo and into the executive mainstream. Indeed, marketing leaders are challenged by a multitude of functional and organization priorities, driven by the changing dynamics of markets and business, to lead marketing as a functional team and organization-wide mindset – to champion customers, lead innovation and drive growth. Marketing leaders must also distinguish their own roles as 'managers' and 'leaders' of the function and of the business, and when to be which, and how to excel at both.

More intelligent leadership	More imaginative leadership
Managing. Management is about making the right decisions, allocating resources and being accountable.	**Leading.** Leadership is about defining a compelling vision, inspiring and encouraging people to follow it.
Functional. Leading the functional marketing team in achieving specific projects and activities.	**Organizational.** Leading the market-driven business strategically, innovatively and commercially.
Coaching. Leaders guide and teach their people, supporting and enabling to achieve exceptional performance.	**Connecting.** Leaders connect people and ideas together, influencing and collaborating for collective success.

Management and leadership are very different yet complementary roles, entirely possible within the same job and person.

- Managers make decisions. This requires rational decision-making. Good managers make the right decisions.

- Leaders inspire action. This requires an emotional commitment from leaders and followers. Good leaders deliver excellent results.

Leaders who inspire the wrong actions will kill the business, and managers who make decisions that aren't implemented are wasting their time. Leaders who love to inspire but will do anything to win people's favour and support, or say yes to their boss or peers for an easier life in order to avoid the more difficult decisions, are unlikely to be successful. Managers who seek to rule by authority, without engaging and motivating people to follow them, or simply see management as maintaining the status quo, will fail too.

In order to lead their functional teams and influence the organization, marketing leaders need to focus on the right, practical decisions that engage people and deliver results. It is often about getting the balance right:

- Leadership vs Management. Knowing when to make a decision, and when to encourage action. Start each meeting with 'What decisions need to be made and who needs to make them?'

- Accountability vs Responsibility. Identifying which activities can be delegated to other people without losing accountability. Indeed, there should be very few activities for which the leader is directly responsible.

- Functional vs Organizational. Deciding which organizational activities to support or enable, and how they can be achieved while also driving functional objectives and, indeed, be essential to the achievement of these.

- Generalist vs Specialist. Leaders rarely need to be experts at everything, or indeed anything, that goes on in their areas. Even when the leader has technical expertise it might be better not to interfere unless necessary.

- Urgent vs Important. Each person, including leaders, needs to distinguish what really matters to them, regardless of other people's agendas. Be in control of your own priorities if you are to achieve significant results.

As marketing's role is increasingly both a function and a business mindset, the marketing leader's role is increasingly up and across as well as down (to use traditional, hierarchical terms). This requires greater focus, stronger influencing and collaboration skills than ever, and recognizing the positive sources of 'power' that marketers can leverage – their market knowledge, customer intimacy, innovation and creativity, as well as the ability to apply this in organization-wide, strategic and commercial ways.

Marketing leaders are increasingly known as chief marketing officers (CMOs); however, they increasingly take on wider roles too, roles without title in the short term, although they may be formalized in the future:

- Functional 'CMOs' – leading and managing the teams and tasks within the organization's marketing function.

- Collaborative 'CXOs' – leading and managing people and processes across the 'outside-in' business.

- Marketing CEOs – leading and managing the business's overall focus, integration and performance.

The average tenure for CMOs at the top 100 brand companies is just 22.9 months, according to research by Spencer Stuart. Compare this with CEOs, who are in their positions on average for 53.8 months, and you start to see cause for concern. While it is partly a reflection of a marketer's versatility in that they can do many roles, it is probably also a reflection of their low boredom threshold. While it means that they quickly progress, it also creates instability in the organization, and lack of a consistent approach to the market.

Sector	CMO tenure (months)	CEO tenure (months)
Apparel	10.0	229.0
Food	12.0	47.5
Telecoms	15.0	37.1
Drinks	25.8	48.1
Retail stores	26.2	60.8
Media	29.3	17.0
Technology	29.9	74.7
Financial services	34.8	45.4

Source: Spencer Stuart

When we consider that the majority of marketing actions are geared to deliver results in future years – through entering new markets, brand building, relationship development and innovation – then most CMOs leave before the true results of these activities are realized. They are therefore not accountable for their performance, or, to look at it positively, they don't get the opportunity to share in their success.

More likely, though, they are encouraged to look to the shorter-term, more tactical, more incremental actions that keep the organization where it is rather than moving it forwards. In some cases, where the CMO has gone for the longer-term wins, maybe they have failed to deliver enough in the short term and so lost the confidence of their leaders who are conditioned to think of marketing as instant deliverables. If they think that marketing is only about driving quarterly sales, then they are unlikely to get stronger brands and innovation.

What's the answer? At one level, marketers need to apply themselves more deeply to the roles, seeing it as a longer-term project rather than just looking for the quick wins and regarding their position as a stepping stone to whatever next. Of course, they do need to deliver today as well as tomorrow, but they need to find the actions that do both. As a professional community we see rapid progression as success, whereas in reality there is often little time to have created such evidence.

Organizations need to see the more strategic contribution made by marketers, and it is up to marketers to educate them by articulating the long-term value of their decisions and actions. We also need organizations to ensure that marketers can have more meaningful, fullfilling roles, where they can make a real difference, can grow themselves over time, and see the longer-term opportunities. At board level, executives are increasingly incentivized to stay with organizations by bonuses that are more geared to future share growth rather than short-term profits. They only get the rewards if they hang around to see the results.

Inspiration 14.1 RICHARD BRANSON

Richard Branson is the epitome of an entrepreneur, best known for the Virgin brand that he founded and still leads. Born in 1950, he has never lost his love of adventure and innovation, his curiosity for what might be, and his passion to make new things happen.

While other leaders might care most about finances and governance, Branson focuses on the customer, a walking incarnation of his brand, working with people across his many businesses to engender the same entrepreneurial spirit and brand values that have served him so well.

His passion is for the customer, much more than the financials. 'I never get the accountants in before I start a business. It's done on gut feeling, especially if I can see that they are taking the mickey out of the customer.'

He first achieved notoriety with Virgin Records, a record label that started out with the unusual *Tubular Bells* by Mike Oldfield and then introduced bands like the Sex Pistols and Culture Club to the world. Known for his wacky exploits used to promote his businesses, Branson is keen on playful antagonisms, exemplified by his 'mine is bigger than yours' slogans that marked the arrival of Virgin Atlantic's new Airbus A340–600 planes.

He is famed for his heroic failures as well as successes, having made several unsuccessful attempts to fly in a hot air balloon around the world. 'Virgin Atlantic Flyer' was the first hot air balloon ever to cross the Atlantic Ocean, and was the largest ever flown. Such escapades almost cost him his life on more than one occasion. Yet the PR value was immeasurable.

He became Sir Richard Branson when he was knighted by the Queen in 1999 for his business prowess and contribution to UK society. Meanwhile, he has guest starred, playing himself, on several television shows, including *Friends*, *Baywatch* and *Only Fools and Horses*. He is also the star of a new reality television show called *The Rebel Billionaire* where sixteen contestants will be tested for their entrepreneurship and their sense of adventure.

In 2004 he announced the signing of a deal under which a new space tourism company, Virgin Galactic, will license the technology behind SpaceShipOne to take paying passengers into suborbital space. The group plans to make flights available to the public by late 2007 with tickets priced at $190,000.

Application 14.1 LEADING MARKETING

What is your role as a marketing leader, a marketing director or commercial director, chief marketing officer or chief customer officer? Indeed, what is the role of a leader compared with that of a manager?

1. Define the essence of your role

Clarify the added value of the CMO, accountabilities and how personally adds value to collective performance.

2. Set clear goals and metrics

Make time to set transparent goals and metrics for the benefit of yourself and team, as much as your boss.

3. Inspire people with your vision

Leaders inspire; managers control … inspire your team and the business with your personal market vision.

4. Connect the best ideas together

Add value by connecting ideas from across marketing disciplines, and other business functions.

5. Coach and support your team

Engage and enable people, taking on a coaching more than directing role, building capabilities and confidence.

6. Champion great marketing

Be the champion of great marketing in your team, business, and market. Build respect and reputation.

Concept 14.1 FUNCTIONAL CMOS

The marketing function is a complex and crucial function to manage. While the '4Ps' – representing products, channels, pricing and communications – provide a useful aide-memoire of what marketing should be doing, it is easy to become dominated by communication.

Of course, people will tell you that there are many more Ps – reflecting anything from people to performance, systems to information, service to sales. However, as Phillip Kotler argues, most marketers are at best struggling to manage two of the 'Ps' effectively.

Advertising still dominates the marketing landscape because it is so tangible and visible: the buzz of advertising campaigns, the visual array of product brochures, the interactivity of websites, the highly impressive events. They are what many people expect of marketers, and what many marketers love to do. Yet the marketing leader who yearns after a strapline to rival 'Just Do It', or a jingle to rival Intel's, really is missing the point. You may laugh, but there are many leaders who see this as the crowning glory of their brand strategies, and their *raison d'être*.

Jaw-dropping, spine-tingling ad campaigns don't necessarily deliver marketing results. Indeed, they are a complete waste of money if you are focused on the wrong markets or customers, or you aren't supported by profitable products or efficient channels, or you don't sustain a price premium or ultimately add value to the business.

Marketing leaders have a responsibility to ensure focus and balance. To recognize the role of communications, but not be dominated by it. To recognize the external contribution that can be made by advertising agencies and the like, but not to be dominated by them.

This requires education too. In a world of media neutrality, CEOs shouldn't expect to see glowing ads on TV as a prerequisite for strong brands. Similarly, leaders need to give their marketers the confidence to do more than write agency briefs and, indeed, do far more of the thinking, planning, creativity, and integration themselves.

Functional CMOs need to apply their leadership and management talents to:

- People and teams. Creative marketers are rarely leading a meek and compliant community; their energy and creativity, charisma and ego needs to be funnelled and connected as a strong focused force.

- Internal and external partnerships. Marketing typically brings together dozens of agencies, and works internally with every part of the business. This is a significant coordination and communications challenge.

- Planning and budgets. With the largest discretionary budgets in the business, marketing needs to allocate its resources wisely, to be more accountable, to ensure that every cent is delivering a profitable return on investment.

- Priorities and integration. It is easy to do more things, and project proliferation is probably the biggest handicap to marketing. Marketing needs to focus on the fewer big initiatives that have the most importance and impact.

- Processes and effectiveness. Particularly in multinational or multi-branded companies, there can be enormous duplication and inconsistency due to lack of clearly defined process, and without common goals and measurement.

- Talent and resources. Everybody thinks they can be a marketer. Yet marketing struggles to attract the best talent in business today. Marketing should be the most exciting, important and rewarding place to work.

- Performance and reporting. Marketing will only be appreciated as an essential business driver if it can articulate its real value to the business, explaining how it drives and what is its actual contribution to the share price.

CMOs need to build teams that understand why and know how to champion customers on behalf of the whole business, to innovate strategically as well as generate derivative products, and to drive profitable growth rather than being satisfied with revenues and market shares.

Inspiration 14.2 JIM STENGEL

Jim Stengel is the chief marketing officer for Procter & Gamble. He leads a team of around 3500 marketers in 150 countries, marketing some of the world's leading brands.

He joined P&G in 1983 and has been moving up the ranks ever since, landing his current position in 2001. He recently topped *Advertising Age*'s annual ranking of 'Power Players', which he attributes partly to his enormous advertising budget, but also to the innovation in its products, processes and communication.

Promoting brands globally can be a daunting task, but he argues that he has achieved his success by focusing on the people. 'Globalization is here to stay, but the challenge is not to let it blind you. You have to be relevant to the local people,' he said. That's why he is always searching for the right strategies, infrastructure, agencies, culture, and people to build the best brands and to bring the right brands to the right people.

'Even something as mundane as doing your laundry is a local habit,' he explained. 'It ranges from cleaning clothes on rocks with open wells in the Philippines to tiny machines that hardly use any water in Europe to the big, top-loading machines in the United States.'

He is largely responsible for returning P&G's marketing reputation, after a number of uncertain years. He has been bold in his actions. An early step was to revitalize P&G's Marketing University training programmes; then he addressed what he saw as an inappropriate dominance of advertising, and fundamental lack of accountability within his function.

Stengel has been an outspoken critic of advertising, and the agencies that extol it. In one 2004 speech, he went as far as to predict the imminent demise of the 30-second TV spot. He argued that the industry had failed to evolve in any meaningful way, and announced that the mass-marketing approach, of which P&G had been a leader, was now dead or soon would be.

He then went ahead and dramatically shifted 20% of P&G's entire communications budget away from advertising to other media. He has experimented with alternative approaches to communication: for example, the Tremor project virally promotes relevant brands to a network of 280,000 teenagers, an audience for which traditional marketing approaches just don't work any more.

Not only this, but Stengel has challenged the lack of accountability in advertising specifically, and marketing in general. 'This is a $450 billion industry and we are making decisions with less discipline than business would apply to $100,000 investments in other parts of the business,' he argued. He immediately put an end to the lazy business model of ad agencies – eliminating payment by retainer or commission and only rewarding agencies on the business results that their communications deliver.

Application 14.2 MANAGING MARKETING

How do you practically manage the marketing function, and its wide range of creative and analytical, strategic and operational activities? How do you manage marketing people who are constantly seeking to do things different or new? How do you ensure marketing realizes its full potential to the business?

1. Define marketing objectives

Define the role and objectives of the functional marketing team, and how each aspect of marketing contributes.

2. Build a talented marketing team

Bring together young and experienced marketing people with talent to think strategically, innovatively, commercially.

3. Develop plans and processes

Develop clear and specific marketing plans, and document the key processes for delivering and managing these.

4. Prioritize resources effectively

Optimize marketing resources (people, partners, assets, budget) to maximize long-term value creation.

5. Focus on what matters most

Prioritize your portfolio focus and tactical actions, strategic initiatives and improvement projects.

6. Manage marketing performance

Manage performance at strategic and operational, team and individual levels, through relevant metrics and rewards.

Concept 14.2 COLLABORATIVE CXOS

The role of the marketing leader, in his or her wider organizational context, is to provide leadership and influence. However, the authority to lead comes from the market and the marketer, rather than a hierarchical or delegated responsibility.

'Outside-in' organizations depend on the market for their guidance, their prioritization and their inspiration. At a strategic level they make sense of the evolving nature of markets, the complexity of structures, blur of borders, fragmentation of audiences, and challenge of competition. At a detailed level, they are driven by a deeper insight into customers, their needs and wants, motivations and aspirations.

Customers give marketers the moral authority to lead the business, to define the priorities and to bring together the resources and activities to achieve this.

While the focus is rightly on profitability in rewarding performance, it is the focus on the source of this success that matters most. In response, marketers must work across every part of the business to ensure focus is on the right markets and customers, that brands are more than skin deep and that their identities come to life with every interaction, and that the promises made are delivered through compelling, consistent and aligned experiences delivered by everybody in the business.

Collaborate CXOs work beyond their function, using their powers of influence to drive focus and integration:

- Market and customer orientation. Ensuring that every part of the business is focused externally, driven by customers and competitiveness. This is more than customer focus, a begrudging admittance that customers are important; rather, it recognizes the outside as the starting point for everything they do.

- Customer and business alignment. Most companies are organized through heritage rather than focus, defined by their products or capabilities. Yet more important is to align the business to the customer – meeting the total needs of an audience rather than having a fragmented approach.

- Brand integrity and activation. Working with people in every part of the business, from customer service to the warehouse, IT support to payroll, to build a better understanding of the brand's purpose, what it seeks to do for people, and how it is different – for employees as well as customers.

- Customer experiences and relationships. Technology has created a proliferation of access points to the organization, increasing the need for consistency of approach and sophistication of customer information sharing. If the customer is to believe they have a relationship with a brand then they expect instant intimacy at every contact point.

- Product and process innovation. Few products can be developed in a vacuum, the ideas and capabilities coming from every part of the business. Few products are launched without changes to operational and delivery process. Few innovations are sustainable unless they involve significant innovation of many parts of the business, not just its products.

- Profitable growth. Profitability is a function of improved efficiency as well as improved revenues. Costs are clearly a challenge for every part of the business, but so is the ability to sustain margins, justifying a price premium at every interaction. Growth is a collaborative challenge too and, perhaps most importantly, requires marketing and sales to work as one, with the shared incentives and rewards to drive it.

As organizations move from vertical silos to horizontal alignment, marketers must be at the forefront of this realignment, encouraging the cross-functional teams, the integrated processes, and shared goals and rewards. Nobody will tell them to do this. They need to be proactive, applying both an energetic approach and a softer influencing style to achieve it.

Leahy joined Tesco as a trainee marketer in 1979. Within five years he had become marketing director for one of its categories, and when marketing was made a board-level position in 1992, Leahy was the man for the job. In 1997, just before he turned forty, he became CEO.

His visionary but pragmatic approach has its roots in a very down-to-earth upbringing. He grew up in a prefab maisonette in one of the tougher parts of Liverpool, yet his carpenter and greyhound-owning father always encouraged his son to do more, studying at Manchester's Institute of Science and Technology, and eventually being knighted for his services to retailing.

In an interview with *The Economist* he reflected that 'I've been fortunate to see all layers of British life. I feel I know personally all customer groups'.

Under Sir Terry, Tesco has transformed from a very average UK supermarket chain into one of the world's largest and most respected retailers. His style can be blunt and analytical, yet he claims to be driven more by his conversations with staff and customers than anything else.

On assuming the lead marketing role, he developed a marketing strategy that put serving customers at its heart. In 1992 he initiated the 'one in front' programme in which a new checkout desk was opened if more than one customer was waiting. This increased costs, but customers appreciated the gesture. He launched Tesco's 'value' range to address price-conscious customers, and internally introduced a 'Would I buy it?' initiative to encourage staff to make their own judgements.

Leahy has also been the architect of Tesco's award-winning clubcard loyalty programme, launched in 1995 and one of the first in retailing. While customers collected points in recognition of their purchases, quarterly statements became a key moment to engage customers more deeply, and the powerful database of over 10 million customers has enabled Tesco to market incredibly personally and intelligently.

In 1997, now as CEO, his 'four pillars' business strategy was a blueprint for even more radical steps forwards – into geographically new markets, new non-food categories, and new store formats. Tesco has grown from around 550 stores at the time to over 2500 by 2005. Tesco Direct was also introduced at the time, building on the highly efficient supply chain to offer tesco.com, which has grown to become the largest and most profitable online grocery business in the world.

This is a CEO who has never lost touch with his customers, and still typically spends a day every week on the shop floor. In 2005 he was named *Fortune* magazine's European Businessman of the Year for 'his stewardship of Tesco through an economic boom and bust and in a hypercompetitive business'.

Leahy is still in the minority of CEOs who come from a marketing background. However, as an ultra-competitive Liverpudlian with Irish roots, he has certainly put his customer passion and marketer's instinct to good effect.

Application 14.3 INFLUENCING THE BUSINESS

How do you influence the business effectively? How do you work with others to champion the customer, drive innovation and profitable growth? What do marketers have that engages people? What gives marketing the right to lead the business?

1. Develop a marketing mindset

Engage the whole business, from leaders to support staff in thinking customer, markets, outside-in.

2. Set the strategic business agenda

Use market, customer and innovation platforms to be driving force of business strategy and decision-making.

3. Champion the customer

Champion customer insight, needs, propositions, experiences and relationships across the business.

4. Innovate the business

Encourage innovation in every part of the business, bringing together teams to drive strategic change.

5. Drive profitable growth

Work with strategy and sales colleagues to target and drive the best growth opportunities, profitably.

6. Become the next CEO

By stepping up to the strategic, innovative and commercial agendas you are well positioned for promotion.

Concept 14.3 MARKETING CEOS

Marketers are increasingly the engine and hub of the business. While today's CEO must also manage the boardroom and investors, he or she increasingly relies on the marketer more than any other function to strategically and operationally drive the business forwards.

Marketing-based leaders are today's organizational lynchpins.

Much is made of marketers not being 'on the board'. This really is a red herring. Indeed, the main board of a public company is increasingly the domain of non-executive directors, except for the necessary attendance of the CEO and finance director. As the Higgs review into corporate governance argued, directors are primarily there to bring a different perspective to the table, to provide a more impartial view, checks and balances, achieved through detachment from managing the business. Higgs therefore encourages more non-exec and fewer exec board members.

What is most important is that boards have a suitable market orientation, that they understand customers and competitiveness, market and customer dynamics, achieved through clearer articulation of plans and performance, injecting more customer insight and creative thinking into their discussions and strategic plans, and giving them the confidence that the marketing leader is actively ensuring their delivery across the business.

Companies would do well to look to marketers to increase the diversity, skills and quality of their non-executive team. Indeed, becoming a non-exec director of another organization might be an excellent way in which senior marketers can learn about corporate governance, and develop themselves for future roles.

Indeed, companies would do well to look to marketers as their next CEO.

Whereas CEOs traditionally have come from a financial or operational background more attuned to safe, steady-state commercial and operational management, companies need more than this in their leaders today. Marketers need to address their common weaknesses, and indeed the perception of these. They must show that they really can be strategic and commercial, collaborative and holistic, that they have the essential talents to steer organizations forwards in complex markets, clarifying direction and focus, unlocking the power of brands and innovation, inspiring people to successfully navigate their way through the fog.

We have already found that companies led by CEOs with a marketing background typically achieve significantly better returns to their shareholders.

Of course, they also need to recognize that CEO roles are not just CMO roles with higher salaries and more power. The additional responsibilities could easily deflect the marketing CEO from also bringing their unique talents to bear – to lead the whole business, not just its marketing activities, to manage costs and revenues, to manage upwards to the chairman and boardroom, to take responsibility for everything from investor relations to property, employee relations and health and safety.

The secret in being a CEO is to recognize that you don't need to do everything yourself, or even to be best at everything. Responsibility is key, but then gathering a great team of people around you, many of who will be more intelligent and experienced in their fields than you could ever be, and ensuring that they work individually and collectively to achieve the business objectives.

In addition to all the more conventional requirements, the marketing CEO is likely to bring the unique attributes and skills that are necessary to lead more effectively:

- Articulate a compelling vision of the future.

- Champion and role model the corporate brand.

- Define market-driven business priorities.

- Ensure that the strategy is market-driving.

- Connect the best ideas and initiatives internally.

- Inspire people through ideas and vision.

Their added value is in bringing a different perspective to the organization, the way in which its many components are coordinated and connected. Marketers can bring a personality to the organization that is often missing in the pursuit of business results and corporate governance. They understand and can easily reflect the brand of the organization, be its human face. Typically, as good communicators, they can articulate visions and strategies, priorities and performance in more human, engaging and inspiring ways.

It is perhaps not surprising that some of the best-known marketing-oriented CEOs have grown their businesses as entrepreneurs – from Steve Jobs at Apple to Charles Dunstone at the Carphone Warehouse, from Richard Branson at Virgin to Phil Knight at Nike. These people intuitively understand their markets and customers, have often single-handedly driven their organizations forwards, and defined their brands in their self-image.

Entrepreneurs are natural marketers who probably never had the patience for big company theory, but they are also smart commercial managers who understand the challenge of finance. They therefore often make the best marketers today. Indeed, the entrepreneurs who are able to take their organizations from start-ups to multinationals are often marketers who can see these bigger challenges and opportunities.

Of course, not every great marketer will make a great CEO, nor will every marketer want to take on these broader and different responsibilities. However, marketers would be exceptional CEOs, and it is important that marketing gains the reputation and credibility to achieve business leadership, whether it is by influence from their functional position or by leadership in name as well as deed.

Inspiration 14.4 MEG WHITMAN

Meg Whitman is a classic marketer who became one of the world's most admired CEOs.

Whitman has been President and CEO of eBay since March 1998. Born in 1956, married to a neurosurgeon, and with two kids, she was recruited by Pierre Omiyhar to implement his vision of the world's leading online marketplace. She is known as one of the most influential and successful American businesswomen of her time.

She grew up in Cold Spring Harbor, Long Island, and after high school attended Princeton University, where she earned a degree in economics in 1977. She completed her education with an MBA from Harvard Business School.

She began her career working at Procter & Gamble from 1979 to 1981, when she built her experience in brand management. She then spent eight years working for the consulting firm Bain and Company, eventually becoming a vice-president.

From 1989 to 1992 she was at the Walt Disney Company, where she ended up as the senior vice-president of marketing for the Disney Consumer Products Division. Whitman then moved to Stride Rite where she was responsible for the launch of the highly successful Munchkin baby shoe line and the repositioning of the Stride Rite brand and retail stores.

She became CEO of Florists Transworld Delivery, the world's largest floral products company. While there, she oversaw its transition from a florist-owned association to a for-profit, privately owned company. She left to lead Hasbro's Preschool Division, responsible for global management and marketing of two of the world's best-known children's brands, Playskool and Mr Potato Head.

Fortune magazine ranked her one of the 25 most powerful people in business in 2004, and *Business Week* has included her on its list of the 25 most powerful business managers annually since 2000. She is also a non-executive director of Procter & Gamble and Gap.

Application 14.4 LEADING THE BUSINESS

What does the CEO actually do? Why is a marketing mindset essential to the role? How do they embrace an outside-in approach to leadership? What does a marketing CEO do differently from an effective CMO?

1. Clarify the role of the CEO

Understand your role as the CEO, and how it is different from your senior colleagues, the chairman and board.

2. Define direction

Define corporate strategy and direction, targeting the best opportunities, and defining the business priorities.

3. Allocate resources

Allocate resources across the business including people and budgets, ensuring people have the right tools to succeed.

4. Inspire people

Inspire people to see possibilities, to innovative, be competitive, energized by customers, and living the brand.

5. Empower experts

Empower your managers to make decisions and deliver results, trusting their judgement and expertise.

6. Engage stakeholders

Ensure effective delivery, compliance and achievement of business results, engaging boards and investors.

What happens after what happens next?

'We are in the twilight of a society based on data. As information and intelligence becomes the domain of computers, society will place more value on the one human ability that cannot be automated: emotion – will affect everything from our purchasing decisions to how we work with others. Companies will thrive on the basis of the stories and myths. Companies will need to understand that their products are less important than their stories.'

Rolf Jensen

'Every man is, in certain respects:

a. like all men

b. like some other men

c. like no other man.'

C. Kluckholm and H. Murry

Genius marketers work in 'double time', creating the future while delivering today, making everyday decisions, taking both small and significant actions that have fundamental implications for the short and long term.

They connect the competing demands of evolving markets and improving services, they combine the extreme objectives of delivering more sales while building brands for tomorrow, and they do this by aligning a more intelligent and imaginative approach to their marketing.

They can only achieve this if they have confidence in where they are going, as well as where they are.

More intelligent futures	More imaginative futures
Insights. We still treat people as averages, and are far from truly understanding them as individuals.	**Ideas.** Insights are not enough. It is the power of original thought that will differentiate and transform business.
Brands. There are few great brands out there that truly reflect and inspire, energize and enable people.	**People.** Business has not yet found out how to unlock the true emotional force of human beings, inside or outside.
Companies. Most companies are still not genuinely customer focused, working outside in for the long term.	**Communities.** People want to be with people like them, to learn and work, to meet and get the most out of their lives.

Each decade becomes known for something, whether it be music and fashion, politics or economics, science or technology. The eighties marked the fall of communism, and the nineties, the rise of our connected world. Since 2000 there has probably been more change than we can yet label. The labelling of an era is in itself a challenge in making sense of it.

Mark Twain said that 'history doesn't repeat itself but it often rhymes'. Cycles can reveal secrets as to how our world will evolve, short and long cycles that influence our markets. Understanding how the future is likely to evolve will determine how we should act now.

We can already see many of the trends that have increasing impact on our conventional markets and ways of marketing. At a market level some of the biggest changes are likely to be around:

- **Borderless economies** – the economy will become more global and connected as expertise evolves in different areas – the consumer products now manufactured in China were often dreamed up in America, interpreted into applications in Europe, and continued east for production. Sony will look west for its inspiration while Ford will look east for productivity. Marketers must reconfigure their roles to understand how, where and when they can add most value to global value chains.

- **Power bases** – nation states will become less relevant economically, socially or politically than corporate states and other virtual communities. From global brands to fashion design, sports teams to media groups, campaigning bodies to terrorist groups, being global and virtual is more powerful than physical location. The World Economic Forum will mean more than the United Nations, Microsoft will be more powerful than the USA, sports more than government elections. Marketing needs to embrace these new power bases.

- **Digital domains** – information becomes more location-specific, easy to embed in any objects, enabling greater access, and tracking and more relevant knowledge. From IPv6, the new Internet protocol with sensors easy to digest, to nano-technologies creating machines made from molecules, what currently requires a laptop to access will soon be all around us. Location-based marketing enables new channels and time-based moments to drive personalization and relevance like never before.

Consumers are changing attitudes and behaviours too:

- **Lifestyle fusion** – more people will flex their jobs to balance their personal interests, and more will choose jobs that enable them to mix these interests with what they do. Ageing baby boomers are still in their creative prime but want to travel and enjoy life, to mix rock music and classical concerts, sportswear and designer fashion. Business will evolve employment models to embrace the best talent, more flexibly on their terms. Marketing must recognize these new macro motivations of business and consumers.

- **Global intimacy** – mobility means that we are part of an increasingly transient populace, travelling regularly for leisure or work. Technology enables intimacy, bringing people with common issues or objectives together, be it doctors providing remote diagnoses across the world, lifetime education with far more diverse subject areas, or personal friendships emerging online where we may have never met people we know best. Marketing can enable this migration through trusted brands as virtual communities.

- **Genetic segmentation** – the rise of personalized screening will enable us to categorize people by their predispositions to certain illnesses and cures, or intelligence and social preferences. As well as the implications for genetic modification, knowing what you are and what you are not will drive new communities of self-interest, lobby groups and social classes. Marketing should tap into this emergent segmentation, with innovation and propositions that engage more personal and profound motivations.

And businesses are changing their structures and roles:

- **Knowledge havens** – India's rise as a technology power is relentless; Singapore is a learning hub, Hong Kong is an eastern gateway. Off-shoring of intangible assets for tax benefits results in the best IP-based teams of multinational companies for brand management or technology research, being found in Swiss mountain villages or Caribbean Islands. Marketers will become more valuable as the intangible asset builders of business, while needing to avoid becoming remote tax exiles.

- **Creative hotspots** – as machines mature in their connectivity and conversations, the workplace will evolve to tap into personal expression and thought. In the same way that technology hubs emerge, entire cities are also reinvented as creative hotspots. Traditional notions of ad agencies will fuse with innovation and design, media and the arts, business and society, profit-making and charitable. Marketers must be at the heart of these hotspots, tapping into talent, with new forms of collaboration for innovation and communication, harnessing the best ideas before anyone else.

- **Customer companies** – as branded companies recognize that their brands are about 'you not me', they also conclude that the majority of their operational activities are non-core to their roles and, indeed, a more virtual basis for partnering with others offers more agility, better customer relationships, and focus on the best opportunities for value creation. Co-creation of new products, customization of existing products, and community building around brands all create customer companies. As customer aspirations rise higher, companies bring exclusivity to the masses, content in all its forms through a diversity of media, a new interpretation of 'value', and recognition that customers are fundamentally in control.

Inspiration 15.1 NIKE

Nike's mission is 'to bring inspiration and innovation to every athlete in the world'.

Bill Bowerman, the legendary track and field coach at the University of Oregon, further defined Nike's definition of an athlete: *'If you have a body, you are an athlete.'*

Phil Knight and Bowerman set out from sleepy Eugene, Oregon, to achieve Nike's mission through 'the service of human potential', which in sporting terms means helping every person to achieve their potential in their chosen field.

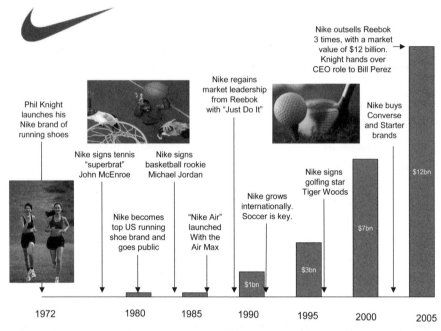

Nike outsells Reebok
3 times, with a market
value of $12 billion.
Knight hands over
CEO role to Bill Perez

Nike regains
market leadership
from Reebok
with "Just Do It"

Phil Knight
launches his
Nike brand of
running shoes

Nike buys
Converse
and Starter
brands

Nike signs tennis
"superbrat"
John McEnroe

Nike signs
basketball rookie
Michael Jordan

Nike signs
golfing star
Tiger Woods

$12bn

Nike grows
internationally.
Soccer is key.

Nike becomes
top US running
shoe brand and
goes public

"Nike Air"
launched
With the
Air Max

$7bn

$3bn

$1bn

1972   1980   1985   1990   1995   2000   2005

Source: Data from nikebiz.com

Nike is now the world's leading sports and fitness company, a key player in every sport, in every corner of the world, employing around 25,000 people directly, and around 1 million more indirectly, all dedicated to the inspiration and innovation of athletes.

Of course, its growth has not been all plain sailing. Most significantly, perhaps, were the negative perceptions of how it ran its Asian manufacturing operations, which Nike has since addressed and, because of its concern, it is perhaps now one of the world's leading sustainable businesses and ethical employers.

Nike's brand, manifest in its 'swoosh' logo, has grown to represent attitude and excellence in the world of sport, standing alone as a brand identifier in recent years. Nike also deploys a wide range of sub-brands to be more relevant to specific audiences – such as Nike Jordan, Nike Woman, Nike Golf, Nike Running, Nike Football and many more.

Perhaps the marketing masterstroke of Phil Knight was when he signed up basketball superstar Michael Jordan. Celebrity endorsement was a new concept, certainly for sports, yet the power of the sports star in reflecting excellence and aspiration is unmatched. This was not simply a cosmetic agreement; Nike works closely with its endorsed athletes to help them achieve their best performances, and in return the athletes work with Nike to innovate new products, and support major events and marketing initiatives.

Nike is probably also as well known for its classic provocations, advertising slogans that capture the essence of the brand, what it believes in and seeks to do for people. With the help of its local ad agency, Wieden and Kennedy, which has itself grown into a globally admired player from its Oregon roots, and many others, Nike is admired for its evocative print and television ads, its product brands, its taglines.

However, Nike has also recognized that its brand cannot be all things to all people, and has both acquired and grown its own portfolio of brands in recent years. Kids are unlikely to label anything cool that their parents think is cool; therefore, Nike uses the Hurley surfwear brand to reach the teen lifestyle.

Similarly, to be taken seriously in the office or upmarket leisure markets, Nike uses Cole Haan as a more formal footwear brand. More recently, Converse, the legendary US brand, joined the Nike stable, while the Exeter Brands Group was created to develop low-cost lines such as Starter and Shaq to be sold through large retailers.

Nike's hometown is Beaverton, not far from the university campus where Knight first gained his thirst for sporting excellence. When you walk up the road to their World Campus, you are shadowed by god-like statues of their most famous athletes – from Michael Jordan to Tiger Woods, Alberto Salazar to Joan Benoit, Carl Lewis to Sebastian Coe – leading to the Mia Hamm building.

The Nike Sports Research Lab, known as 'the kitchen', lies at the philosophical and physical heart of the brand, the business and the campus. Enter the lab and you are confronted by 13,000 square feet of Nike design expertise. There's a hardwood basketball court, artificial soccer pitch, and 70 metres of synthetic running track.

There are usually a handful of Nike sporting stars on hand to help the innovation process. Perhaps French footballer Thierry Henry will be kicking a ball, captured by high-speed video cameras recording 1000 frames per second. Or marathon world record holder Paula Radcliffe will be pounding the treadmill, as Nike scientists distinguish her kinematics (motion analysis of her foot) from her kinetics (the ground reaction forces and loading rates).

Every technology from muscle scanners to breath analysers, graphic design systems to thermal imaging devices are deployed in the pursuit of sporting excellence. Nike is about product leadership that enables its consumers to perform at their highest level. Everything from the structure of shoes, to the durability of textiles, the comfort and aesthetic appearance of its products matter. Nike is not about compromise, it's about breaking barriers, always at the frontier between what is possible and what is currently impossible.

Nike is constantly searching for the edge, to move forwards, to evolve or, as it states in its book of *Nike Maxims*, issued to all Nike people, to 'amplify what's good, change what isn't':

From	To
elite sports	active life
big	big and strong
resource hoarding	resource sharing
slow	fast
process quicksand	process agility
innovation	innovation (cubed)
athlete icons	athletic heroes
exploitive	supportive
no and maybe	maybe and yes
advertising	communicating
isolation	alliance
brand awareness	brand respect
complacent	aggressive
consensus	courage

Source: *Nike Maxims*

Nike's annual report to shareholders captures the essence of a genius brand. Rather than being dominated by figures and graphs, the report is articulated in pictures and stories. The goal itself is not to make the sportswear or deliver the best returns to shareholders (Nike has more than doubled the S&P growth over the last decade), although these might well be the result. There is a bigger, more inspiring and more relentless goal:

> 'Speed: our idea of a good investment ... The margin between first and fourth in modern 100m races has been as little as .005 of a second ... Our calculations tell us that Nike Swift apparel can deliver a 1.13% improvement in times.

> Nike Swift technology took us 36,000 hours to develop. So it wasn't all that fast in development. But it's fast everywhere else. And it's only one of the many, many things

we do to help athletes go faster. To a lot of athletes 1.13% more speed could be the difference of a lifetime.

'To us it's just good business.'

The report describes the performance of a genius brand, one that is driven from the outside in, one that has a disciplined focus on what matters most for customers and shareholders, but with a creative spirit to do it differently and better. Phil Knight concluded his final report to shareholders with the anecdote:

'Nike remains a kid at heart. Just a few weeks back, on the Michael Johnson Track at World Headquarters, we celebrated the 50th anniversary of Roger Bannister and his royal performance as the first to crack the 4-minute mile.

Providence was ours that day. Michael Stember won with 3:59.4 – matching exactly the good doctor's time set 50 years earlier ... It was a magical day for more than 2000 screaming Nike employees crowding the track.

This is the Nike that will always be.'

Source: Nike Annual Report 2004

Application 15.1 FUTURE SENSING

How do you make use of the future? How are your markets and customers, business and marketing, likely to evolve in the future? What should you be doing today to prepare for, survive and thrive in that future?

1. Develop a forwards orientation

Culturally encourage a curiosity of, and understanding of your future markets, looking forwards not backwards.

2. Explore the future context

Explore future market scenarios, technologies, environment and society over the next 10–50 years.

3. Explore the future customer

Explore the emerging needs and aspirations, beliefs and behaviours of customers over next 3–10 years.

4. Explore the future business

Explore the future nature of business models, products and channels, partners, and ways of working.

5. Explore the future marketing

Explore new ways of marketing, from memetic viruses to satellite zipping Explore the new ways of marketing.

6. Decide what matters most today

Interpret what is most certain, and what you should start now. Act today with the potential of tomorrow in mind.

Concept 15.1 INTELLIGENT MARKETS

Marketing must harness the power of intelligent markets, not only markets connected by always-on technologies, but also markets that can increasingly think. Intelligent markets can mobilize themselves as communities with a common cause, with the self-initiating structures that help them to find their own structure, order and power.

In the past, markets were made up of many individuals who each had a separate transaction or relationship with a company, or at least its brand. Imagine the millions of people who use the same product but don't know each other, or who shop in the same supermarket but never speak. In the past, companies have been the main organizing force within markets, while customers have been somewhat Neanderthal in their isolated, unconnected behaviours.

Markets are increasingly organized and civilized. While there has always been regulators creating rules, encouraging competition, policing undesirable business practices, customers have not themselves had a voice to challenge business, to exert pressure on them, to drive change.

Today we see intelligent markets with more voice and power, not just in terms of being able to buy anything anywhere, to check out the best prices online, and to read about what brands are really like inside, but also the power to make or break the fundamental reputation of brands and the companies that manage them:

- Consumers distrust increasingly sophisticated marketing techniques and react against them. Increasingly intrusive telemarketing has been greeted by their banning by consumers at websites like donotcall.com.

- Blogs have become online soapboxes set up by anybody, and accessible to everybody with one click of the mouse, and they are increasingly vociferous in their commentary of brands. One dissatisfied customer can tell a million others.

- Media commentators can fundamentally influence customer attitudes and behaviours, raising issues fairly or unfairly about organizations or their products, their ethics, their fairness, their reliability, their value.

- Lobby groups are increasingly vocal and professional, covering anything from environmental to political issues, running sophisticated marketing campaigns themselves, often with more ingenuity and impact than a brand's own marketers.

- Technologies can raise issues and create backlashes at alarming speed. Like a computer virus can spread across the world in minutes, so can market forces; brands can turn from heroes to villains within 24 hours.

Marketing needs to work with the changing nature of markets, not against them. Public relations, for example, is a far more sophisticated, all-engaging challenge today than it ever was about column inches in the press. It is about harnessing public opinion, customer perceptions and employee morale as a positive force, respected and engaged. Market research should provide insights into the deeper values and perceptions of customers rather than just their product needs. Customer relationships are about listening and working together to improve what really matters, rather than a one-sided attempt by companies to cajole people into buying more.

RFID (radio frequency identification devices) drive a whole range of possibilities of how marketing could be more intelligent in response to technology-enabled markets. The billions of devices now under production could revolutionize our shopping experiences, enabling electronic wallets to replace the need for checkouts, sending individualized incentives to your mobile phone as your browse the aisles, tracking goods purchased to their new homes and, at the moment of disposal, flagging the need for replenishment. But, of course, it could go well beyond this, both in terms of the ways in which suppliers could track and incentivize customers and in transforming customer experiences in everything from personalized menus in restaurants to supply chain efficiencies and precision-timed logistics.

But it is the rise of the intelligent customer that is most interesting. Customers are beginning to realize their power through price comparisons, customization, and through demanding fundamental solutions to their problems – on their terms. We are likely to see the rise of 'gateway' brands, as opposed to 'ingredient' brands, and 'customized' rather than 'productized' companies that fundamentally act on behalf of the customer.

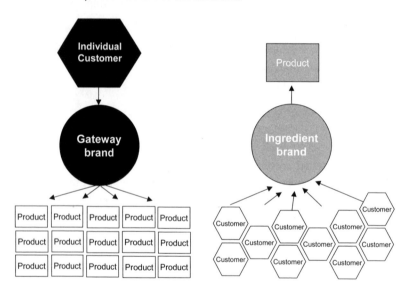

Gateway brands don't have any products but they do know their customers deeply, understanding their needs and issues and then going out to find the right ingredients to solve their problems, impartially negotiating the best deals with ingredient brands to create the unique perfect solution to the customer's problem. Gateway brands are totally on their customers' side. Their brands reflect their values and their processes are driven by customers who come to them rather than waiting to be bombarded with irrelevant promotions.

They may seem a little like intermediaries, but gateways are the principals – they are the only brand the customer sees, cares about and trusts. They will be information rich, with customer service at their core. Their expertise is in problem solving and relationship building. They will be the power hubs of the intelligent markets, redefining the power bases, the market structures and the sources of value.

Inspiration 15.2 NOKIA

Nokia is at the forefront of our rapidly evolving, global and connected society. Its vision, its mobile technologies, and their innovative applications, are changing the way we think and learn, communicate and transact at an unbelievable pace.

Yet the origins of Finland's largest company, and the world's largest communications equipment manufacturer, is far more grounded in nature. Indeed, Nokia's story is a fabulous one of business evolution and adaptation.

Nokia was founded in 1865 as a humble wood-pulp mill by Fredrik Idestam. The company expanded to produce rubber products in the Finnish town of Nokia, and soon embraced its name. At the end of the Second World War, Nokia acquired Finnish Cable Works, a producer of telephone cables.

In the 1970s Nokia became even more involved in the telecoms industry by developing the Nokia DX 200, a digital switch for telephone exchanges. In the 1980s, Nokia introduced a range of personal computers called Mikromikko, which later merged with ICL, and began developing mobile phones for the NMT network.

However, the company ran into serious financial problems in the 1990s and streamlined its manufacturing of mobile phones, mobile phone infrastructure and other telecommunications areas, divesting itself of other items such as televisions and personal computers.

Nokia now sees itself as a multimedia player, recognizing the potential of the handset to be much more than a phone – it is an information and entertainment, computing and commerce device too. While it openly admits to losing some ground in recent years, to the challenge of the likes of Samsung and Motorola, Nokia is refocusing its efforts to regain leadership.

Indeed, it sees the market moving in cycles of industrial-based innovation, more grey and cornered, technical and rational, through to more design-led styling, more colourful and smooth, human and emotional. The implication is that Nokia is preparing to take us, aesthetics and all, into a new generation of more intimate communication devices.

Perhaps Nokia succumbed to what it sees as some of paradoxes of market success, such as:

- As markets mature, the less engaged customers become. They accept and expect you, rather than being thrilled by the newness.

- The more popular you become, the more difficult it is to be cool. Ubiquity does not sit well with stating your individuality.

- The larger you become, the less personal you can be. Yet at the same time consumers are looking for deeper relationships with their brands.

Nokia's brand is clearly and simply about 'connecting people' and the possibilities that better connections enable.

Application 15.2 BRAND BLOGGING

Blogs are everywhere as individuals seize the platforms and freedom of the Internet to express their views, instantly and direct. Brands should be part of these conversations too – leading the bloggers, engaging them in constructive dialogue. How can you use blogs to make your brand mean and matter more to people every day?

1. Create a brand blog

Create an online 'blog' for your brand,
a dedicated website first-hand log that
is informative and updated daily.

2. Develop a brand personality

Develop the blog with personality,
articulate ideas in simple language, and
be transparent about your issues too.

3. Offer a view on the world

Talk about the world of your customers,
take a perspective on their issues,
add insight and provocation.

4. Address your anti-blogs

Encourage and respond to blogs that
are anti your brand, encourage dialogue
and turn criticism into opportunities.

5. Add more value to people

Become part of your customers' world
adding value beyond transactions, and
connecting with them in new ways.

6. Stand up for what you believe

Become a thought leader, campaigner
and voice of your customers' world.
Be bold and brave in your beliefs.

Concept 15.2 INSIGHTFUL BRANDS

Brands need to do more for people. Brands are still largely used as the identities that distinguish one similar proposition from another. This is commodity thinking. Brands need to do more than tell the difference; they need to reach out to people, to be there for longer than the transaction, and offer more than their functional benefits.

- Brands that define you.

- Brands that people can hang on to.

- Brands that add value.

- Brands that provoke and inspire.

- Brands with original thought.

- Brands that do something extra.

- Brands built on humanity and humility.

- Brands to live your life by.

Brands are about people, not products; they bring together communities as well as companies, reflecting the aspirations as well as the motivations of their audiences, educating rather than just delivering, connecting people with a common interest or aspiration, doing the unexpected rather than just meeting expectations and stirring emotions as strong as those when you fall in love.

Yet most brands don't do this. And don't work.

There are significant implications too. Insightful brands with the power to cut through the noise and complexity of markets to truly engage their audiences, and also the power to drive attitudes and behaviours that result in more purchases at higher prices, cannot make compromises.

Indeed, compromise is the biggest weakness of brands today. They try to be nice to everyone. They try to meet the needs of everyone, young and old, rich and poor, mainstream and marginal. When they compromise they lose their insight, their relevance, their uniqueness, their power.

Great brands polarize people. Some people love them, others hate them.

But that's OK. As long as the people you want to love them do. Of course, to gain acceptance and trust, a brand has to deliver its promise, in every way, every time. This requires clarity inside and out, alignment and passion. It also means that the same brand has to engage and inspire customers, employees and shareholders. And because great brands polarize, it means that not everyone will enjoy working with, or want to invest in, a great brand.

To succeed in the future, brands need clarity of purpose, the strength of their convictions and belief in themselves, as well a bit more humility. Leaders need this too, to stand by the brand, to accept the knocks alongside the acclaim. Indeed, organizations, leaders and brands are inextricably linked. Brands need to come to life, with a human face, delivered by real people, to succeed or fail depending on their attitudes and behaviours every day.

Indeed, brands that are about customers, rather than suppliers, will bring together people who share similar values and aspirations. These people are likely to want to be with each other too, which was never the case when all they had was common product purchases in common.

Brands that reflect customers create communities, they act as the organizing force for bringing like-minded people together, typically around the applications for which the brand is associated. Teflon could bring together cookery fanatics, Fisons could bring together keen gardeners, and Castrol could bring together car fanatics.

Indeed, customers are never likely to want to have relationships (in the true sense) with companies, but they may want to have relationships with each other. Communities are dynamic structures that evolve over time as they normalize around common values and beliefs, structures and conventions, and gradually become more democratic and civilized.

Brands can help their related communities to take shape, to provide resources and structures, as well as the values and beliefs, acting as the functional and emotional hub of the community. The brand remains highly visible and relevant to the community. It doesn't need to force itself on it – in fact, the opposite applies. Customers can recognize whom to thank, and conveniently turn to when they need something.

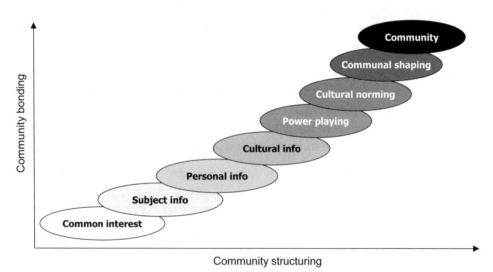

Hewlett-Packard created the online HyPe gallery that brings together graphic designers with a passion for their art, providing them with a platform to exhibit, meet, perform and share their ideas and issues. In some cases it has even provided a springboard to commercial success. Of course, the designers know what the big H and big P mean, and what they can do; the difference is that they now want to go to HP to find out more, and they are now more likely to choose them, and recommend them to others too.

Brand communities are built on brands about you. Forget campaigns, channels and relationships – with some thought and action, this is a better way to engage people.

Inspiration 15.3 DYSON

How often have you said 'I could have designed that better myself'? James Dyson does, constantly. He likes to make things work better. Since 1970 he and his research team have developed products that have achieved over $5 billion sales worldwide. After early success with the 'Ballbarrow', a wheelbarrow with a ball rather than a wheel, Dyson turned his attention to the suction of vacuum cleaners.

In 1983 – after 5127 prototypes – Dyson emerged with the first bagless vacuum cleaner, based on his studies of cyclone towers generating a centrifugal force more than 100,000 times greater than gravity, removing even the tiniest powder particles of dirt.

The first Dysons were actually sold to Japan under the G Force brand, and became a status symbol, selling for $2000 each. Using the revenues from the Japanese licence, a decade later Dyson opened a research centre and factory in Wiltshire, in the west of England.

Scientists worked on the cyclone technology until they had achieved a further 45% improved suction. Dyson also wanted to create a more intelligent vacuum cleaner, so he installed three on-board computers and 50 more sensory devices, and 60,000 hours of work later, the range of Dyson cleaners as we know them today was launched.

These development years tested Dyson's resolve and, almost bankrupt, he struggled to keep up the ownership of his patents during the long time to market. Indeed, 1999 saw his landmark victory over Hoover, which he claimed had tried to imitate his invention and infringed his patents.

After 14 years in the making, Dyson products are now sold in 22 countries worldwide, as well being exhibited in most of the world's design museums. Indeed, it was a fortuitous appearance on the hit TV show *Friends* that established Dyson as the must-have household accessory across America, and secured the inventor's success.

Application 15.3 PASSION BRANDING

How can your brand truly engage with its community? Or, indeed, how can it create a community out of people's passions that have never been connected? How can you reinterpret brands based on what matters most deeply to customers? How can this re-energize the business? How can brands become positive structures of society?

1. Discover your customer passion

Work with your customers, watch them, talk to them, join them to understand what they really deeply care about.

2. Reflect how you enable it

What is it about your brand, proposition or solutions that really matters and connects with their customers' passion?

3. Rearticulate your brand appeal

Rearticulate your brand to share the passion of chosen customers (being special to all of them is impossible).

4. Re-energize your own people

Re-energize your employees with this sense of purpose, building a new culture that connects with customers.

5. Re-engage with customers

Redefine your propositions, solutions and experiences to deliver this new focus practically and innovatively.

6. Bring them together in new ways

Great brands bring people together, building new communities of interest, redefining brands as social structures.

Concept 15.3 INSPIRED MARKETERS

Genius marketing is only achievable if marketers have the confidence and capabilities, ambition and inspiration to make it happen. These marketers need to be able to raise themselves, their thinking and doing, in order to exploit the complex markets intelligently, rather than be subservient to them, to develop insightful brands rather than settle for the mainstream, functionalized sameness. What we all hate.

Inspired marketers:

- See what everybody has seen ... but think what nobody has thought.

- Have the same skills and tools ... but do what nobody else has done.

- Face identical challenges ... but succeed like nobody has before.

Anybody can achieve this. The Russian scientists were wrong: there is no such thing as a genius gene. Thomas Edison was right: it really is about 99% hard work, guided by a little inspiration. It's the inspiration that matters, be it finding a role model who shows that the extraordinary is possible, the catalyst to push you into doing what you've just never quite got round to doing, or the flash of insight that opens up a whole new stream of thinking.

Whatever the source of inspiration, the hard work matters too. It's about recognizing that the extremes in the way we work are complementary rather than competitive. There is no such person as a purely left brain or right brain person, one who is creative and another who is analytical. These are just excuses for what we know best, or have been led to believe matters most.

Genius is about embracing the extremes, and finding positive reinforcement.

It's about combining right and left brain thinking so that the creativity enhances the analysis, the intelligence stretches the imagination. It connects the opportunities that come outside-in with the capabilities that work inside-out. It's about finding the solutions that deliver more successful results today and tomorrow.

Genius marketers embrace the extremes with curiosity and confidence, with the willingness and talent to combine such diverse disciplines as:

- Cash flow analysis and memetic messaging.

- Scenario planning and media integration.

- Social anthropology and investor relations.

- Regression analysis and creative disruption.

- Strategic thinking and collaborative team play.

Genius marketers are inspired by contradiction, by problems, by paradox, by the unknown, by what doesn't yet make sense.

They are 'frontier people' living on the edge between what is perceived to be possible and impossible, between markets and business, between customers and products, between today and tomorrow.

It is perhaps not surprising that entrepreneurs often make the best marketers, with the intuitive passion and vision to do what hasn't been done, without the comfort and conventions that surround marketers in most big companies. Richard Branson and Michael Dell, Steve Jobs and Phil Knight.

Big companies need to embrace more entrepreneurial marketers and leaders too, giving them the space and respect to try new things, to challenge the conventions of yesterday, to create a new space to operate in. This brings with it inevitable risks, as well as rewards. Conventional wisdom says that the people who start companies are rarely the people to lead them in maturity. However, these four disprove that belief, although they are all smart enough to surround themselves with the right mix of conventional and unusual talents.

The inspired marketer's challenge is not the theory. There are plenty of models and techniques for marketing, and indeed most academic research appears to get stuck in the detail rather than move forwards. The inspired marketer's challenge is not operational either. Doing the wrong things well is probably worse than just doing the wrong things. It needs the right thinking and new ways of doing. To embrace the extremes, to take people with you, and deliver extraordinary results.

Like the burning rubber on Bill Bowerman's waffle iron, genius is the inspiration to think the impossible, and the confidence to make it profitable.

Inspiration 15.4 INNOCENT

'Sometimes it's the simple things that make you happy. Waking up on a sunny morning. Folding a map correctly the first time. Beating your Mum at arm wrestling. Or just drinking a smoothie. Our smoothies contain only the purest and freshest fruit. No concentrates, preservatives, or additives of any kind. And they're made and delivered daily. We could try to make it more complicated but that would mean less time to sleep and eat. Two more simple things that we hold dear.'

Label on one of Innocent's Pure Fruit Smoothies

Innocent is the young but fast growing 'tasty little drinks' company from London, founded by three friends – Rich, Jon and Adam – who gave up their jobs in the worlds of advertising and consulting in order to pursue a healthier lifestyle.

Back in the summer of 1998 the friends were struggling to get their idea off the ground. They had developed some great recipes but had so far failed to attract investors to the idea of a drinks business based entirely on pure, premium, perishable fruit.

They decided to put their fate in the hands of customers. With £500 worth of fruit, they set up a stall at a local music festival to make and sell their smoothies. They also put out two bins with a sign saying 'Do you think we should give up our jobs to make these smoothies?' The 'Yes' bin filled up far quicker than the 'No' bin, and they resigned from their jobs the next day.

While natural fruit is the heart of their business, being natural – or innocent – informs every aspect of what they do. From the choice of stationery and their offices at Fruit Towers to the cheery person who greets you if you call the Banana Phone.

As their business has grown from 3 to 60 people, making 80,000 smoothies every day, with a turnover of close to £20 million and a market share of just over 50%, they still focus on the detail. 'Sell by' dates on bottle tops are replaced by 'Enjoy by' dates, and while 25% of their plastic bottles are recyclable, they say 'we're working on the rest'. Thickies (yoghurt and fruit drinks) now complement the original smoothies, alongside a range of Juicy Water.

The similarities to Ben and Jerry's, the ice cream pioneers from Vermont who eventually sold up to Unilever for $326 million, are all there – delivery vans dressed as cows and grass meadows, a charitable foundation, a live jazz festival called 'Fruitstock'.

However, there is much more to Innocent. They really are inspired by what they do, and their company is an inspiration too.

Of course, they're a business, and fully aware of the commercial and competitive realities of the world. However, their passion is 100% on making 'really nice drinks'. The pocket-size, and cartoon-illustrated 'company rule book' captures the spirit of the brand in eight 'rules':

1   **Work hard, play hard.** 'Just think of innocent drinks as your one healthy habit – like going to the gym but without the communal showers afterwards.' You can always visit their own gym at innocentgym.co.uk.

2   **Always ask an expert.** 'When we started this business we didn't know anything about it, and we still don't know that much, so we just ask customers what they want.'

3   **Thou shalt not commit adultery.** 'We call our drinks innocent because we refuse to adulterate them in any way … 100% pure crushed fruit; no concentrated juice, no additives; no nothing.'

4   **Have global aspirations**. 'We want to make the best drinks in the world, ever. That means getting the best ingredients in the world … Alphonso mangoes from India, Queen pineapples from Vietnam. Vanilla beans from Indonesia.'

5   **An apple a day** '… keeps the doctor away, so imagine what 3/4lb of fruit will do. The director of the Centre for Nutrition and Food Safety says "Innocent drinks are very good for you". Doesn't mince his words, that professor.'

6   **Don't believe the hype.** 'We've won lots of awards for our drinks, but we're going to pretend we haven't ... We just want to produce lovely drinks. And save up for a day out at the seaside.'

7   **Try to keep your work and emotional life separate.** 'It's a good rule, but we're sorry, we can't. We love making drinks, we love drinking them, and we especially love everyone who buys them.'

8   **Don't waste time** '... reading boring bits of literature like this. Life's too short ... However, if you're ever bored you can call us on our Banana Phone, or e-mail us at iamabitbored@innocentdrinks.co.uk.'

Application 15.4 THE FIVE BALLS

While we have focused largely on the business attributes of a marketing genius, the marketer is clearly an individual, and an inspired marketer derives that energy from all aspects of their life and well-being.

Paula Radcliffe, the world record holder for the marathon, uses the analogy of five balls to reflect on her unbelievable success in obliterating the competition in her first three marathons, knocking almost four minutes off the previous record time. She pushed the boundaries to the limit, training 150 miles per week, lifting weights well beyond her own, jumping into an ice cold bath after each run to help stimulate her blood flow. Yet all this seemed wasted when she failed to finish the Olympic marathon in Athens.

In trying to rationalize her excellence, but misfortune, she mused that life is about juggling five balls in the air. They are health, family, friends, integrity and career. However, these balls are not the same; the important thing to remember is that the career ball is made of rubber but the others are more fragile.

You can take more risks with the rubber ball. You may try to throw it through higher and higher hoops because if you do drop it, it will eventually bounce back. Normally, this ball does not suffer long-term damage. The other four balls need to be looked after more carefully. If you drop one of these it will be damaged and it may even shatter.

In sport, athletes constantly take risks with that career ball, throwing it higher and higher, pushing themselves into the unknown to get an edge on their competitors, to strive for excellence, to realize their potential.

In business, and in striving to become a marketing genius, it is no different. Indeed, Brian Dyson, the CEO of Coca-Cola Enterprises uses the same five balls analogy to inspire his marketers to greater things. He urges his people to recognize and achieve balance in themselves, as a route to achieving personal and marketing excellence. He encourages them thus:

- Don't undermine your worth by comparing yourself with others. It is because we are different that each of us is special. Don't set your goals by what other people deem important. Only you know what is best for you.

- Don't take for granted the things closest to your heart. Cling to them as you would your life, for without them, life is meaningless.

- Don't let your life slip through your fingers by living in the past or for the future. By living your life one day at a time, you live all the days of your life.

- Don't give up when you still have something to give. Nothing is really over until the moment you stop trying.

- Don't be afraid to admit that you are less than perfect. It is this fragile thread that binds us to each other.

- Don't be afraid to encounter risks. It is by taking chances that we learn how to be brave.

- Don't shut love out of your life by saying it's impossible to find. The quickest way to receive love is to give it; the fastest way to lose love is to hold it too tightly: and the best way to keep love is to give it wings.

- Don't run through life so fast that you forget not only where you've been, but also where you are going. Don't forget, a person's greatest emotional need is to feel appreciated.

- Don't be afraid to learn. Knowledge is weightless, a treasure you can always carry easily.

- Don't use time or words carelessly. Neither can be retrieved.

- Life is a journey to be savoured each step of the way.

Radcliffe, for one, has used the story of the five balls in good times and bad – to maintain a sense of balance and humility while all the world went crazy about her stunning world record-breaking performances. She also used them to put failure into perspective and to pick herself up again, in her case by rebuilding her reputation only months later by winning the New York City marathon.

The genie: Becoming a marketing genius

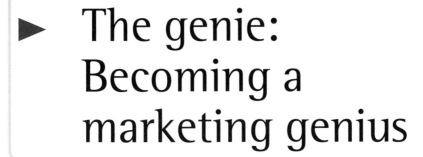

PART 5

The genie: Becoming a marketing genius

'Come to the edge. We might fall.
Come to the edge. It's too high.
Come to the edge.
And they came, and he pushed.
And they flew.'

Christopher Logue

'The moment one definitely commits oneself, then providence moves too. All sorts of things occur to help one that would never otherwise have occurred. A whole stream of events issues from the decisions, raising in one's favour all manner of unforeseen incidents and meetings and material assistance which no man could have dreamed would have come his way. Whatever you can do or dream you can do, begin it. Boldness has genius, power and magic in it. Begin it now.'

Goethe

Diagnostic of a marketing genius

A simple diagnostic approach to understanding how you and your team could achieve 'marketing genius'. Learn where you are now, your strengths and weaknesses, and how to track your progress over time.

The starting point is to recognize the four dimensions in which you need to think more intelligently and imaginatively in order to achieve genius.

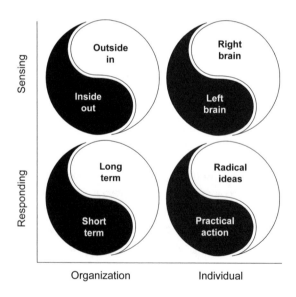

Two of these dimensions require an organizational approach, while the other two are about the individual. In both cases, there are aspects which are more sensory, in that they determine how they understand and are stimulated, and other aspects which are more about the response, how they frame solutions and drive action.

Genius space = Outside in + Inside out

This is the orientation by which an organization senses opportunities.

Does your organization start by thinking outside in, or inside out? What is the starting point for strategies, decision-making and management? Are you more driven by the opportunities and challenges of the market, or the efficiency and improvement of capabilities?

'Genius marketing' requires both orientations; however, outside in is the newer approach and more essential in today's markets.

Genius time = Long term + Short term

This is the timeframe in which an organization responds to and measures success.

Does your organization start by considering its long-term or short-term objectives? What is the relative importance of these timeframes when making decisions and investments, and when measuring and reporting performance? Are you working more to maximize long-term value or short-term profitability?

'Genius marketing' requires both timeframes, although the long term matters most and is the context in which to address the short term.

Genius thinking = Left brain + Right brain

This is the mindset by which an individual senses issues and understands them.

Do you start by thinking rationally or creatively, rigorously analysing specific facts, or do you explore the possibilities and bigger picture? Is your thinking linear and progressive, quantifying issues and opportunities, or is it more holistic and random, seeing the possibilities and bigger picture?

'Genius marketing' requires both mindsets, although the right brain creates the quantum leaps and uniqueness that wouldn't otherwise exist.

Genius doing = Radical ideas + Practical action

This is the action bias with which an individual responds to issues and adds value.

Do you have a bias to ideas or action, to contribute more by the power of your thought, or by the practical application of ideas into effective business action? Is the output of your thinking more visionary, innovative, strategic and long term, or is it more grounded in today, tactical and short term?

'Genius marketing' requires both action types; fundamentally it needs radical new ideas, which can then be implemented successfully.

A marketing genius must embrace the extreme alternatives and achieve new balance in all four of these dimensions. One of the main reasons why marketers might not achieve this is that they focus so much energy on achieving excellence in one extreme, that they lack the energy or capability to also achieve the other.

Balance, as in the famous yin-yang, is about positive reinforcement rather than neutralization; it is about ensuring that $1 + 1 = 3$ rather than $1 - 1 = 0$.

Indeed, the first step is to recognize that the dimensions exist, and the extremes within them. It would be easy, and probably common, to spend a whole career driven by the conventions of business, completely unconscious of these alternatives and needs.

Indeed, 'space–time' was a fundamental principle of Einstein's understanding of the physical world around us; such different aspects of nature as distance and time are actually connected and can trade off, and reinforce, each other.

In genius marketing, marketers need to work to ensure that the 'space–time' context in which their organization does business is in place, as well as taking personal responsibility for how they and each of their colleagues then engage their 'thinking–doing' in order to deliver those extraordinary business results.

Genius marketing

If we now bring together the first two dimensions that work at an organizational rather than individual level, we can explore some of the implications in more detail.

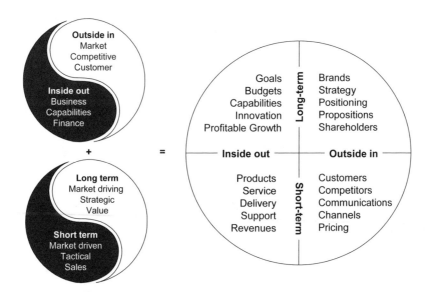

Genius marketing is about working in all four quadrants, although some will be more unusual than others, both for the marketer and the business at large.

Most significantly, genius brings a more outside-in perspective to the short- and long-term thinking of the business. This is why customer focus (OI+ST) is not enough, as markets themselves morph at significant pace and the hotspots of today could be the black holes of tomorrow.

Market shaping strategies (OI+LT) are therefore much more important to organizations today. And while the business as a whole, and the strategy and finance team may well be looking to the future (IO+LT), it is the market perspective that matters most, and where marketing can add significant value, becoming the driver of business direction and focus.

The strategic difference is that future markets are chosen more on the strength of their economic opportunity and brand genetics than the increasingly virtual capabilities of today. When considering the practical marketing actions, to be relevant and valued in today's world, everything from brands to propositions, communications to pricing should start from an external perspective.

Brands (OI+LT) are built over time to reflect the needs and aspirations of chosen audiences, rather than the company or its products. These audiences are more sustaining than the products that service them. Communications (OI+ST) are initiated by the specific needs of customers, within the competitive context of today.

Performance is measured in terms of the long-term value created for stakeholders, most significantly shareholders (OI+LT), although this is only achieved by creating value in a mutually reinforcing cycle for customers, driving improved margins and sustainable growth. Of course, profits still matter (IO+ST), but only as a means to this end, working in double time to deliver today, while creating tomorrow.

Of course, this can only happen if the marketers who drive it can achieve genius too.

Genius marketers

We now connect the second two dimensions, focusing on the way in which the individual senses and responds to business challenges and opportunities.

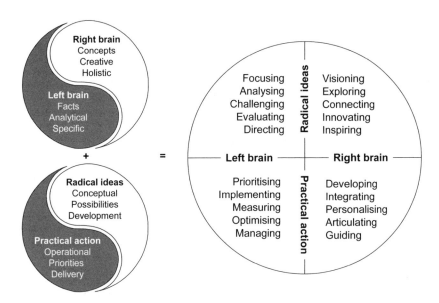

Genius marketers again work in all four quadrants, although their personal capabilities and preferences for work might be in some areas rather than others.

Perhaps even more significant is the importance of focusing on those aspects that people have been conditioned to think – convention suggests that people who are radically creative struggle to make their ideas happen practically, or that highly analytical people could never have an innovative thought in their mind. This is nonsense and, while stereotypes are hard to break, the impact of people who can connect these perceived anomalies will speak for itself.

Of course, there is a question as to whether any one person can ever be good at all of these aspects, or whether it is more about bringing teams together that have the diversity of skills and experiences to cover all the bases.

The real genius marketers, like the most successful entrepreneurs, really can do it all. Not because they necessarily have huge technical experience, but because they appreciate the importance of all dimensions and can make the connections themselves.

Developing market strategies through rigorous analysis (RI+LB) will always be limited by where you limit your context, whereas in fast-changing, blurred markets, adjacent markets rapidly become the same market, and it requires the exploratory mind (RI+RB) to see this bigger picture. Complexity, of course, can be analysed into many components, but if not connected (RI+RB) they will not make much sense.

Success, of course, is only achieved if the radical ideas can be made reality. However, implementation cannot be a standard process (LB+PA) in competitive markets; it requires constant rethinking and creativity. While marketers have perhaps relied too much upon their agencies for their thinking, they now need to take the lead (RB+PA). As marketing gets more multi-faceted, more individualized and more complex itself, then integration matters as much as task execution.

Leadership exists in all quadrants, adding value in different ways in each.

Understanding your potential
As is evident from the previous pages, diagnosing your team and personal potential as a marketing genius has many facets. Indeed, even the most genius of marketers will not succeed if they are unable for whatever reason to influence the organization to embrace this too. A

detailed genius diagnostic for your organization, team and individuals is available, but requires more explanation and support than is realistic to achieve here.

There are 12 attributes against which to profile your team's marketing activities – to map where you are, want to be, then to identify the most significant gaps for improvement (see Marketing Map).

At a personal level you can also evaluate your own marketing actions, to understand how you can add most value today, and where you need to improve or work with somebody who comple-ments you. There are similarly, 12 attributes of marketing genius in which to evaluate yourself and your genius potential (see Marketer Map).

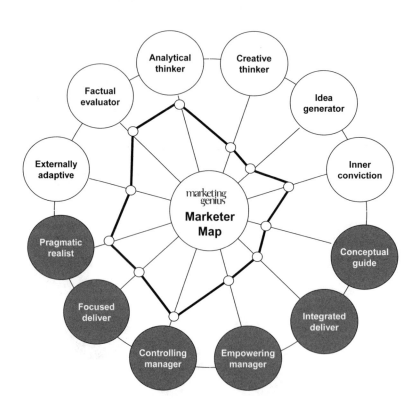

Challenges for the marketing genius

Marketing genius, or rather the complexity and competitiveness of markets today, poses some significant challenges for every business and their marketers.

So how do you apply genius to your strategies and brands, marketing and innovation, communications and experiences?

The strategy challenge

1 *Creating the future.* Marketing must shape the future, as well as delivering today. By sensing the emerging opportunities, market and product innovation drive future revenue streams, and brands and relationships make them more certain.

2 *Making sense of blur.* Marketing must define its context, where and how it is to compete amidst blurred boundaries, evolving regulators and unpredictable change. Market strategy is the starting point.

3 *Doing fewer things better.* Marketing must choose where to focus effort amidst the bewildering array of opportunities, as markets and segments fragment, technologies evolve and ideas proliferate.

4 *Finding the high ground.* Marketing must clarify its difference as a compelling brand proposition, the big idea that cuts through all the noise and imitation, convergence and commoditization.

5 *Making the right decision.* Marketing must make better decisions. Few marketers have clear business criteria on which to make the right decisions strategically or tactically.

The brand challenge

6 *Building power brands.* Marketing must harness the brand in all its manifestations to build awareness and reach, trust and affinity. There are lots of names and logos, but few truly great brands emerging today.

7 *Engaging customer passions.* Marketing must engage human emotions more deeply. Sharing a passion that matters to the specific target audience, helping them define themselves, recognizing you can't be everything to everyone.

8 *Being the real thing.* Marketing must be authentic and transparent. Whatever you say, you must do. In today's transparent world, words and actions are closely watched for consistency and delivery.

9 *Building coherent structures.* Marketing must bring coherence and support to brand architectures. Corporate and operational brands, product and ingredient brands must work better together.

10 *Focus on the value creators.* Marketing must manage market, brand and product portfolios actively, finding and nurturing the value creators, addressing or eliminating the value destroyers, not annually but every day.

The customer challenge

11 *Reverse engineering.* Marketing must market on customer terms. Power has shifted from company to customer, from surplus supply to surplus demand. Customers have high expectations, and want nothing less than perfection.

12 *Everybody is different.* Marketing must target with precision. Customers are more different and individual than ever. Segmentation is complex, needs and behaviours change, targeting is hard.

13 *Speed dating.* Marketing must work out what kind of relationships it really wants. Satisfaction is expected. Loyalty is rare. Customers are promiscuous. Few really want a relationship with you.

14 *Brand communities.* Marketing can tap into passion networks. Consumers don't care about products; they care about themselves – babies, sports, work – helping to build new communities which tap into their passions.

15 *Privacy is an opportunity.* Marketing can turn privacy into a positive. Communication overload and intrusion has created of backlash in use of personal information. However, permission is the start to a dialogue a customer actually wants.

The communications challenge

16 *Campaigns don't work.* Marketing needs to create background awareness without blanket selling. Campaigns are done by companies promoting what they want, when they want. Customers don't buy them any more.

17 *Embrace more media.* Marketing must capture disparate customer bases. Broadcast media proliferation has driven audience fragmentation. 'Customizable' and interactive. Complex and expensive.

18 *Compelling propositions.* Marketing must sell the benefits clearly. Only clear and compelling value propositions stand out, turning a brand into a relevant promise. Targeted and tailored, rather than generic to everyone.

19 *Creative neutrality.* Marketing must apply impartial logic to creativity. Marketers are still obsessed with television ads. It's a brave person that chooses not to do them. Be more open minded about which media, and what leads.

20   *Get more out of agencies.* Marketing must find new ways to work with creative agencies. Agencies should work together serving clients, compensated for quality of ideas as well as, or more than, their implementation.

The channel challenge

21   *Think innovatively about channels.* Marketing must innovate its routes to market. Channels were not sexy – warehouses and transport. Technology changed that, and channels are now ripe for innovation.

22   *Designing the experience.* Marketing has a great opportunity to differentiate through distribution. Channel models are changing with intermediaries needing to add more value, elaborating the customers' experience.

23   *Multi-channel fusion.* Marketing should design its channels, not rely on others. Multi-channel solutions create customer choice and convenience, but would be even better if they were designed to bring the best bits together.

24   *Embrace new business models.* Marketing should innovate strategically. How the business makes money can be significantly innovated for market and financial impact, like Dell's 'built to order' model, customization with negative working capital.

25   *Go beyond the website.* Marketing has yet to embrace channel technologies in innovative ways. Digital formats have hardly started to be exploited, and can do much more to improve efficiency and the customer experience.

The pricing challenge

26   *Don't be afraid to charge more.* Marketing should add more value to customers, and charge them more for it. Changing the peer group, the customer context to judge value is one way. Yet few marketers are actually responsible for price.

27   *Change the frame of reference.* Marketing must get into customer heads. The perceived value of benefits relative to competitors is in the buyer's mind. Improve the benefits, and change the competitive context.

28   *Price transparency.* Marketing can no longer hide within sectors and countries. Prices can be compared online between suppliers and markets. Price becomes primary, and discounting reduces margins.

29   *Find better incentives than price.* Marketing can do better than money off. Yes, seek to incentivize trial and change behaviour. Yet coupons only appeal to discount seekers, and create expectations for the future.

30   *Loyalty cards aren't loyal.* Marketing has lost sight of what loyalty is really about. Loyalty points are fun, but also quite meaningless. Compare a '2 for 1' grocery offer with the 1–2% discount equivalence of a typical points scheme.

The innovation challenge

31   *Be the innovator.* Marketing should drive innovation in the business, within products but much more too. More than creativity, it solves a real problem, with commercial results. Analysis focuses creatively on what matters.

32   *Innovate the market itself.* Marketing should innovate after launch too. Innovation focuses too much on the product or service, with too little regard for the market or customer, and what happens at each stage after launch.

33 *Embrace anthropology.* Marketing uses research as a prop, like a drunk uses a lamppost. Good research stimulates ideas, rather than fuelling prejudice. Anthropology is one of the simplest and most insightful techniques.

34 *Design can cut through.* Marketing should embrace the power of design of products, or any aspect of business, as a critical tool. One of the biggest emotional engagers, yet it is either seen as an afterthought or not seen as marketing.

35 *Differentiate laterally.* Marketing must champion the total customer experience. Products are quickly copied. Experiences are much harder to copy, but also take much more effort to make happen.

The performance challenge

36 *Think like an investor.* Marketing has a great story to tell the analysts. Investors look to the long term, where cash will come from beyond the next three years. The answer is largely in marketing's hands, but rarely do they connect.

37 *Communicate with investors.* Marketing drives the future cash flow. Businesses create long-term value for shareholders through capital growth and dividends. Capital growth depends on investor perceptions, hence the need for communication.

38 *Raise the financial bar.* Marketing needs to understand what really makes money. Profits help, particularly if they exceed investor expectations. However, marketing without focus can destroy as much value as it creates.

39 *Limited satisfaction.* Marketing shouldn't be fooled by a rush to delight the customer. Our customer-focus conscience still rates highly. It matters like hygiene, but is no guarantee of loyalty or profitability.

40 *Know which metrics matter.* Marketing needs to find the key measures of success. Lots of data, but few marketers measure the right things. Few connect inputs and outputs, and understand the most important drivers of value.

The people challenge

41 *Drive the boardroom agenda.* Marketing needs a strong mindset in the boardroom, whether or not in person. There is a low marketing IQ on most boards. Strategy and decision-making needs 'outside in' market thinking.

42 *Take marketing to the masses.* Marketing must move from function to process. Marketers are stuck doing their Ps, or at least one of them. Yet marketing disciplines must drive and connect everything. Marketers must leave their comfort zones.

43 *Become the business driver.* Marketing must get strategic and commercial. Marketing will drive the business through proof of its value, strategic and innovative leadership, and engagement in its priorities.

44 *Embrace business skills.* Marketing needs new types of marketers. Marketers need the leadership skills to drive strategy, the innovation skills to catalyse the future, commercial skills to prove it works.

45 *Leadership is more than management.* Marketing needs intelligent and creative leadership. Management is about making the right decisions; leadership is about inspiring people. Both matter, but it's not easy to be both.

The implementation challenge

46 *Leapfrog.* Marketing can often piggyback its way to market. Connecting your brand with another already loved by a target audience, fusing the values and value of both brands and propositions through affinity marketing.

47 *Create non-intrusive hellos.* Marketing must learn to influence customers without intrusion. Creating the background presence – to build awareness and shape preferences – without intrusion. Reputation management is key.

48 *Be the consumer's guide.* Marketing needs to help customers make sense of marketing. With limited time, consumers don't want to be experts, or to work hard; they want advice, support on what is best for them. Free, instantly.

49 *Marketing guerrilla.* Marketing shouldn't be afraid to usurp the conventions. Surprise tactics to challenge a competitor's campaign, such as foresighted purchasing of advertising space, can have a big impact at little cost.

50 *Embrace the network effect.* Be it word of mouth, or an e-mail to friends, viral transmission is still the best form of marketing around. Networks have infinite value, and grow exponentially with use. We believe our friends more than any marketer!

Who is a marketing genius?

Genius list 1: 50 genius brands

From online retailer Amazon to Spanish fashion merchant Zara, from established giants like Coca-Cola to emerging players like Canada's Jones Soda, which are the best brands around that every marketer can learn from?

1   Amazon: service personalization and unending choice

2   American Express: brand positioning and personal relationships

3   Apple: product and market innovation, and personality brand

4   Audi: brand heritage and customer experience

5   BlackBerry: market innovation and memetic connections

6   Bloomberg: account management and market leadership

7   Boden: great product quality and customer loyalty

8   BMW: brand experience and consistent delivery

9   Coca-Cola: brand leadership and customer loyalty

10   CNN: disruptive marketing and global reputation

11   Disney: customer passion and service delivery

12   Dyson: product innovation and premium positioning

13   eBay: radical innovation and business model

14   Enterprise Rentacar: differentiation and relationships

15   Freixenet: brand heritage and premium positioning

16   Google: market innovation and constant innovation

17   Gucci: customer relevance and brand reputation

18   Guggenheim: radical innovation and public relations

19   Harley Davidson: brand heritage and passionate community

20   Hurley: customer relevance and individual personality

21   Ikea: innovative business model and market growth

22   Innocent: brand passion and authentic business

23   Intel: ingredient branding and customer relationships

24   Jet Blue: niche positioning and innovative proposition

25   Jones Soda: radical branding and product customization

26   Krispy Kreme: brand reputation and customer experience

27   Lego: segment propositions and affinity branding

28   Lexus: premium branding and service delivery

29   Microsoft: market leadership and product innovation

30   MTV: content development and channel integration

31   Nike: brand passion and product innovation

32   Olympics: customer partnering and brand reputation

33   Panera Breads: service experience and customer loyalty

34   Paul Smith: product differentiation and niche positioning

35   Pret A Manger: brand activation and customer service

36   Porsche: niche marketing to profits through design and brand

37   Real Madrid: global branding and personality development

38   Samsung: product innovation and new market entry

39   Sky: content development and rights management

40   Starbucks: market entry and brand experience

41   Starck: product innovation and radical design

42   Sony: concept innovation and brand management

43   Spain: brand repositioning and reputation management

44   Stella Artois: premium branding and packaging design

45   Tesco: customer strategy and efficient delivery

46   Tiger Woods: personality endorsement and management

47   TY: product innovation and customer loyalty

48   Visa: global leadership and channel relationships

49   Westin Hotels: ingredient branding and product licensing

50   Zara: local positioning and speed of innovation

Genius list 2: 50 genius marketers

From Apple's design guru Jonathan Ive to CEO Phil Knight, who developed Nike from nothing, from Frappucino's Scott Bedbury to irreverent ad man Trevor Beattie, who are the best marketers alive?

1   Scott Bedbury: putting the Just Do It into Nike and Frap into Starbucks

2   Trevor Beattie: unruly, irreverent, innovative advertising creative

3   Jeff Bezos: from Wall Street to Amazon, a pure play visionary

4   Johnny Boden: charismatic leader of online clothing company Boden

5   Richard Branson: intrepid global explorer and brand portfolio leader

6   John Browne: recognizing that brand was the core to BP

7   Clay Christensen: creating the innovator's dilemma of disruption

8   Michael Dell: challenging the IT market model and going direct

9   Jean-Marie Dru: the TBWA advertising chief and author of *Disruption*

10   Charles Dunstone: entrepreneur who created a telecom intermediary

11   James Dyson: designer who recognized vacuum cleaners don't need bags

12   Michael Eisner: putting magic back into Disney people and brands

13   Niall Fitzgerald: driving the growth and focus in Unilever

14 Simon Fuller: responsible for hugely successful entertainment brands

15 Bill Gates: with the vision of a PC in every home, on every desk

16 Martin George: marketed British Airways out of its turbulent times

17 Seth Godin: from Yahoo to Purple Cows, spreading ideas with blogs

18 Stelios Haji-Ioannou: happy to make anything easy and orange

19 Gary Hamel: championing the path to innovative growth

20 Jonathan Ive: the design genius behind Apple's smooth grooves

21 Kevin Kelly: seeing the network potential of the connected world

22 W. Chan Kim: making sense of markets through blue ocean strategy

23 Philip Kotler: the father of modern and holistic marketing thinking

24 Nirmalya Kumar: connecting marketing and business strategy

25 Steve Jobs: the marketing visionary of *Toy Story* and iPods

26 Jean Noel Kapferer: brand master, recognizing the value of brands

27 Phil Knight: runner and accountant, turning billionaire entrepreneur

28 AG Lafley: transforming P&G by making the customer the boss

29 Terry Leahy: ensuring that every little helps make Tesco successful

30 Martin Lindstrom: engaging all your senses in the world of brands

31 Malcolm McDonald: academic with the vision to write a cartoon book

32 Rob Malcolm: focusing his drinks portfolio on what matters most

33   Julian Metcalfe: putting passion into the sandwich business

34   Keith Mills: capturing the loyalty of customers through cards and data

35   Geoffrey Moore: crossing the chasm, into tornadoes and mainstream

36   David Neeleman: creating the USA's premium airline with low-cost fares

37   Michael O'Leary: creating Europe's no-frills airline with low-cost fares

38   Don Peppers: missionary of the one-to-one future and value of customers

39   Richard Reed: threw in his advertising job to make tasty Innocent drinks

40   Fred Reicheld: the doyen of customer loyalty, and how it makes money

41   Kevin Roberts: the Saatchi and Saatchi man with the *Lovemarks*

42   Maurice Saatchi: the advertising intellect that redefined a generation

43   Howard Schultz: from Moby Dick to every street corner, a cup at a time

44   Paul Smith: quirky and mischievous, and worshipped in Japan

45   Martin Sorrell: the financial wizard behind the leading creative agencies

46   Philippe Starck: poetic Frenchman who turns products on their heads

47   Jim Stengel: disciplined and accountable leader of the FMCG world

48   Peter Van Stolk: the frustrated skier who gave us turkey and gravy soda

49   Meg Whitman: classically trained marketer who led a retail revolution

50   Dan Wieden: half of agency W&K, and the advertising brains of Nike

Genius list 3: 50 genius innovations

From the printing press to text messaging, from waffle soles to self-heating drinks, from the Windows operating system to MP3 digital music, what are the best innovations?

1   Air from Nike: the platform for a distinctive product range

2   Aspirin: branding in a highly competitive market

3   ATM cash machines: banking at more convenient times and places

4   Barcode: hyper-fast checkouts, hyper-efficient replenishment

5   Beer widget: enabling you to have a real head wherever you are

6   BlackBerry: innovative, inseparable, indispensable,

7   Clockwork radio: low-tech solution for a high-tech age

8   Digital cameras: redefined the photography market in a year

9   DNA analysis: finding your true identity

10   DVD: more content, less space, better quality, charge more

11   E-mail: what would work be without this – remember paper memos!

12   Fibre optics: enabling information to make the world go around

13   Flash memory: revolutionizing content transfer between devices

14   Flat screen: space saving and aesthetically pleasing

15   Gel pen: the smoother, brighter, tactile writing machine

16   Gel drinks: nutritious meals on the run, or in outer space

17   Gore-Tex: the original fabric that breathes and keeps the rain out

18   3G: much hyped, overpaid, and eventually delivering results

19   JPEG: images that move across systems rapidly

20   Integrated chips: the constant challenge to get more from a silicon sliver

21   iPod: the indispensable lifestyle accessory that changed an industry

22   Loyalty points: far better than dealing with paperclipped coupons

23   Lycra: putting stretch, shape and durability into your clothes

24   Microwave ovens: transforming cooking and eating experiences

25   Mobile phone: always in touch wherever you are

26   Modem: ensuring that data connects from networks to devices

27   MP3: enabling downloaded music to take off

28   Nanotechnology: creating machines out of molecular particles

29   Oyster card: London's new travel and payment smart cards

30   Palm Pilot: your life in your hand, organized and accessible

31   PDF: protecting and sharing knowledge like never before

32   Personal computers: from mainframe to usability, essential to life

33   Plasma screens: adding aesthetics and picture quality indoors and out

34 Post-it Notes: from hymn books to process mapping

35 Ready meals: moving from the unhealthy to the nutritious

36 RFID tags: retailer inventory control, or consumer behaviour tracking

37 Satellite imaging: seeing objects and distances which used to be sci-fi

38 Self-heating drinks: cans that serve hot coffee with a pull of the ring

39 Shrink wrap: bringing hygiene and preservation to the kitchen

40 Smart Car: Mercedes and Swatch's designer little cars

41 SMS/Text: instant messaging, personal and discreet

42 Solar panels: making the most of natural resources

43 Sony Walkman: transformed a generation of people and products

44 Space Shuttle: from amazing spectacle to daily activity

45 Swatch: transforming an industry, and redefining a watch

46 Tupperware: enduring plastic boxes sold through pyramid parties

47 Voice-mail: intensely frustrating and essential messaging

48 Voice recognition: technology becomes human, fast and convenient

49 Web: imagine a world without the Internet, a decade seems a long time

50 WiFi: Wireless connectivity for a truly mobile world

Genius list 4: 50 genius concepts

From affinity marketing like Capital One to the customer communities of Huggies, from Intel's ingredient branding to Hotmail's viral communication, what are the best marketing ideas?

1   Adjacent markets: natural places for brand extensions

2   Affinity marketing: connecting your brand values with another's

3   Ambient marketing: using the surroundings as active media

4   Anthropology: watching what people actually do

5   Auctions: a more democratic approach to pricing

6   Brand: the most core, valuable and energizing business asset

7   Brand management: managing the total customer experience

8   Business models: how all partners interact and create value

9   B2B and B2C: each has a lot to learn from the other

10   Category management: managing categories rather than products

11   Celebrity endorsement: putting extreme humanity into brands

12   Chaos theory: everything is complex and nothing is certain

13   Communities: bringing people together with common purpose

14   Cost of capital: the minimum return required by investors

15   Cost of sale: separating brand investments from selling costs

16   Customer value: understanding the perceived value to customers

17 C2C: enabling customer-to-customer transactions

18 CSR: being a more responsible organization and brand

19 DCF: using discounted cash flows to make more strategic decisions

20 Direct marketing: getting connected with direct channels and media

21 Disruptive technologies: challenging leaders with inferior solutions

22 Double time: creating tomorrow while delivering today

23 Dynamic pricing: using pricing more flexibly and changing in time

24 Guerrilla marketing: opportunist marketing (without littering the streets)

25 E-marketing: embracing technology, from web to WiFi, text to telematics

26 Econometrics: the statistical analysis of marketing and consumer impact

27 Economic profit: the real profit, operating profit less cost of capital

28 Ethical marketing: marketing with integrity, promoting ethical solutions

29 Ingredient branding: the compelling force inside somebody else's brand

30 Intangible assets: brands, relationships patents that create future profits

31 Killer applications: concepts that grab imaginations and market share

32 Lifetime value: the sum of future revenues from loyal customers

33 Loyalty points: rewarding purchase frequency and tracking behaviours

34 Market chasms: mind the gap between early adopters and mainstream

35 Market strategy: where and how to compete, core of business strategy

36 Marketing strategy: how to implement the business strategy

37 Metrics: the chosen key measures and targets for business performance

38 Multi-channel management: managing channels in an integrated way

39 Media-neutral marketing: unbiased choice of communication media

40 Neural networks: market research that quantifies human emotions

41 One-to-one marketing: building relationships one at a time

42 Permission marketing: communicating on customers' terms

43 Portfolio management: managing the range of businesses or products

44 ROCE: the return on capital employed, using investors' money well

45 ROMI: the return on marketing investment, short or long term

46 Scenario planning: strategic planning that considers future possibilities

47 Segmentation: clustering together and targeting similar customers

48 Trusted agents: intermediaries who act on behalf of customers

49 Value-based marketing: making decisions based on economic value

50 Viral communications: exploiting networks with contagious messages

Genius list 5: 50 genius inspirations

From books like *The Monk And The Riddle* and gurus like Geoffrey Moore, to websites like BrandChannel and blogs like Seth Godin's, and visual companies like Xplane and the innovators of IDEO, where should you go to be inspired?

1   *Authentic Business*: Neil Crofts describes a more enlightened approach

2   *Brand Child*: Martin Lindstrom explains how to market to kids

3   *Celebrity Sells*: Hamish Pringle explores the cult of personality

4   *Crossing the Chasm*: Geoffrey Moore captures the main market

5   *Good to Great*: Jim Collins takes one step to good, another to great

6   *Leading the Revolution*: Gary Hamel drives growth through innovation

7   *One to One Enterprise*: Don Peppers applies B2B thinking to B2C

8   *Purple Cow*: Seth Godin on a mission to make everything different

9   *The Monk And the Riddle*: Randy Komisar's fable of a growth company

10   *Welcome to the Creative Age*: Mark Earls and his banana marketing

11   *Blink*: the book of the zeitgeist from *New Yorker*'s Malcolm Gladwell

12   *Advertising Age*: the US leading voice of the marketing industry

13   *CMO Magazine*: everything for US market leaders (cmomagazine.com)

14   *Fast Company*: funky focus on the cool brands and businesses

15   *Harvard Business Review*: best of new thinking (hbsp.hardvard.edu)

16   *The Marketer*: radical views on the marketing agenda from the CIM

17   *Strategy and Business*: more business ideas (strategy-business.com)

18   Brand Finance: making the connections between marketing and finance

19   Flytxt: redefining text-based marketing for consumer brands

20   IDEO: radical innovation company that will take you for a 'deep dive'

21   Innosight: Create new market disruptions with Clay Christensen

22   Henley Centre: new ideas and visions with customer foresight

23   Marketing NPV: making sense of ROI marketing (marketingnpv.com)

24   Neurosense: the leading neurological marketing consultancy

25   One Minute Customer: customer-thinking company (theomcgroup.com)

26   St Luke's: creative agency that believes in a balanced approach

27   Strategos: innovative growth from Gary Hamel (strategos.com)

28   The Foundation: creators of customer companies (thefoundation.biz)

29   Wieden and Kennedy: advertising agency to the leading brands

30   Xplane: explaining the unexplainable through the power of pictures

31   AMA: bringing together the US marketers (marketingpower.com)

32   ANA: the leading network of American advertisers (ana.net)

33   EMC: bringing together Europe's marketing networks (emc.be)

34   IPA: voice of UK's advertising agencies (ipa.co.uk)

35   Marketing Leadership Council: closed network of leading companies

36   Marketing Science Institute: bringing together academic ideas (msi.org)

37 Marketing Society: the UK marketing leaders (marketing-society.co.uk)

38 Allaboutbranding.com: aggregator of the best brand articles

39 Adslogans.com: every marketing line that has ever been used

40 Beinghunted.com: what's cool in the world of fashion

41 Brandchannel.com: everything about brands and branding

42 Brandrepublic.com: marketing new portal from Haymarket group

43 Customercapital.org: measuring business through customer eyes

44 Marketingprofs.com: latest marketing ideas and articles weekly

45 Marketingsherpa.com: more marketing ideas and articles weekly

46 Philippe-starck.com: the mind and madness of the innovator himself

47 Sethgodin.com: permission-based blogger with a passion to be different

48 Shapetheagenda.com: emerging ideas in marketing from the CIM

49 Trendwatching.com: what's hot and happening on the streets

50 Wikipedia.org: everything you need to know and can add yourself

Recharge

In many ways this book reflects my own marketing journey so far. It brings together the many ideas and experiences that I have gained by working with amazing teams of people along the way.

In the early days at British Airways they included Mike Batt, Martin George, Terry Daly, Jonathan Dutton and Roy Langmaid. There was the great team at PA Consulting Group including David Cook, Mark Thomas, Jonathan Hogg, Tim Isaac, Peter Barrett, Nicole DeMartino and Adam Forbes.

At the Chartered Institute of Marketing they included Mike Johnston, Dianne Thompson, Tess Harris, Laurie Young, John Coke, Annabel Pritchard and many others. Most recently, they have been David Haigh and others at Brand Finance; Charlie Dawson, John Vincent and the team at The Foundation.

Along the way there has always been the advice and stimulus of Rita Clifton, Alan Mitchell, Phil Dourado, Hugh Burkitt, Hamish Pringle, Janet Hull, Simon Benham and Brendan Barns.

I have learnt much from all of them, and hope you find it valuable too.

Most of all I would like to thank my wife Alison, my daughters Anna and Clara, and my Mum and Dad, for all their love and support, and to whom I dedicate this book.

You can keep up to date with genius marketing and marketers – learn more about achieving Marketing Genius, the latest ideas and actions of genius brands and their people, new events and services, by visiting the new Marketing Genius website:

www.MarketingGeniusLive.com

Index

advertising 290–91
Agent Provocateur 275–6
Amazon 293–4
American Express 230
Apple Computer 36–8, 103–4, 146,
    201
Apple PowerBook 233–4
ARM Holdings 222
Armstrong, Neil 209
Audi TT 237, 264

balanced scorecard 341–3
Beecham, Sinclair 154
Belsay Hall (Northumberland)
    213–14, 215
Berners-Lee, Tim 301
Bezos, Jeff 293–4
Black & Decker 204–5
Blackberry 201–2
Bleustein, Jeff 253
BMW 159, 166–7, 206, 250, 254
Bowerman, Bill 105, 423
Brabeck, Peter 376–7
brand 3, 25–6, 139–68
    activation 156–7
    architecture 161–2

awareness 27
blogging 434–5
definition 139, 150–51
development 140
enabling people to do more
    144–6
equity 147, 164, 167–8, 343
extensions 158–61
gateway 432–3
impact 163–5
ingredient 432
insightful 436–9
intelligent/imaginative 140
living the brand 152–4
management 382–3, 384
passion 440–41
passion branding 440–41
powerful 140–41
reflecting/engaging people
    142–4
short-/long-term value
    146–7
tattoo 320
value-based analysis 164–5
Branson, Richard 148, 400–401
Brin, Sergey 26

British Airways 206, 245–6, 319,
    380–83
Browne, John 158
Buffett, Warren 102
business innovators 374, 385–6
business models 220–23, 224–5
business-to-business (B2B) 125,
    324, 326
business-to-customer (B2C) 324,
    326

Cadbury Schweppes 82, 83, 337–8
Café Direct 184–6
campaigns 90
Carlson, Jan 143
Centrica 316–17
change drivers 30–31, 42
chief executive officers (CEOs)
    413–15, 417
chief marketing officers (CMOs)
    398–400
    collaborative 398, 408–9
    functional 398, 403–5
    length of tenure 398–9
    marketing 398, 413–15
    see also leadership

Christensen, Clay 204, 206
Cirque du Soleil 217–18
Club World (British Airways) 245–6
Coca-Cola 74–7, 221, 448
Cohen, Jack 238
collaborative CXOs 398, 408–9
communication 24, 40
    effective 236–8
    genius 463–4
    integrated 290–93
competition 25, 227–327
    black holes 34
    cool places 34
    hot spots 33
    white spaces 34
competitive advantage 34, 134–5
competitive positioning 135–6
complexity 1, 23–54
    competitor-collaborator
        distinction 30
    coping with 27, 32–3
    drivers of change 30–32
    inside out/outside in 24
    making sense of 25
    perspective 24
    structural/behavioural changes
        33
connections 5, 279–304
    changes 280–83
    channel integration 299–300
    channel inversion 296–8
    integrated communication
        290–93
    intelligent/imaginative 280
    mapping 288–9
    market networks 301–2, 304

media integration 294–5
conversation 236–8
core competence 115
Corre, Joseph 275
cost of capital 130
creative catalysts 211
creative disruption 204–9
creativity 86–7
customer 3–4, 169–96
    behaviour 35–6
    capital 363–6
    champions 374, 379–80
    changing 171
    companies 188–91
    coping with complexity 32–3
    decision-making 229
    ethnography 195–6
    expectations 57
    experiences 42
    focus 188
    foresight 172–3
    intelligent/imaginative 170
    loyalty 317–20
    memetics 251–2
    needs 180–81
    partnering 324–6
    predictability 25
    product brand 154
    research 174–8
    responsibility 182–4
    responsible marketing 186–7
    script 243–5, 246–7
    segmentation 170–71
    transparency 172
    trust 172
    winning 231

customer management relationship
    (CMR) 308
customer relationship management
    (CRM) 58, 68, 172, 188–91,
    305–27
    customer affinity 313–15
    intelligent/imaginative 306
    loyalty 317–20, 322–3
    partnering 324–7
    relationship mapping 311–12
customer value 73–4
    see also shareholder value;
    value; value-based
    marketing
customer value propositions (CVPs)
    230–31
    customer memetics 251–2
    customer messages 243–5
    customer scripts 246–7
    development 241–2
    intelligent/imaginative 230
    neuro marketing 247–50
    perceived value 233–8
    value perceptions 232
cycle times 41–2, 44

DaimlerChrysler 321
De Bono, Edward 208
decision-making 117–19
Dell Computer Corporation 212,
    283–8
Dell, Michael 283–5
Dell's Direct Model 286–8
design 263–5
    function and form 267
Diageo 344–50

Disney *see* Walt Disney Company
Disneyland 273
distribution channels 296–8,
    299–300
  genius 464
Dogs and Stars Chart 349
Drucker, Peter 199
Dyson, Brian 448
Dyson, James 439–40

eBay 51–2, 221, 416
economic profit 130
economic value 65, 70–71
Einstein, Albert 86, 99–100
Eisner, Michael 152
employees 57
    corporate brand 154
Enterprise Rentacar 131–2
entrepreneurs 444
expectations 2, 55–84
    delivering today/creating
      tomorrow 56
experiences 5, 253–78
    being intuitive 270–71
    benefits-based 255
    customer theatre 272–5, 276–7
    forms 274–5
    how to do it 270
    intelligent/imaginative 254
    knowing what to do 270
    mapping 256–7, 261–2
    personal service 268–70
    why do it 270

frontier people 443
Fuller, Richard Buckminster 263

futures 7, 419–49
    borderless economies 421
    brand blogging 434–5
    business structures/roles 422–3
    creative hotspots 423
    customer attitudes/behaviours
      421–2
    customer companies 423
    digital domains 421
    five balls analogy 447–9
    genetic segmentation 422
    global intimacy 422
    insightful brands 436–9
    intelligent markets 430–33
    intelligent/imaginative 420
    knowledge havens 422
    lifestyle fusion 422
    market level 421
    power bases 421
    sensing 428–9

game changing 42
Gardner, Dr Howard 250
General Electric (GE) 206–7
genius 2, 85–107
    analytical thinking 91
    attributes 89–93
    born or made 88
    brands 462, 469–72
    catalysts 8, 461–8
    communications 463–4
    concepts 47880
    conviction thinking 93
    creative thinking 90–91
    definition 93–7
    distribution channels 464

doing 454–5
dual thinking 91
holistic thinking 92
implementation 467–8
innovation 465–6, 475–7
inspiration 480–83
intelligent/imaginative 86
lab 8, 452–60
marketers 472–4
marketing 455–6
observational thinking 91
original thinking 90
people 467
performance 466–7
potential 458–60
pragmatic thinking 92
pricing 465
profile 97–8
role 87–8
source 8–9, 94–6
space 453
stimulus 88
strategy 461–2
thinking 453–4
time 453
use of creativity 86–7
visual thinking 93
volume thinking 92
genius marketers 99–102, 457–8,
    472–4
    imagination 101
    impact 102
    intelligence 9–100
Gillette 160
Gladwell, Malcolm 229
Google 26–9

growth drivers 375, 389–90
growth management 394

Harley Davidson 272
Hewlett-Packard 313, 439
Higgs review 413
holistic approach 59
Hotmail 40
HumanSigma approach 68

IBM 160, 231
Ikea 223–4
Illy 313
iMac 37, 201
Innocent 444–7
innovation 4, 197–225
    concept change 215
    context change 214–15
    cosmetic change 214
    creative catalysts 211
    creative disruption 204–9
    definition 198–9
    development 212–17
    early adopters/mass market gap
        200–201
    genius 465–6, 475–7
    intelligent/imaginative 198
    managing 388
    pathway 202–3
    reframing 219
    sources 199–200
intangible assets 360–61
Intel 314
intelligent markets 430–33
intuition 270–71
investor relations 366–7

iPod 37–8
iShuffle 38
iTunes 38

Jensen, Rolf 237
Jenson, Bill 25
Jet Blue 119–21
Jobs, Steve 38, 100, 103–4
Johnson & Johnson credo 137–8
Jones Soda 257–61

Kaman, Nick 146
Kamprad, Ingvar 223
Kelleher, Herb 237–8, 307
King, Lord 380
Knight, Phil 102, 105–7, 423
knowledge management 58
Kodak 29, 159
Krispy Kreme 302–3
Kroto, Sir Harry 263

Land Rover 125, 313
Lazardis, Mike 202
leader vs follower approach 125
leadership 7, 329–417, 395–417
    balanced 397–8
    collaborative CXOs 408–9
    influencing the business 411–12
    intelligent/imaginative 396
    managing marketing 406–7
    roles 397, 398, 401–2
Leahy, Terry 240, 410–11
lean thinking approach 68
Levi's 146
Lindstrom, Martin 32, 320
loyalty cards 319–20

loyalty ladder 319, 322–3

McDonald's 220
Macintosh *see* Apple Computer
Malcolm, Rob 347, 350
management 396–7, 402
market
    focus 129–31
    mapping 34–6, 39
    networks 301–2
    new 42
    perspectives 123–6
    posture 124–5
    power 48–50
    segments 25
    selection 127–8
    shaping 42
    space 29
    speed 40–44
    value 77–8
    vortex 47
Market Radar 35
market research 174–8
    analysis/ordering frameworks
        176–7
    approaches 175–8
    data collection 174–5
    interpretation 175
market strategy 115, 121–2
    choices 116–17
    dimensions 116
marketers 6–7, 369–94
    brand management 384
    business innovators 374, 385–6
    business priorities 370–71
    CEO perceptions 372–3

challenges/opportunities 371–2
customer champions 374,
   379–80
functional activities 373–4
genius 472–4
growth drivers 375, 389–90
imperatives for change 375–6
inspired 442–4
intelligent/imaginative 370
managing growth 394
managing innovation 388
managing markets 378
role 374–5
marketing
   affinity 308, 313–15
   CEOs 398, 413–15
   description 55–6
   genius 455–6
   managing 406–7
   metrics 340–43
   optimization 352–3
   outside-in perspective 56–9
   peripheral function 55
   reporting 357–63
   responsible 186–7
   reverse 54, 282–3
   scorecards 351
   shaping strategies 56
Marketing Society 370–74
Marshall, Colin 380
Mauborgne, Renee 217
media integration 294–5
memes 248–50
Mercedes 320–22
Metcalfe, Julian 154
Metcalfe's Law 31

Microsoft 60–63, 159
Mini 250–51
mission statement 67, 202
Mitchell, Alan 290
Moore, Geoffrey 31, 200
Moore's Law 31
MTV 298–9
Multiple Intelligence Theory 250

Neeleman, David 119–21
Nestlé 376–7
networks 31, 40, 301–2, 304–5
neuro marketing 247–50
new product development (NPD)
   216–17
Nike 105–7, 143, 146, 423–8
Niketown 272
Nokia 433–4
Novartis 114

Ohga, Norio 263
Operating and Finance Review
   (OFR) 359–62
operating profit 80
outside-in strategy 56–9, 115, 408

Page, Larry 26
Panera Breads 309–11
partner development 324–7
PayPal 52
Peppers, Don 306
performance 6, 331–67
   customer capital 363–6
   genius 466–7
   incentives 58
   intelligent/imaginative 332

measuring 333–7, 340–43
optimization 352–3
reporting 357–63
scorecards 341–3, 351
value-based marketing 338–9
personal service 268–70
Philips 314, 386–7
Picasso, Pablo 101
Pixar 103
portfolio analysis 132–3
power profile 53
Prêt a Manger 154–6
Procter & Gamble (P&G) 192–5,
   405–6
product development 43, 216–17
product life cycle 130
profit 72, 130
propositions 4–5, 229, 230–31
   see also customer value
      propositions (CVPs)

Radcliffe, Paula 447
radio frequency identification
   devices (RFID) 431
Rees, Serena 275
Regus 222
Reicheld, Fred 317–18
relationship marketing 5–6, 306–7
   see also customer relationship
      marketing (CRM)
Research in Motion (RIM) 201–2
return on investment (ROI) 355–6
revenue driver 80
risk/reward 35
Roberts, Kevin 37, 144
Roddick, Anita 263

Rogers, Martha 306

Sarbanes Oxley 358–9
satisfaction scores 81
Saxby, Robin 222
scenario development 35
Schultz, Howard 44, 143
Sculley, John 103
Sears 147
Seymour, Richard 264
Shaich, Ron 309–10
shareholder value 57, 58, 65, 66,
    70–72, 80
    see also customer value; value;
        value-based marketing
shareholders 57–8, 147
Shell 314
Six Sigma 58
Sky TV 126–7
Smirnoff 74
Smith, Paul 265–6
Sony 144
Southwest Airlines 307
stakeholders 58, 64
Starbucks 44–6, 143, 268
Starck, Philippe 101, 104–5
Stella Artois 354–5
Stengel, Jim 405–6
Stolk, Peter van 258–61
strategy 3, 111–38
    choices 127–8
    competitive positioning 135–6
    definition 112–14
    direction/perspective 123–6
    focus of effort 129–31
    genius 461–2
    inadequacy 112–13
    intelligent/imaginative 112
    leaders/followers 125
    making choices 117–19
    market 115–17, 121–2
    market advantage 134–5
    outside in 115
    portfolio analysis 132–3
    types 113
Sunderland, John 82

3M 209–11
Taylor, David 158
Taylor, Jack 131–2
technology 205
    see also innovation
telemarketing 32
Tesco 238–41, 410–11
Thomas, Freeman 264
Total Quality Management (TQM)
    58, 189
total shareholder return (TSR)
    71
Toyota 67–8, 160

Unilever 129

value
    creation 58, 64–7, 69,
        130
    destroyers 130
    disciplines 134
    drivers 80
    perceived 233–8
    see also customer value;
        shareholder value;
        value-based marketing
value propositions see customer
    value propositions
    (CVPs)
value-based marketing 79–83,
    338–9
    see also customer value;
        shareholder value;
        value
Virgin Group 148–50
Virgin Mobile 212
VW Beetle 264

Walt Disney Company 159,
    390–93
Welch, Jack 40, 206, 238
Whitman, Meg 416

Zara 178–80